Seagulls in my Belfry

Seagulls in my Belfry

The very personal story of a Naval career

Rear Admiral C.C. Anderson, CB

The Pentland Press Limited
Edinburgh • Cambridge • Durham • USA

First published in 1997 by
The Pentland Press Ltd.
1 Hutton Close
South Church
Bishop Auckland
Durham

British Library Cataloguing in Publication Data.
A catalogue record for this book is available
from the British Library.

ISBN 1 85821 461 0

Typeset by CBS, Felixstowe, Suffolk
Printed and bound by Antony Rowe Ltd., Chippenham

This book is gratefully dedicated to
Pam
who shared so much of it with me but
was refused advancement to Leading Rate
because she was 'a bad influence on
the mess deck'.

Parts of this book have already
been published in *The Naval Review*,
to the editor of which, as always,
my thanks

CONTENTS

PROLOGUE

Six years old, I stood on the jetty at Boulogne with my mother, staring at the British destroyer alongside. The guns and torpedoes, the sleek lines and the grey paint, had an atmosphere of deliciously sinister power and danger. As we watched, the Quartermaster shambled aft to the Officer of the Day, saluted and said, probably, 'Four o'clock, sir. Pipe Hands to Tea?' The OOD looked at his watch and nodded. The Quartermaster saluted again and withdrew.

'Gosh!' I thought. 'They even salute each other when they ask the time.' And from that minute onwards my future was settled. I had, said an aunt, bats in the belfry. No, said my mother. Seagulls.

For the rest of the holiday I could think of nothing else. Home again in Ireland the years passed and I went to prep school announcing that I was a Navy candidate. The Headmaster was torn between the urge to acquire the kudos of another entry to Dartmouth and the realisation that my meagre academic potential, particularly in maths, was hardly likely to get me there. And failure for his school was unthinkable.

At the age of eleven, another destroyer came into Dun Laoghaire harbour and sailors with flapping bell-bottomed trousers strolled along the sea front. I spent all day just looking at them with a queer tight feeling in my stomach and, when the ship opened to visitors, I was the first on board. A kindly sailor took charge of the eager little boy and to this great man I confided the secret of my future. We explored the whole ship and when, reluctantly, I had to go, 'Goodbye, mate,' said my sailor. 'See you in the Navy.' I walked home on top of the world and, a year later, my application was sent in to their Lordships.

The statement sounds simple. The truth was more complicated. The Headmaster, convinced quite reasonably that I was mathematically moronic, was uncooperative. My mother had no idea how to set about taking the step and it was left to a Godfather with a vaguely military background to solve the problem. 'Write to Gieves,' he said, and to those famous Naval tailors we wrote.

1

Gieves replied by return with a little book entitled *How to become a Naval Officer*. It was blue with the title in gold and it told us all we needed to know. It told us how to apply and what interviews and exams were involved. It showed photographs of the Royal Naval College at Dartmouth and described the food, routine and curriculum. No bishop ever studied the Bible with more emotion than me as I read and re-read that little book. In particular, there was a sentence describing the great moment when the successful candidates gathered on Paddington platform to catch the special train to the Naval College for the first time. 'The motley crowd of schoolboys has become a uniformed body of Officers.' It was heady stuff to a dedicated twelve-year-old.

The interview was held in the Admiralty and we knew all about it beforehand. Everybody did in those days. 'The Admirals' would ask you the number of your taxi to test your general power of observation. So we all arrived with a taxi number firmly in our heads – though most candidates had come by Underground.

I went in to the ordeal to be faced at once by disillusionment. The glorious array of uniforms I had expected to confront was absent. Instead, behind a long table, sat a few men in ordinary civilian clothes including one who, horror of horrors, wore an ecclesiastical dog collar. The rest, I knew, must be 'The Admirals' but how had a parson crept in? He was, presumably, the Headmaster of one of our more distinguished public schools but I was not to know that. I took against him and my adrenalin rose. This probably saved me.

'The Admirals' started affably. Why did I want to join the Navy? (How could I answer such a silly question!) Had I ever been on board one of HM ships? I told them of the Dun Laoghaire destroyer and a schism at once arose. Some said no ship could have visited the Irish Free State and I must be mistaken. One claimed she was there for one reason, another claimed another. I suggested she had come for our annual fair and the whole Board laughed. Somehow the ice was broken and we all got on splendidly till it came to 'the Parson's' turn. I glowered. Perhaps he misunderstood my look and was human after all because, unexpectedly, he said, 'Fie, my lord, fie. A soldier and afraid?'

'Afeared,' I muttered.

Dog Collar stopped dead and there was a sudden silence. 'Are you telling me, boy, that I'm mistaken?'

'Yes, sir.'

A slight snuffling noise came from one of the Naval officers, who had his face in his hands and seemed to be shaking. The silence grew. Dog Collar was not shaking but gave the impression that he was. The President of the Board suddenly said, 'Send for a Shakespeare,' and an interminable wait ensued. Nobody spoke. I thought frantically back to *Macbeth*. We had done it only that term and I had played Lady Macbeth in the school production. I knew her lines.

An Admiralty messenger came in with a copy of the *Collected Works of Shakespeare* dredged up from some unlikely corner. Dog Collar snatched it and searched with an air that showed us all how contemptuously familiar he was with the play. Slowly he declaimed –

'Fie, my lord, fie. A soldier and – afeared . . .'

There was another silence broken only by the same peculiar snuffling noise. I wilted.

Dog Collar looked at me with loathing.

'What's eleven times three hundred and twelve?' he snapped.

I guessed I had not been a success but this was really too much. I had come to discuss the Navy with Admirals and here, instead, was a parson laying bare my most dangerous weakness.

'I'm sorry, sir,' I quavered, 'but I thought the educational exam came later.'

The snuffler was now almost sobbing. Dog Collar had swollen slowly up like a huge bullfrog. Again the President came to my rescue.

'All right, Anderson,' he said. 'I think you'd better go now.'

Sketching a salute as my mother had advised me to, I ran from the room.

With the unexpected news that I had passed my interview a period of intense activity set in at school. The Maths master took to screaming and this so disconcerted me, because he pinched my ear as he did it, that I became mildly neurotic and quoted the school's Latin motto as 'A table in a healthy body'. My mother spoke to the Headmaster and suddenly everybody became strangely patient and gentle. When the time came to attend the written exam and I left to catch the mailboat to Holyhead, the Headmaster actually gave me a present. I unwrapped it to find it was a slim volume, amusingly illustrated, giving the salient dates of English history in short, pithy verse.

Gieves had sent me all the details of the requirements for taking the exam, even including the equipment in the way of rulers, dividers, etc. which I should need to use. Of the two hundred who had undergone the interview with The Admirals some sixty had survived for the academic test. These sixty, and their parents, had all been invited to take tea with Gieves after the ordeal was over in order to be measured for their uniforms. Only thirty-seven would eventually enter Dartmouth but Gieves, efficient to the end, were taking no chances.

The exam was even more dreadful than I had expected. The Latin was full of unaccountable full stops. At the end of the Maths, I suddenly realised that I had done all my multiplication back to front and I barely managed, before the paper had to be given in, to add a pathetic personal note to the Examiner explaining that I had just seen what I had done but lacked time to correct the faulty sums. Geography concerned itself almost exclusively with Korea, a country of which, in those happy days, nobody had ever heard. However, as History was taken at the same time as Geography, I pretended I had had no time to tackle the latter and concentrated solely on the history. It demanded a standard of knowledge that I obviously lacked but here my Headmaster's understanding suddenly bore fruit. I already knew his little book by heart and I wrote a series of erudite essays which, though they may have born little relationship to the questions, were studded with facts and dates, all brief but deadly accurate.

My mother collected me from the front door of the examination hall and carried me away to the hotel in which Gieves were to give us tea. In the taxi, the full implications of my failure burst upon me and I dissolved into mutinous tears. To go to be measured for a Naval uniform would, under the circumstances, be more than I could bear. I refused to go. But my mother was adamant. If I had thrown away my future at least we might as well salvage something from the wreckage even if my nearest approach to the Navy was to be a free tea from Gieves.

We arrived. In the hotel lounge was a grand piano on which Gieves had erected a pyramid of Naval Officers' caps. Shiny peaks, huge gold badges, there they sat – symbol of all I craved for and could never have. I stared at them, stricken and heartbroken. A card on the wall announced that the others, who would go to Dartmouth, would be the Exmouth Term.

Sharing our table was the mother of an obviously clever and able boy who was taking the whole occasion in his easy stride. How, she asked, had I found the exam? Oh? Her son had considered it rather easy. But perhaps I was good at games? So few people were brilliant at both. Oh, I wasn't a great games player either? Ah well, still waters normally ran deep. Her boy was lucky. He was captain of both cricket and rugger at his school. While the mothers fought their deadly battle I looked at the other boy and hated him. I was still very close to tears.

The other mother said how much she had enjoyed talking to us. She hoped she would have the pleasure of meeting us at Dartmouth next term. She and her son departed, trailing glory. I never saw either again.

I returned to Ireland and my prep school. Every day was grey and there was no point in living. Spent and exhausted from their earlier efforts the masters ignored me and left me alone in class – a small, silent, miserable child at the desk in the corner.

One day we were doing Latin and I was summoned to see the Headmaster. Somehow I knew this was it. My way took me through the lavatory at the end of the playground and there I paused and prayed in a way I had never done before and never have since. At the entrance to the hall, the Headmaster's wife, carving knife in hand, stood by that day's joint, looking helplessly at my mother who, in her turn, was crying. The Headmaster's face, as usual, betrayed no expression but the tableau told me all.

I sauntered up. 'Well,' I said, 'What's the matter? I told you I'd failed.'

'You haven't,' said my mother, 'You've passed.'

She showed me the letter she was holding. It was from Gieves and said that, in view of my success in passing into the Navy, they were putting our valued order for my uniform in hand. They offered their respectful congratulations and looked forward to the privilege and pleasure of attending to my needs during the years ahead.

I had the grace to pause in the lavatory on my way back and say a fervent thank you to my Creator. Then, on air, I re-entered the classroom to meet a total and pregnant silence.

'Splendid,' I announced loudly, 'No more bloody Latin.' And so the school got the news.

Their Lordships' official letter a week later could only be anticlimax.

Chapter 1

DARTMOUTH

On 30 April 1930, 'the motley crowd of schoolboys now a uniformed body of officers' gathered on Paddington station with their parents. At thirteen years old, few had worn stiff white collars before and our inexperience showed in the gleamingly visible new front studs and the individualistic knotting of the ties. The marvellous caps, retrieved from the grand piano by a provident Gieves, were so large that, if we had not had prominent ears, only our huge black boots would have been visible below. We were very proud but there was palpable emotion on the platform. Now dreams had become actuality and we were all a little afraid of the unknown. All of a sudden, parents realised that they were delivering up their small sons to the strange and awful majesty of the Navy and that the same small boys would never return. As the train pulled out there came the sense of finality that there is when a ship draws away from the quayside, the gap of water widens, and the empty horizon claims its own. Much must happen before the leavers and the left are together again as they were only that morning.

Lieutenant Commander 'Poop' Edwards, our Term Officer, Nicholls, our Term Cadet Captain, and Favell, our Cadet Captain, travelled down in the train with us but were not sighted on the journey. At Kingswear, however, these Godlike creatures appeared and were joined by Chief Petty Officer Taylor, an old pensioner and the Exmouth 'Term Chief' who would be our father confessor, mentor and 'sea daddy' for our whole time at the College. CPO Taylor, short, weatherbeaten and almost completely square in shape, sized up the crowd of nervous little boys who emerged from the train and greeted us with the Navy's eternal and ubiquitous solution to any shambles.

'Get fell in,' he commanded.

Somehow we were sorted out and shepherded down to the yellow funnelled steamboat which took us across the river. Dominating the town of Dartmouth on the other side, huge and rather lovely on its hill, stood the red brick and white stone college which was the Navy's womb. Fertilised by the prep school seed, its gestation period three years and two terms, from it were delivered in due course the future sea officers of Britain. Most, had they been able to develop naturally through public schools, would have chosen very different careers by the time they reached the age of eighteen. They might have been successful business men or charming failures, actors or artists, judges or criminals – but at twelve years old they had opted for the glamour and prestige of a Naval career and the Navy never gave them the chance to change their minds. A mixture of savage discipline, ruthless mental processing and the simultaneous development of extreme idealism produced a standard young Naval Officer for the Fleet, which then continued the process. Few, very few, total misfits fell by the wayside. The remainder emerged toughened, strengthened and good. Their professional standards and their devotion to duty were of the highest order. They accepted themselves as Naval Officers unthinkingly because they had never had the opportunity to consider anything else but under the imposed veneer were the men who could have made a success of so many other things and this brought a rich variety of character and intellect to the Royal Navy which was markedly lacking in the other two services.

Now, naive and vulnerable, thirty-seven thirteen-year-olds faced The System.

The Exmouth Term had 'got fell in' at the Sandquay landing stage below the College. The first day of the Summer Term was unseasonably hot but the regulations required us to join in British Warms (summer and white cap covers did not start till 1 May and on 30 April it was therefore still winter) and, in these heavy coats and our unaccustomed stiff white collars and big boots, clutching our suitcases, we started the long march up the countless stone steps of the steep hillside. By the time we reached the top we were soaked with sweat and already exhausted.

The Exmouths were marched straight to the dormitory to dump their suitcases and I sank down wearily on my bed.

'GERRUP,' roared the Chief. 'Gawd, what's the matter with you, then? Tired already? You aren't even started yet! Down to the gunroom, all of you. Come on then. MOVE YOURSELVES! SHAKE UP!'

We hurried down to the gunroom, a large square room with wooden floors and backless benches. This was to be our home. Here we settled and were addressed by Those Set In Authority Over Us.

First CPO Taylor, his square shoulders set, his fierce voice entirely belied by the very human twinkle in his kindly, tired old eyes. Now, pay attention. We were to call him Chief. If we treated him fairly we'd find he was all right. If we didn't – he paused for a threat which failed entirely to materialise. If we were in any trouble or wanted advice we should always go to him. Now sit up smart because the Commissioned Gunner was going to have a word with us.

The Commissioned Gunner came in and the Exmouths froze alertly. The Commissioned Gunner had that effect.

Now, pay attention . . . We were in the Navy now. Childish things were behind us. Discipline. Dig out. Discipline. That was his job and he was a terror. But if we played ball with him we'd find he was all right. If we didn't – he paused, glared round and the message came through loud and clear. Meanwhile, if we were ever in any trouble or wanted advice we only had to get fell in outside his office and he'd deal with the problem. Now sit up smart because our Term Officer was going to address us.

'Poop' Edwards came in with the mystique of two and a half stripes. Spry, alert, immaculate and gentle by nature among term officers who sprouted fierce 'buggers' grips' on either cheek and chased their terms mercilessly.

'Now, pay attention,' he began. He was our Term Officer – in sole charge of our training, our wellbeing and our welfare. We'd find it all pretty hard at first but we had to learn discipline. We were in the Navy now and childish things were behind us. We were Exmouths. The Exmouths had always been the best term in the college. We must be too. Meanwhile, if we were ever in trouble we must never hesitate to come to him at once. His cabin door would always be open to those who wished to see him. He meant it. Dear Poop: too kind and too gentle to go far in the Service. But, when he left us after that first talk, every new Exmouth felt he had a substitute father in this strange and frightening place.

Finally Nicholls stood up. Tall, dark, composed. Going To Sea in the Summer.

Right, pay attention. Life and routine in the College. There are eleven terms each named after a famous Admiral. The others are Grenville, Hawke, Blake, Drake, St Vincent, Duncan, Rodney, Hood, Benbow and Anson. He was an Anson. Favell, our Cadet Captain and his assistant, was a Hood. There was no Nelson term to avoid jealousy. Nelson was too great. Each college term we would move up one gunroom until, in our sixth term, we left the Junior College and became Senior College. The five terms comprising the junior college lived in D Block, their gunrooms lining the long passage outside in ascending order of seniority. When we moved down that passage we would be passing senior terms' gunrooms and when we did that WE DOUBLED. The lavatory was called the 'Heads'.

We would wear lanyards round our collars, ends tucked into breast pockets with our keyrings on them. As we got more senior, the knots in our lanyards would be lowered so that the length of the bight to the knot indicated a cadet's seniority. He had no doubt that we understood that, as first termers, our lanyards should nearly choke us. We had no pockets in anything except our blazers. Hands in pockets of blazers was the privilege of the Senior College.

Blazer collars could only be turned up by the Senior Term and members of college teams.

Finally, discipline. He and Favell carried little notebooks. Every minor transgression was noted and the transgressor given a Tick. When we had gained four Ticks we would be beaten with four cuts of a cane the first time and with six thereafter. Most important of all was guff. Failure to double smartly past a senior gunroom was guff. To wear white shorts when rowing or blue shorts when sailing was guff. Hands in blazer pockets or a collar turned up was guff. To stand in one particular part of the Quarterdeck gallery was guff and so was any conduct liable to incur the displeasure of a senior cadet. Speaking under any circumstances to a senior cadet was guff of the most formidable. Guff was the responsibility of the two Chief Cadet Captains alone. There was no excuse and no appeal. If one committed guff the Chief Cadet Captain would arrive one night, the culprit would be turned out of bed and six cuts would be delivered on the spot. Guff was Mortal Sin.

We probably realised we had joined one day before the rest of the college. This was because the new term started with Divisions on the Parade Ground the first morning and by then the Exmouths must look like proper cadets and not like a bunch of dressed up schoolboys. So we would now adjourn to the parade ground to be licked into some sort of shape so that he could hold up his head among his friends when they returned the next evening. Now – Move. Come on. Shake up.

The Parade Ground and the Parade Ground staff . . . Get fell in. Tallest on the right, shortest on the left. Quick march, double march. Halt. About turn. Quick march. DRESS BY THE RIGHT. Head up, chin in, chest out, stomach in, left, right, left, right, left, right. Halt. Stand still. By the right, quick – wait for it – . . . MARCH. Heads up. Swing them arms. Bags of bull then. Oh my Gawd! HALT. ''Ow are we ever going to face the College?' The Commissioned Gunner almost in tears. Many of the Exmouths too, soft feet blistering in the big, unaccustomed boots, the stiff white collars now limp.

Supper. Happy old pensioner steward. ''Ere y'are then, me lucky lads . . . The Roast Beef of Old England . . .' Supper at prep school was nothing like this. This was Master's food. We were grown up. We were in the Navy now . . .

Afterwards Nicholls continued our instruction. 'This is the wash place. That's the cold plunge. You start every day by jumping into it and I want to see you come out wet all over. Toilet gear here. Soap on the left. Toothbrush on the tumbler facing east and west.' (Which was north even?)

Back to the dormitory where we learned how to fold and stow our clothes in our sea chests – an immaculate display which would have impressed even the Guards. Then the chests lined up plumb line straight. Finally the windows.

'Half open north. Shut south.' At exactly twenty-five minutes past nine – 'Say your prayers.' The Exmouths knelt reverently by their beds. At exactly half past nine – 'Turn in.' Finally, some minutes later, 'Books away. Lie down.' We lay rigidly to attention on our backs as the Officer of the Day appeared for Rounds and the measured tread of the little procession passed down the centre gangway of the dormitory.

Then, at last, the lights turned off. Soon we learned that the worst part of the day, the beatings, started then. But that first night, in our innocence, we relaxed between the sheets.

Already we had changed from the erstwhile prep school boys of that morning on Paddington station. We had new values and new expressions. We were mentally and physically exhausted and yet exalted too. We were suddenly no longer children. We were in the Navy now . . . It was going to be tough but that was what we wanted. In the morning we would dress in uniform, in blue and gold, the colours of the sea. All life ahead was our chosen adventure. Meanwhile the Exmouths slept.

The bugle call Reveille (which must be pronounced 'Revally' said Nicholls) woke us in the morning, followed instantaneously by CPO Taylor's single bellow of 'TURROUT!' A cold plunge (we had yet to learn how it could be faked, particularly in the icy depths of winter). Breakfast and the Parade Ground again. Tours of the College learning our way around – and back to the Parade Ground. Then off to the piano and sing a scale. Half a dozen new trebles for the church choir. And back to the Parade Ground.

By tea time we were marching like a drill squad of eager little penguins, arms swinging stiffly high above the shoulder, eyes almost shut with our grim concentration, bodies rigid and jerky with effort and pride. The lovely, slow and relaxed Naval marching would develop over the years but this was a beginning. We would do for Divisions next day – just.

That evening the rest of the Cadets returned and suddenly the College, which we had almost begun to think of as ours alone, came to life. The long passages filled with formidable looking senior cadets, strange officers and masters. We observed that cadet seniority could be gauged by the lowness of the lanyard, the shortness and tightness of white flannel trousers which shrank in the wash as their owners' legs grew, and the battered, seaworn appearance of the caps. Really senior cadets spliced extra pieces into their lanyards so that they could be worn even lower and longer than God had intended and their gold cap badges had weathered to the colour of old pewter. To lower the knots of our lanyards by a millimetre would be guff and so unthinkable whilst our trousers had yet to meet their first soap suds and hung overlong and flowing round our great boots. But our caps . . .! Suddenly the glorious sight on the Gieves piano became a symbol not of glamour but of

Aged 13. The Gieves Cap.

newness and we started playing football with the beautiful things across the gunroom floor and rubbing the golden badges on our sleeves to take away the blatant lustre . . .

Slowly time gained momentum and the days began to slip by. The routine became routine. Thirty-seven small boys became thirty-seven cadets who were, indeed, The Exmouth Term – a corporate body with a mind and soul of its own. And as we settled down, so the standard was raised and tightened. Ticks began to shower upon us and each evening, after 'Books away – lie down,' Nicholls and Favell advanced grimly down the dormitory with their fell little notebooks.

'Barnes – your cap badge was crooked at Divisions. Tick!'

'Fraser-Harris – your chest is slack. The socks are crooked. Tick!'

'Blake – you're getting pretty slack generally. You want to shake up – Tick!'

'Anderson – you moved in bed during Rounds last night. Tick!'

Each Term occupied two dormitories separated by a 'flat', or landing, with the Term Officer's cabin and steps leading down to the wash basins, lavatories and showers. This 'flat' was the seat of justice. The Hawkes – third term, tough and ineffably senior – were directly below us and took only some ten days to earn their first punishment. As we were dozing off we were jerked awake by the horrible sound, like a juicy muffled whip crack, of a cane biting into a taut behind. One, two, three, four, five, six. Measured and slow the cuts fell and the sound came loudly up a double flight of stairs, across the flat, through the door and down the whole length of the dormitory. Four beatings in all and then merciful silence. Suddenly, Ticks mattered. Night after night we lay awake listening to the Hawkes being beaten – and then our own turn came.

Luckily for the Exmouths, 'Poop' Edwards held to the lonely view that merciless beating of small boys was not necessarily good for their souls and he had restricted first beatings to only two cuts and subsequent ones to four – though even he was powerless to prevent the mandatory Chief Cadet Captains' six cuts for guff.

However, from the nature of the system, the more carefree and happy-go-lucky Exmouths soon clocked up four Ticks and then another four and we got quickly into the habit of lying rigid in bed after Rounds, watching the light in the flat between the two dormitories. Until it was turned off we could not be sure that beatings were over for the night and we were safe to go to sleep. One could well be beaten for many offences without the formality of earning all four Ticks and, until the light was switched out, we were all vulnerable. On rare occasions it was left on by mistake and then nobody slept till merciful exhaustion took over.

After I had earned three Ticks I found the strain of waiting for the fourth unbearable. All the next day I heard in my mind the sickening sounds of the nightly executions. By now the Exmouths were well away and the Hawkes seemed to be beaten in mass, six cuts after six cuts resounding through the Block.

That night, I brought things deliberately to a head. After cleaning my teeth, sick with guilt, I placed my brush on the tumbler facing west and east instead of east and west. Then I turned in and lay waiting for outraged justice to descend.

Favell appeared at the far end of the dormitory and made his slow way from bed to bed, dispensing Ticks as he went.

'Anderson, your toothbrush is facing west and east.'

'Yes, Favell.'

'Tick!'

'Yes, Favell.'

So this was it. Uninterestedly I watched Nicholls make his rounds. Suddenly he was beside my bed.

'Anderson, your D.194* was sculling round the gunroom.'

I could only stare at him in horror.

'Tick!'

Merciful God – I had five!

Rounds came and went. The dormitory lights went off. Those in the flat stayed on. I lay and trembled. Alphabetically, I should be first. Someone else was called. Several beatings. The lights went off. I had not been called. They had not had time to add up the latest Ticks.

Next day my shame, guilt, fear and anxiety over-rode prudence and I told Nicholls what I had done. The day dragged interminably till 'Say your prayers,' 'Turn in,' and 'Books away, lie down.'

Rounds.

The dormitory lights out and the door shut. Flat light left on.

The door opened.

'Anderson, turn out.'

I hopped out of bed and went through the opening ceremonial.

Feet into the open-heeled canvas slippers. Slap slap of slippers running down the suddenly interminable centre gangway between the chests. Favell holding the door open for me (unusual courtesy!) Nicholls tall and disapproving holding The Cane – bamboo nearly as thick as his little finger. Attention in front of Nicholls. Trembling uncontrollably.

'Anderson. You've been pretty slack. You've got four Ticks That's two

---

* *a small note book*

cuts for a first beating. But you've got five which should make it another four cuts. And not only that, you got your fifth Tick deliberately by flagrant and wilful disobedience of orders. I'm not sure it's not mutiny. Do you realise under the Naval Discipline Act you can be shot for that? Even if it's not mutiny it's certainly guff [worse, much worse!]. So I reckon you should have twelve cuts at least. However, since it's your first beating I must follow your Term Officer's policy. Two cuts. Bend over. That's not good enough. Touch your toes.'

A pause, then a sudden anguish of liquid fire across my pyjama clad behind. Then the same again and it was over.

'Turn in.'

I had been told by some misbegotten humorist that Cadet Captains admired you if you showed your nonchalance by going for a pee after a beating.

'Nicholls, may I go to the Heads first, please?'

Blank amazement on Nicholls' face.

'I suppose so.'

I went.

That morning we had had our first fainting at Divisions and when I got back to the dormitory everyone thought I, too, had fainted. Explanations left me a term hero. Next day when we all bathed (naked) in the college swimming baths I, too, had joined the club of the average junior college cadet whose backside carried the great purple, yellow, black or blue welts of the cane. From that night on until my seventh term I never went to bed without asking the Cadet Captains whether I had done anything during the day to earn a beating. Neither they nor I saw anything remarkable in the question.

There was one more arrow in the disciplinary quiver which, like beating, thirteen-, fourteen- and fifteen-year-old cadets could not avoid. This was the Term 'strafe' and it came to us in about the fifth week of our first term.

After prep, instead of being left to make our usual noisy way to bed, Nicholls stood up to address us in the gunroom.

We had, it appeared, become generally slack. Our discipline was slack. Our marching was slack. Our appearance was slack. Our lanyards were too low. Our self esteem was too high. So we were going to have a strafe. From that moment, no more Ticks would be given. An offence, no matter how minor, would be visited by a beating and it would consist of six cuts. Our breakfast period the next morning, and our dinner hour, would be spent on the Parade Ground after the hastiest of meals. Every spare minute of the day (such as we had) would be equally constructively filled. In the meantime, we had exactly five minutes to be turned in. CARRY ON! SHAKE UP!

A blackguard rush from the gunroom and up the stairs to the dormitory. Clothes wrenched off and immaculately folded according to the requirements.

Exactly five minutes by stop-watch, the last Exmouth scrambling into bed. Both Cadet Captains inspecting the chests, picking up the most minute defects. Then two minutes to be dressed in daily uniform. Another inspection. A cap badge crooked. Several lanyards too low. A boot not tightly laced and tied.

Two minutes to shift into blue sports rig.

One minute into white sports rig.

Three minutes to shift into blues (the extra minute to allow for the still unfamiliar stiff white collar). By the time it was finished our chests were a shambles of unfolded clothes frenziedly hurled off as we changed. Ten minutes to be turned in. And we needed every one of them to get our entire wardrobe folded back into place as neatly as if it had just arrived from Gieves. Another inspection of the result and, finally, the flat light left on after rounds and a long time passing before darkness and silence. Strafes lasted two or three days and, at the end, we were sore bottomed and mentally and physically exhausted.

It was tough. Indeed it was very tough. But it did us no harm. Beatings and strafes were accepted as a necessary part of the new life to which we were still totally dedicated. In every other way our idealism was carefully cultivated. 'When You Get To Sea' was the leitmotif of all our instructors' lectures. 'When you get to sea, of course, you'll find this and that' . . . Seamanship was learned in the Seamanship room with its huge working models of a battleship's forecastle or down on the Dart under oars and sail. The Engineering workshops were superbly equipped and there we did our practical work, interspersed with lectures on everything from boiler tubes to ventilation systems. All that we should meet 'When We Got To Sea'. From every window one seemed to look out across the entrance to the Dart. There were the two big white troopships waiting for autumn and the trooping season to the furthest corners of the Empire. In the vee of the Devon hills, blue and infinitely tantalising, lay The Sea.

Nicholls and the Ansons went off for a cruise in *Forres*, the old sloop attached to the College, and came back green with sea sickness but infused with new glamour. As the Summer Term drew to its close, they were allowed to wear their sea-going cadets' uniform. Real superfine like the Term Officers wore with pockets in the reefer and slits at the back. The Eleventh Term Ansons were nearly there – living proof that a time would come when we too, like the last Exmouths, would really Get To Sea.

On the last night of our first term, my ticket to Ireland in my private till, it swept over me that I was leaving Dartmouth and going home. It would be nice. It would be splendid. But quite overcoming my pleasure was, somehow, the unreasoning fear that something might happen to prevent my returning. I had passed into the Navy. I had lasted my first term. But I still felt I only had my toe in the door. To return in my own right, to have new Ansons doubling past the Exmouth gunroom, not till all this had come to pass could I really feel I belonged. At the end of my first term, my highest ambition in the Navy was to return for my second.

There was always a carrot round the corner at Dartmouth and as the terms slipped by the stick grew less. By the fifth term, we had stood all we could of beatings, strafes, D Block and the Junior College. But now the Senior College opened its arms to the Exmouths. This offered not only an infinity of new dignity, epitomised by our being able to put our hands in our blazer pockets, but was marked by two major events in our careers. Firstly, we gained a new Term Officer. Secondly, we crashed through the adolescent barrier into puberty.

The passing of 'Poop' was a moment of genuine sorrow to the whole Exmouth Term. By Dartmouth standards he had been very gentle and the obvious kindliness and sympathy of the man had been our strength and shield in our early terms. But now we had grown old enough to need a stronger hand. It was at this psychological moment that Poop left us and St John Cronyn arrived.

St John Cronyn was a short, stout, infuriated tub of a man, his purple face topped by an equally purple bald dome, fringed with a sort of bristling monk's tonsure. His flow of obscene language was a spray of abuse which galvanised us into activity at the same time as it delighted us. His gin bill was reputed to be astronomical and he was a seaman to the ultimate of his being.

A story was told of him that, serving on the Mediterranean station, he had suffered greatly from toothache but refused to allow the errant tooth to be extracted. Eventually, he went down with tonsillitis and entered the Naval Hospital at Bighi to have his tonsils removed. The crafty dentist crept in and, while the formidable patient was safely under the anaesthetic, seized the opportunity to whip out the cause of the dental trouble while the doctor got at the tonsils. Cronyn never forgave the medical profession nor trusted them again. Finally, the time approached for him to go home. Traditionally, he stood on the Quarterdeck looking across Grand Harbour to the alluringly lit P&O liners, with the soft notes of dance music floating across the water and filled, everyone knew, with beautiful planters' daughters who would solace hungry Naval Officers going home. Soon his turn would come – and then he went down with appendicitis. He was taken back to Bighi and wheeled once again into the familiar operating theatre. The surgeon lifted the sheet, scalpel in hand and there, tied to the only possible place, was a large P&O label – 'Wanted on Voyage'.

This, then, was the officer who had come to relieve Poop Edwards. He took us down to the river to see what we were made of. I found myself bowman of a whaler with a large, plump Exmouth at the tiller. The wind was strong – stronger than would have been considered safe before but this was St John Cronyn. Cronyn called us alongside the pontoon and we altered course accordingly. We were running free, right before the wind, and we were going fast. The gap of water narrowed and narrowed as I stood placidly in the bows with a boat hook waiting for the moment when the mainsail would be lowered and the boat, losing way, turned neatly round and alongside. Still we tore at the jetty with no orders from the coxswain. I turned enquiringly and saw him sitting rigid, his face a frozen mask of horror, literally paralysed with fright and quite unable to speak or move as the terrible thing which was about to happen struck home to his helpless mind.

We hit the jetty at right angles still going fast. I was catapulted straight ashore, masts and sails came down with a crash and the water began to lap lethargically in through the large hole in what had been the bow.

On hands and knees I looked up at St John Cronyn standing above me. He had not moved but he was even more puce than usual. In a soft whisper he began. 'Jesus Whipped . . .!' The voice rose slowly to a scream of splendid and terrible abuse. The Chief Yeoman stood behind him with a rapt look in his eyes, his lips moving silently as he memorised some of the better words and phrases. The cadet coxswain cringed beside his tiller as the tide took over and carried the sinking whaler slowly away. I stayed where I was. It seemed safer.

Finally, the outburst ended and a nervous Exmouth who had been waiting anxiously in the background stepped forward and gave his best salute.

'Sir,' he said, 'One of the blueboats has lost its oars and is drifting down river to sea.'

Cronyn regarded him with real interest for a moment. Then, 'You have a face like a pancake,' he said conversationally and walked away.

That night he addressed us in the gunroom. We were useless, hopeless, horrible ullages. We had the mentality that signalled the Admiralty, 'Am being fired at. Request Instructions.' In future, cutters would sail with a reduced crew of four and without a rudder. Whalers' crews would consist of two cadets only. We were going to become seamen if he killed us in the attempt which certainly wouldn't kill him. As for beatings he had no use for continuous minor corporal punishment. No Exmouth would be beaten in future unless he'd really asked for it. For anyone who did, the minimum would be twelve cuts.

From that minute onwards, the Exmouth Term took a great leap upwards in performance and morale. He made us really good and we knew how good we were. Self confidence, seamanship and *esprit de corps* were our hallmarks.

We were experiencing our first lesson in great leadership.

Puberty came with nearly as big a shock. There was little homosexuality at Dartmouth because the system prevented it. Even the term above us, only four months older, was completely cut off by the barriers of guff. We doubled past their gunroom. We never spoke to them. There was no contact with cadets outside our own term at all.

The result was that we developed together. What was good was 'clean'. A cadet who grew up a little early was 'foul'. We were not foul. We were a clean term. We found our 'foul' element totally repugnant.

Then, one evening, in the gunroom, one of the 'foul' Exmouths was seen showing something to his cronies. It turned out to be a nudist magazine. There was a sudden explosion of emotion and lynch law developed among the infuriated mob. The magazine was ceremonially burned. The Cadet Captain's sea chest was raided, his cane procured and we beat the owner of the foul publication. Then we turned on another cadet whose bed had been creaking nightly after the lights were turned out and we beat him too. We were the outraged, excited, fascinated mob which had once burned martyrs and our cause too was overtly religious. But it tipped us over the edge. Next morning nothing was said about the outburst but, overnight, the Exmouths, as a term, had become 'foul'.

Foul perhaps because age had overtaken us. But we remained as idealistic as ever beneath it all. Beside our gunroom was the beautiful chapel and, in the flat outside, the College War Memorial. I stood there alone one Sunday evening and looked at the names in the Book of Remembrance. In World War I, the college had been cleared and all cadets had gone straight to sea at the commencement of hostilities. Here in the book were their names and the ages when death came to them.

Name after name of fifteen-year-old boys, beautifully inscribed in the hallowed pages. I looked and thought. They were my age. It could have been us – the Exmouths. I thought of my friends and a lump came into my throat. Thank God that in 1932 war was unthinkable. But what a Service and what a cause to serve. I felt humble yet inspired as, later, I stood in front of the long dormitory mirror where we normally stood in threes, squashing the spots on our faces. I looked not at my face but at my uniform. The lanyard half way down. The battered cap with its pewter coloured badge. All that was now me. I felt deeply thankful for the proud path I had chosen to follow.

Our Senior year came and the best of us were chosen to be Cadet Captains for other terms. In our last term, we faced the horrors of the Passing Out exam which covered the whole syllabus for all we had learned our whole time at the College and so was a fairly demanding academic hurdle. The words 'When You Get To Sea' took on a new meaning.

On Sundays, the Senior College went to farms. Each farm was held inviolate by the group of cadets who always went there and when one Went To Sea one turned one's farm over to the fifth term who were about to enter the Senior College. At first we played the gramophone, sat in a Devon parlour by a roaring log fire and ate a huge tea of scrambled eggs, bread, jam and a vast bowl of Devon cream. The room and the tea cost two shillings a head. Now, however, beer appeared after tea, surreptitious smoking took place and the first whispers came of Mr Niblock's Secret. Mr Niblock, the formidable Commissioned Gunner, had, it appeared, a secret which he divulged to cadets on their last evening in the College before they Went To Sea. Security was so important that even the existence of the secret must not be discussed outside the Senior Term. It fascinated us and even the Passing Out exam paled into insignificance.

Our sea-going uniforms came and the Exmouths strolled past lesser gunrooms followed by worshipping eyes. A hand, slipped casually into a reefer pocket, drew an almost audible sigh. Our lanyards hung deep down to our navels. Our gunroom lockers were covered with virtually every silver cup and trophy the College had to offer. The Exmouths had indeed been a good all-round term and Poop would have been proud of us.

On the last night of all, the Passing Out exam over, our trunks packed and the College virtually behind us, we were sent for one at a time by the Commissioned Gunner.

The lights inside the big Main Entrance where he had his office were turned low and the shadowy Quarterdeck, with its statue of the King between the two Colours, was in gloom. Alone, Mr Niblock sat in his sanctum with one light low on his desk.

'Anderson. Shut the door. Come here.'

I tiptoed across to stand beside him. Now I had truly finished with Dartmouth. I was about to learn Mr Niblock's secret.

Slowly and with infinite mystery he opened a drawer and took out a large, black, shining object shaped like a rugger ball with a flat end. Reverently we both regarded it.

'Do you know what it is?'

'No, sir.'

'That,' said the Commissioned Gunner, 'is an elephant's testicle. You may touch it,' he added simply.

Awestruck, I put my hand on this desirable trophy and felt a sort of soft hardness.

'Send in Barnes,' said Mr Niblock as I crept, respectfully, away

It was not till we reached the West Indies two months later that I found elephants' testicles, coloured green, all over every coconut tree.

Chapter 2

HMS FROBISHER

Just seventeen, the Exmouth Term joined the Cadet Training Cruiser, HMS *Frobisher*, in early January 1934. Chatham dockyard was a dirty litter in the rain but, to us, our ship looked superb.

We shambled up the gangway, drinking in the newness of it all, to be greeted by an infuriated little Gunner's Mate on the Quarterdeck.

'Get fell in!' he was yelling. 'Come on, move yourselves. Salute the gangway then. Pick yer feet up. Move.'

Automatically, the Exmouths got fell in. This was old, familiar stuff. But now, besides us, were new, strange faces. Cadets with gleaming gold cap badges and caps which still looked wrong on their heads. Cadets who had obviously never learned to salute anything, let alone a gangway as we had instinctively done. These were the 'Pubs', the special eighteen-year-old direct entry straight from public schools. As green to the Navy as the Exmouths had been what seemed so many years before.

Petty Officer Mould, the Gunner's Mate, was barking, yapping and nipping like an angry little sheep dog herding peculiarly stupid and slothful sheep and gradually he got us sorted out. Port Watch and Starboard Watch. Parts of Ship. Foretop, Maintop, Forecastle and Quarterdeck men. Guns' crews. Abandon ship stations. By the time he had finished even the Exmouths were bemused but we soon sorted things out. For the Pubs life was agony.

The second afternoon, leave was given in the dog watches from four o'clock to seven o'clock. This symbolised our new status. At the College all towns, even Dartmouth, had been strictly out of bounds. To go ashore to the exotic temptations of Chatham on a winter's afternoon was indeed emancipation.

On the way back, I got lost in the dockyard. At first I was not worried but as time slipped by I realised I was in danger of that ultimate in Naval sins, breaking my leave. I began to run and became more lost than ever.

Darkness had fallen and the rain teemed down. Tripping over railway lines, knocking into bollards in the gloom, falling over wires, I fled about the yard until I turned a corner and there, thankfully, was *Frobisher*'s gangway. Up I sped to be greeted by the small, sinister figure at the top.

'Yer late!'

'Yes, Petty Officer Mould.'

'Yer three minutes late!'

'Yes, Petty Officer Mould.'

'Get fell in on the Quarterdeck.'

I was a defaulter, a leave breaker, a man with a mark on his conduct sheet. Still sobbing for breath I repaired aft. A pause, then Petty Officer Mould appeared with the Officer of the Watch.

'Cadet Anderson, OFF CAPS! Cadet Anderson, sir. Did remain absent over leave three minutes, namely from 1900 to 1903.' The Officer of the Watch was my Divisional Officer. He looked at me and took in the soaked figure, the flushed cheeks, the still panting breath, the agonised, shamed eyes.

'Petty Officer Mould, what time do you make it?'

PO Mould looked at his watch. 'Eleven minutes past seven, sir.'

The Officer of the Watch consulted his own wrist. 'I make it exactly eight minutes past. I think you're a little fast.' He glared at me. 'Don't run things so tight again. We can't have this sort of slackness when we get to sea. Case dismissed.'

'Cadet Anderson, ON CAP. Case dismissed. Right turn. Double March.'

Behind my back Petty Officer Mould tore off his gunnery salute to the Officer of the Watch and their eyes twinkled. Both understood each other perfectly.

We sailed the next day, the cadets working the ship, or rather the Dartmouth cadets working ship after a fashion and the Pubs getting in everyone's light. We felt very proud of ourselves until we cleared the Medway and met a full gale in the Channel. After that, class consciousness fell away as we were all impartially sick.

For four days and nights I ate nothing and learned only that one can still vomit with an empty stomach.

At half-past five every morning, 'Reveille' went on the bugle and the voice of Petty Officer Mould was loud on the messdeck. ''Eave oh, 'eave oh, 'eave oh, lash up and stow. Wakey, wakey, wakey, rise and shine, the morning's fine. Come on, me lucky lads, let's 'ave yer. Sun scorching your eyes out! 'Eave oh, 'eave oh, 'eave oh! Show a leg and shine!' Stumbling out of our pits we lashed up our hammocks with the regulation seven turns and went up on deck into the howling darkness as 'Both Watches for Exercise' was piped.

'Scrub forrard. Scrub aft.' Petty Officer Hendy, the foretop PO, walked in front of us, sluicing the deck with a fire hose. A draggled, vomiting line of miserable cadets followed him, blue with cold, scrubbers hardly moving in

When the gap of water widens . . . Frobisher sails for West Indies

their shaking hands.

'Come on then, lads, put some weight behind it. Keep in line. Scrub forrard. Scrub aft.'

On the fifth morning I was able to take some steaming hot cocoa and a rock hard ship's biscuit before going up to Both Watches. Suddenly the sea air seemed crisp and splendid and I found I was feeling well.

As we got our squeegees out to mop up the decks, a breathtakingly beautiful dawn broke across the horizon and the darkness of night became suffused with a wonderful array of reds and golds and yellows. I stared entranced at the sheer glory of it – and realised that two sailors were also standing beside me, leaning on the handles of their squeegees, watching.

The great, tossing, turbulent Atlantic waves slowly became visible as we stood there, silent and awed in the face of so much beauty. I waited to see how they would express the deep emotion I felt. There was a long silence. Then:

'F-----g sun,' said one.

'The bastard,' replied his mate. Had I learned something?

Gradually the weather improved, the sun shone on blue waters, the first flying fish appeared and we gave up thick blue seaman's sweaters for a white shirt and shorts. At night, the messdeck was deserted and we slept on the upper deck.

Petty Officer Hendy was delighted and, once a week, instead of scrubbing decks we holystoned them. This consisted of the row of cadets on their knees, clutching the holystones in their hands and scrubbing the deck with them as Petty Officer Hendy backed slowly in front, hose in one hand and great gobs of sand in the other which he spread liberally on the wet teak, chanting as he did so, 'Little drops of water, little grains of sand. Give 'em to the caydets and they make the decks look grand.' The sailors sang ''Oly, 'oly, 'oly every Friday morning. Down on our f-----g knees our song shall rise to thee . . .' Or, sometimes, 'The sea is His and He can have it for His hands prefer the dry land . . .'

The foretop locker was presided over by an old 'stripey', Able Seaman Foad, fearsomely tattooed and known as the Loch Ness Monster. He dispensed cleaning gear – bluebell for brightwork, cotton waste, buckets, scrubbers and holystones. He also dispensed good advice and old sailor's yarns. Lucky indeed was the day spent sitting at Able Seaman's Foad's knee helping him with a wire splice.

Silly questions got short answers. 'Please, Able Seaman Foad, why does Admiralty Brown* have one side all rough and the other glazed and shiny?' 'One side's for Officers, son, the other for matelots.' But normally he was a

---

* *issue toilet paper*

veritable fountain of philosophy and good advice.

'You remember, lad, wot matters is keeping of yourself clean. You'll see a smartly dressed matelot going ashore, bell bottoms flapping, but if 'e ain't lived clean – oh, young sir, wot 'orrible things them trousers do conceal! Every leave I goes home to my poor ol' f-----g widdered mother and she says "'Arold. 'Ave you bin clean?" And I says "Yes, ma." And I've always bin able to. But you, you're a young Officer. And you remember that Officers can go anywhere matelots can and a lot of places matelots can't. And them's the worst ones 'alf the time. But if you can go 'ome and face your f-----g mother and say you've been clean you'll be doin' all right, lad.' His foretop locker held a big sign: 'Work like Helen B. Merry' and he had been all round the world but hardly ever set foot on foreign soil. He was a 'dhoby firm' in every ship he went to and, while his mess mates went ashore, he stayed on board making a few pennies extra by washing their clothes in a bucket on the Upper Deck.

We had left Chatham on a wet and windy day in January and we spent two long weeks crossing the Atlantic till we felt we had been at sea all our lives. Then, one forenoon, we came to Trinidad. The sea was a flat, glazed blue. The sun beat down from a cloudless sky. Ahead, the first misty suggestion of land showed on the horizon. I climbed to the foretop and watched, delighted, as we threaded our way through small green islands covered with palm trees and fringed with white beaches. No sailor can ever have lived who does not remember vividly the magic of his first tropical landfall.

Anchored in the harbour, Quarterdeck awnings were spread and the duty cadets dressed in their gleamingly new white uniforms. Around us gathered a crowd of bumboats full of laughing, black faces. Ashore, dominating the town, floated a Union Jack. We had made an interminable journey across the changing faces of the sea, England and all our past seemed another lifetime altogether, a new, more colourful, world was about us – and that old, familiar flag was still there. It was quite the most overwhelming impression of them all and my first understanding of Empire.

First run ashore in our cadets' shoregoing plain clothes 'uniform' of blue blazers and grey flannel trousers. Black hands thrusting shark bone walking sticks, coral bowls and seaweed fans in our faces. Black urchins about seven or eight years old dancing round us crying, ''Allo Johnny. You f--k? Then f--k off!' and going into peals of laughter. Others earnestly offering us their sisters. 'Very clean, Captain. Very good. Very jig a jig. You like, eh?' The Exmouths were faintly shocked but tried to look worldly.

In Barbados I had my first, very innocent, love affair with a shy girl who thought that when I suggested leaving the dance to look at the stars that was all I had in mind and then felt so embarrassed at her own naivety that she kissed me without being asked instead of resisting an advance I should never have known how to make anyway.

By the time the cruise was over, we had visited many of the West Indian islands. We had attended cocktail parties on board and ashore, disported ourselves on Caribbean beaches, learned how to bargain with the natives, danced at Governor's balls held in our honour, landed as a battalion under arms in a tropical dawn, found ourselves drunk on unaccustomed rum punches and gin slings, and grown from boys to young men.

When we sailed for home we had found our sealegs and we were relatively useful members of the ship's company. The ratings now accepted us as fellow workers who could do their fair share of the day's chores and cadets, sailors and marines laboured affably together on terms of mutual affection and respect. We talked, laughed, argued, questioned and discussed. And all the time we learned about the Navy, our job and the men we should one day lead.

But one thing only the sea could teach us and this lesson we learned half way across the wintry Atlantic Ocean. The glass began to drop horribly, the wind to rise. All through the night the motion increased and by dawn we found ourselves in a world gone mad. Vast towers of rushing water bore down on the ship and flung the cruiser physically sideways. Nobody was allowed on the wrecked upper deck and all unnecessary work came to a halt. It was the worst Atlantic storm for thirty years and all day we lay wedged into whatever safe corners we could find, listening to the hideous din of wind, sea and the smashed furniture and crockery which went crashing from side to side as the ship lurched, pitched and rolled. This was weather to make mere seasickness laughable. We started tired from a sleepless night, we became hungry when meals were impossible to produce, we went on to sheer physical and mental exhaustion from the actual strength and effort involved in holding on in this lurching, noisy madhouse of a ship. We entered the last stage of thin hysteria where we wanted to scream out loud for just one moment of sanity, of quiet, of a still, steady world where one could dare to let go and even stand up.

The aftermath of the storm found the weary survivors emerging to view, startled, the shambles of what had been our immaculate *Frobisher*. Through the wreckage went the Commander and his Chief Boatswain's Mate, axes in hand, smashing in the bottom of the few remaining undamaged boats. At least, when we entered the Fleet Regatta, all our boats would be new.

The Exmouths did one more cruise to the Baltic, where I lost my heart to a beautiful blonde student in Bergen, and then our cadet time was over.

In September, in all the glory of my white midshipman's patches, I joined HMS *Achilles* in the Home Fleet.

Chapter 3

HMS ACHILLES

This is, perhaps, the moment to consider the Fleet in which we were to serve. To put it in perspective, it must be remembered that the Exmouths had gone to Dartmouth only fifteen years after Fisher had finally retired. All Lieutenant Commanders and above had World War I medals and had served in 'Fisher's Navy'. His spirit and his legacies lived on.

Fisher and Beresford had left the Service bitterly divided into opposing camps. Indeed, it is hard to see how the Navy had ever earned the title of the 'Silent Service' when one reads the public fulminations, in and out of Parliament, of Lord Charles Beresford, or the bitter autobiographies and published correspondence of Fisher and Percy Scott. All the megalomania and spite at the highest levels of the Service were paraded before an avid readership in the Press.

The result of the reaction to this state of affairs was that, to my generation, the Press, publicity and politics were anathema. Even more so, criticism of a senior officer or his decisions was considered unpardonable disloyalty.

Perhaps no great revolution is achieved without extremism. Fisher was certainly an extremist but he had 'dragged the Navy into the twentieth century by the scruff of its neck' and his reforms, and those of Percy Scott in gunnery, had just managed to turn the decorative Victorian fleet into a reasonably efficient fighting machine. Even so, the Navy, having lost the opportunity offered at Jutland, had ended the war for the first time in remembered history without inflicting a decisive defeat on the enemy.

However, this failure had been glossed over by the glorious moment when the German High Seas Fleet finally steamed into the Forth to surrender and, although the lessons so painfully learned were being studied in Staff Colleges so that the faults would never be repeated, the Navy as a whole remained more than satisfied with itself.

Unfortunately, post war economies and the long years of depression meant that most ships were of wartime vintage and largely obsolescent. Living conditions for the sailors were primitive and, in the older destroyers, even

Officers had no bathroom, while washing for ratings, of bodies and clothing, was usually done from buckets on the Upper Deck.

Food was adequate in the bigger ships where the Paymaster Commander worked out menus and the meals were properly prepared by professional cooks. But the system of 'Canteen messing' in smaller ships left the sailors to provide their own food and its preparation was in the hands of the young, and totally unqualified, rating euphemistically called 'Cook of the Mess'. Moreover the money allowed, but not spent, was returned to the sailors as 'Mess savings'. Poorly paid as they were, the older married men, who naturally had the most influence, preferred to economise on food in order to draw the money. The result was that food in small ships was not only bad but inadequate.

The hierarchy was essentially feudal and enjoyed both the benefits and the faults of such a system. The Officers were the products of Dartmouth and the English public schools, with all their strengths and weaknesses. If, perhaps, some remained mentally as eternal prefects, chasing the fags and retaining all the mores of the sixth form, it can at least be argued that such an attitude built and governed an Empire. It was fine providing you were not one of the fags. The great strength of the average Naval Officer was his idealism, total dedication and complete acceptance that the requirements of the Service took precedence in every way over his own interests, great or small. Among the Officers, the Executive Branch formed an inner elite. Although Paymaster and Engineer Officers were indistinguishable from Executive, apart from their coloured stripes, they were still not eligible to be members of the United Service Club. If a nautical crisis arose in a ship's boat and the Commander (E), the Paymaster Commander and an executive Midshipman were present, it was the Midshipman who would be in command. In the pre-war Navy one knew one's place and woe betide even a wife who stepped into a boat after a lady married to her husband's senior.

The sailors, on the other hand, came from the opposite end of the social spectrum. There was a minority of men from Home Port families with a tradition of Naval service but, mostly, ratings simply joined to avoid the unemployment ashore. In any foreign navy they would have been indoctrinated with the glorious history of their service but, in the Royal Navy, it never occurred to anybody that there might be any benefit from such an unBritish attitude. The mystique of tradition belonged to the Quarterdeck and the Messdecks were left to lump it.

This they did with remarkable fortitude, a certain cynical philosophy and a deliciously sardonic sense of humour. Basically, just as the Officers' background enabled them to give orders naturally, so sailors accepted taking them equally instinctively. The top and the bottom of the class structure have always got on well together. Indeed, the sailors carried the system to extremes.

An incompetent Officer if popular ('a proper gentleman') would have his shortcomings tolerated and would even, to a large extent, be 'carried' by his ratings as far as they could. But the few 'Upper Yardmen', young ratings promoted direct to commissioned rank and always of sterling worth, would find every form of obstructionism placed in their way. ('He's not a proper Officer. He's no better than me!')

The weakness of the system was two-fold. Firstly, although a good Officer was rewarded with an affection and respect out of all proportion, the damage which could be done by a bad Officer was considerable. Some, lacking humility or even basic good manners, adopted an arrogant, bullying attitude which naturally caused extreme resentment in defenceless sailors and, if the culprit was in a key position, could ruin a ship. Others believed that a sharp, aggressive attitude showed their keenness and led to promotion. Certainly, such bad handling of men was no bar to the higher ranks. The ineffable Collard, who had provoked a mutiny in Portsmouth Barracks as a Lieutenant, again became infamous as a Rear Admiral, for the Royal Oak courts martial.

The British working man, well led, is without peer. Badly led, or driven, he can be the most bloodyminded in the world. In ships, unlike the Army, Officers and men must live and work in close company. Where there is good leadership and team spirit, this is an abiding strength but, where there is friction, it is exacerbated by the proximity. Alcohol, apart from the daily tot, was totally prohibited on the mess decks. A noisy, late night Wardroom drinking party could be heard clear across an anchorage. Many Officers believed that sailors appreciated wild conduct on their part and, in happy ships, this was, to some extent, true. In others it simply led to resentment.

The second weakness of the system was that the highest levels had lost touch with sailors' difficulties and opinion. Perhaps this was natural. Modern management techniques had not been dreamed up and, in any case, there was little challenge to Naval management when unemployment ensured a constant supply of manpower which could be dealt with by the Naval Discipline Act.

Industrial psychology was unheard of. Leadership was something born in every good Officer. Driving was a very acceptable substitute. Their Lordships and Wardrooms in general were well satisfied with the state of affairs in the Navy and could foresee no problem. Neither could the Officers of the old Indian Army. They had Cawnpore. We had Invergordon.

It must be stressed, however, that when this unsavoury episode was over everyone wished to forget it as quickly as possible.

Looking back, it is, perhaps, too easy to criticise from modern standards. On the whole, the Fleet was in good heart, morale was high and there were far more happy ships than unhappy ones. The standards were those of the day and, as such, they were accepted. If life was sometimes rough and the cry of the 'Roll on my f----g twelve' too often heard, the Navy was still better than the hunger and hardships of civilian unemployment and, most acid of tests, plenty of ratings signed on for pension, giving a well balanced, experienced rating structure with a hard core of excellent Chief and Petty Officers and splendid old 'Stripeys' like Able Seaman Foad.

The general picture, then, was one of dedicated Officers and highly professional, long service ratings. What the Fleet lacked in efficiency was largely due to factors outside its control.

Behind all shortcomings lay the Treasury dictum, established in 1919 and renewed every year thereafter until 1933, that it must be assumed that 'the British Empire will not be engaged in any great war during the next ten years'. Such a ruling was death to any hope of modernising the Fleet. Apart from destroyers, only the battleships *Rodney* and *Nelson* and five Leander class cruisers had been built since the end of the war-time construction. It also meant that, hampered by the need for economy and with no obvious threat to plan or prepare for, Commanders-in-Chief had no great drive or urgency in their programmes. Training and thinking were still based on the lessons so bitterly learned at Jutland. Some, like the need to fight at night, remained very relevant but, on the whole, the Navy was preparing for another massed Fleet action when there were no suitable enemy battle fleets available to fight. No preparations had been made for the real threat from over and under the sea.

This, then, was the Fleet in which the Exmouths were finally to Go To Sea. I joined *Achilles* on 3 September 1934 and, as I did so, a page of history was already turning. The Treasury dictum had at last been quashed. Hitler was taking power in Germany. New ships were about to come to a Navy which was on the verge of awakening from fifteen years of peacetime sloth and shortage. It was time. There were five years to go to the day.

HMS *Achilles* was lying astern of *Frobisher* in Chatham dockyard when I joined her. Painted in dark Home Fleet grey, businesslike and modern, she was one of the five new Leander class cruisers, four of which made up the Second Cruiser Squadron. I paused on the jetty and eyed her with delight.

For the first time, no cries of 'Get fell in' greeted me as I joined. Instead I was gravely saluted over the gangway and a side boy despatched to collect my luggage from the taxi. I was really an Officer at last. It was a heady experience – but the pride was to be short lived. Junior Midshipmen may have been technically Officers but they were also the only section of the whole Naval community who had no rights at all.

First came a briefing by the Sub Lieutenant, a small, slight, pedantic youth who interviewed the new Midshipmen in his cabin next to the gunroom, fingertips together, a disapproving look on his face. He did not, it appeared, believe in beating 'the young gentlemen', but . . .

The Commander was more direct, for his philosophy was simple. 'You're here to learn,' he said, 'and if you don't you'll remain on board till you do.' Every night a Midshipman went Rounds with the Commander, who had the habit of picking some awkward pipe half hidden in a gloomy corner and demanding to be told its purpose. Ignorance involved an automatic week's stoppage of leave and Junior Midshipmen went ashore very little from *Achilles*. Our Snotties' Nurse was the Navigator, a long, thin, formidable man with the expressionless face and eyes of a snake. He was deeply religious and over his bunk, from which his Midshipman 'doggy' had to turn him out at all hours when at sea, there hung a simple statement: 'This is the day which the Lord hath made. Let us rejoice and be glad in it.' I should have quickly thrown a seaboot at it had I been awoken at irregular intervals night after night, but the Navigator lacked any human weaknesses. He was an ice cold machine with no interests outside the Service and he required from us the same ruthless efficiency he required of himself. When we failed him our leave was stopped. We hated him but we respected him. When we left *Achilles* and suffered from lesser men we learned how good he had been for us. Looking back over the years, I know I can never thank him enough for what he made of such unpromising material.

My first day in the ship, some business took me into the Yard past *Frobisher*.

A diminutive, angry little man was abusing a sheepish group of new Pubs on the Upper Deck. 'Petty Officer Mould,' I hailed delightedly. He turned about, doubled smartly down the gangway, approached, halted and tore off the Whale Island salute. 'SIR!' He stood rigidly to attention, teaching me a last silent lesson. I was an Officer and must behave accordingly. 'Petty Officer Mould' . . . suddenly I was embarrassed and became a little pompous. 'Your voice seems to be getting hoarse. You need a beer. Perhaps you would care to join me in *Achilles* at tot time?'

Another salute. About turn. A scream from the jetty which froze the group of cadets, left at attention. 'Stand STILL!'

He came at noon, and in the *Achilles* gunroom pantry, we drank beer and I let him know how much I had appreciated him. Although our roles were suddenly reversed we could talk freely and now, over a glass, neither side felt the least embarrassment. It was quite natural to us both and neither even thought that it might be a tribute to the Service and its training.

That night I had the luxury of a hammock boy to sling my hammock in the gunroom flat but, beforehand, came the agony of dinner. Like that first day at Dartmouth, once again I was fumbling with an unfamiliar stiff shirt and studs. Another Exmouth had joined with me and we entered the gunroom together and asked for a half pint of bitter, drinking it respectfully in the background while our elders and betters gathered round the Sub. At last we sat down to dine. The Sub rapped the table with his President's gavel and said grace. Soup was served and the Sub paused in his conversation to say, 'Perhaps the atmosphere is a little close. I think we'll have the punkah louvres open.' The Marine attendant turned to the ventilating trunking which ran under the deckhead and opened the three little louvres which directed a blast of fresh air into the Mess. It was, we found, a nightly ritual at dinner and one which was shortly to cost us dear.

Meanwhile, the Leading Steward appeared at my shoulder. What would I drink? Consternation. Was I being asked to choose some esoteric wine? Supper at home in Ireland tended to be sardines on toast and nothing had prepared me for this.

'Port,' I muttered hopefully, clutching onto the thing I knew went with dinner.

'Of course, sir,' murmured the voice, so quietly that nobody could hear my gaffe. 'I'm sorry, sir. I meant with the meal. Perhaps a little beer?' I accepted thankfully, knowing he'd saved me out of the kindness of his heart. The dinner continued. Four courses. The King's health drunk seated. Fruit and port. Greatly daring, the other Exmouth and I took cigars and a glass of crème de menthe. Junior Midshipmen's wine bills were restricted to 15/- a month and spirits were not allowed. 'Sticky green' was therefore the universal gunroom liqueur except for the Subs who, being over twenty, were allowed a brandy and a wine bill of no less than £2.

The Sub had observed our emancipation without approval. 'Breadcrumbs,' he said and we knew enough to put hands over our ears. He made some disparaging remarks about Junior Midshipmen then added, 'You may put your hands down now.' But even we were not quite so ingenuous and we remained as we were. Baulked, he looked at us with even more distaste and slowly raised his fruit fork to where a beam would have been in ships of old. We knew this one too and left the Mess. It was the end of our first dinner.

Achilles sailed next day, met the rest of the Home Fleet and carried out a mock invasion of the Humber.

I was in charge of a cutter and the pride of this first command kept me going through two days and nights without sleep. On the third day, thick fog came down and the Fleet anchored off the mouth of the Humber. The Commander-in-Chief was 'Paddy' Boyle. The sailors adored him and told, with relish, a fund of stories of which he was the hero. He was always referred to as 'Paddy' till he succeeded to the Earldom of Cork and Orrery when he was immediately known as 'Old Cock and Orifice'. This great man had just anchored his Fleet from the flagship *Nelson* when a Grimsby fishing trawler hove out of the fog. It was in the pause when, upon anchoring, the signalman on the bridge had stopped sounding the siren but the side boy had not yet closed up on the Quarterdeck and started ringing the bell which denoted a ship at anchor as opposed to under way. The Commander-in-Chief was just about to leave his bridge after a final look at the fog when the trawler appeared, saw the great grey steel side of the flagship only yards ahead, and put the wheel hard over to avoid a collision. The skipper, from his diminutive bridge, yelled at the face above him, 'Why don't yer ring yer f.....g bell?' The Commander-in-Chief looked courteously down and replied, 'Because I'm not a f.....g bicycle!' By morning, somehow, the whole Fleet was relishing the story.

I learned the power of the same grapevine some days later. In Hull, my leave had been stopped by the Commander, a matter of fine distinction because it had already been stopped by the Navigator. However, my friend had been ashore and, on our joint behalf, had bought two highly varnished sixpenny pipes from Woolworths. Wishing to save ourselves the discomfort of 'smoking them in' we had filled them, lit them and stuck them in the gunroom punkah louvres which obligingly blew smoke through till the bowls were suitably carbonised. By dinner time the atmosphere in the mess was pretty pungent and we knew exactly what would happen so we made suitable preparations. After all, Junior Midshipmen were supposed to be 'rorty' and the Sub had made it clear that he valued traditionalism.

Grace. Tomato Soup. The fingertips disapprovingly together. 'Perhaps the atmosphere is a little close. I think we'll have the punkah louvres open.'

The Marine attendant, his face a perfect blank, opened the first and a ping pong ball shot out straight into the Sub's tomato soup, splashing his immaculate stiff shirt the colour of blood.

No flicker of expression crossed the Marine's face but his normally studied movements took on an unexpected urgency as he moved quickly to the other two and released the little balls we had so carefully laid and trained.

The Sub Lieutenant was really very cross and we were taken into the bathroom, bent over and given twelve cuts each.

Achilles sailed in the night and the next morning, possibly emotionally exhausted by what he had suffered, the Sub went back to sleep after his call and was late relieving the Gunnery Officer for the Relieve Decks (0730-0830) watch. He blamed me for not calling him properly and, after Guns had dealt with him, he came aft seeking vengeance. So I got another twelve cuts in the middle of breakfast. I returned to the Mess, aggrieved, and someone asked me if it had hurt to which silly question I replied curtly that I didn't know because I hadn't been paying attention. The Sub, entering the Mess behind me, found this remark peculiarly offensive because he took it as a slight on his physique so he took me back to the bathroom and gave me another dozen on the spot, requiring me to stand up between strokes and report that I had been paying attention and it had hurt. Thirty-six cuts in twelve hours was a record even for those days.

That afternoon, I had to take my cutter away to recover a torpedo. As I sat gingerly down in the sternsheets, a hollow groan of pain came from one of the sailors somewhere forrard and we all burst out laughing. From that moment onwards I could do no wrong with 'the troops' and over and over again they saved me from my own incompetence.

'Midshipman,' said the Commander once. 'Why is your cutter not ready for hoisting?'

Before I could mutter some excuse for my forgetfulness, a quick voice came from the Leading Hand standing beside me. 'Officer told me to do it, sir, but we've just cleaned the boat so I left it at the boom till they finished hosing down the deck. All ready now, Mr Anderson, sir. I'll get it seen to right away.' Frustrated, the Commander went and my leave was saved.

One night, I found myself with a pinnace full of drunken libertymen to bring back from Weymouth pier to the ship, out at anchor in the bay. It was a big responsibility for a boy at any time. In bad weather, boats had been lost with heavy loss of life through poor handling or seamanship on the part of the Midshipman in charge. The normal drill with drunks or a noisy boat load was to turn the boat with the sea slightly on the bow so that sheets of spray came over and soaked the recalcitrants with icy water till they sobered up sufficiently to be taken alongside the gangway. But on this night sea conditions were bad enough to occupy all my concentration without the dangers of a load of libertymen who were howlingly, screamingly drunk in the open fore-part of the pinnace. I had to establish some form of order and discipline before I left the pier and started out to the open sea. I shouted, threatened and cajoled but was greeted with derisive laughter and jeers by the few who even heard me. Finally I turned to my Leading Seaman coxswain in utter desperation. 'What shall I do?' I asked.

He peered forward into the dark mass of milling men and said, 'Leave it to me, sir.' Then, clambering along the side of the canopy, he picked out a few of his more sober friends. 'Look, Scouse, given us a hand. We can't start off with this f-----g lot like this and its f-----g rough out there. 'Ere, Lofty, make Spud pack it in. Come on, lads, play it fair. You'll only get Mr Anderson beaten again.' Gradually, the din quietened down. An anonymous voice called. 'OK, Andy, give 'er the gun, boy. Orf we f-----g go!', and a thin cheer followed. Suddenly they were all alcoholically on my side, unanimous in the precarious dignity of carefully behaved drunks.

'Thanks, Coxswain,' I said.

He grinned. 'That's all right, sir. The lads don't mean no harm. Half of them aren't drunk at all really. But they don't feel it's been a proper run ashore, like, unless they get filled with beer and raise hell. If they can't afford the beer, they'll still play up 'cos then they reckon they must be enjoying themselves so they think it's been a fair run anyway.'

Achilles was a good, efficient ship and a reasonably happy one – for all except the Junior Midshipmen. We learned our job professionally. We learned to understand and deeply to appreciate the British sailor, but in *Achilles* I lost all traces of the sentiment which had been my strength since that far off day in Boulogne.

It was particularly sad because it was so unnecessary. After all, we were intelligent, dedicated young men filled with a genuine desire to become good Officers. Strict discipline we would have accepted without question (Dartmouth had seen to that), and hard work hurt no one. What demoralised us was that we were expected to take real responsibility one minute and yet we were treated the next like particularly silly and irresponsible children. The result was that our self respect and self confidence were undermined. Midshipmen had to learn, and to learn one must make mistakes. Careless mistakes should certainly be jumped on but, equally, to bring out the best, even in a horse, there is a need for occasional merited praise. Of praise or encouragement we had none. Midshipmen, it was considered, responded only to the perpetual fear of punishment, and every transgression was ruthlessly stamped upon.

Late one night, coming back in my pinnace, soaked and exhausted, I let my coxswain take the boat to the boom while I went below and flopped, thankfully, into my hammock. The next day I was sent for by the Navigator. Why had I not completed my job? I mumbled some excuse and he looked at me consideringly with his expressionless snake eyes. Then he said simply, 'You will carry out any duty, at any time, to the best of your ability, until it is completed and, if necessary, at the cost of your life.' I gazed at him speechlessly. What can one say to that? But it stuck in my mind and this sort of thing did have one benefit because it gave me a built-in guilt complex which has remained with me throughout my life, leaving me incapable of tackling any job in a casual or slap-happy manner. To a man of instinctively lazy habits, this has been an abiding strength. At least we learned that nothing but perfection, and then a bit more, was acceptable to the Naval way of life – a state of mind which, generally inculcated, was probably largely responsible for the high standards which Naval Officers took as natural in the world war then just over the horizon. And, perhaps, for a fighting Service that is sufficient justification.

In September 1935, I returned from summer leave to find an air of mild excitement and purpose in *Achilles*. Normally the Home Fleet went inevitably to Scapa Flow, Invergordon and Rosyth in the autumn, the West Indies in the spring, and British seaside resorts and the Baltic in the summer. Now the autumn cruise had suddenly been cancelled and, from Chatham, Portsmouth and Devonport, the whole Home Fleet was to concentrate in Portland. Italy was expected to invade Abyssinia and, if she did, we were probably going to war.

The news was taken calmly, the general reaction being that this was a pleasant and rather stimulating break from routine. The Fleet assembled, awnings were spread, Saturday rounds carried out in all ships and leave piped. The flap started that evening.

The recall was flashed on cinema screens, shouted by Naval patrols above the hubbub in the pubs and passed rapidly round the streets. On Weymouth pier I found an astonishing scene. Hundreds of libertymen were milling round while the boats and drifters from the Fleet queued at the landing steps to pick them up. An open air dance had been abandoned and the band's microphone was being used by the Naval Provost Marshal to control the chaos.

Large numbers of holidaymakers stood watching and, as I arrived, someone was just starting to sing 'Tipperary'. It was taken up by the whole crowd and a mood of Great War euphoria swept through the throng. The sailors, thoroughly appreciative of their part, began to kiss the girls and the girls wept happily and promised to meet them in Abyssinia as nurses. Lumps came into everyone's throats except the Provost Marshal's. Gradually the numbers dwindled until only the *Achilles* drifter was left. We cast off last and, when we drew away from the shore, the holidaymakers were singing 'There's a long, long trail a-winding'. As I stared back at the receding shore line, the song wavered and died as the crowd of civilians realised the drama was over and we had all gone. Somewhere in the background dance music started up but nobody turned away. They just stood staring after us in silence.

When we arrived alongside *Achilles*, the ship was already under way and the rest of the Fleet had sailed.

I wrote home describing the scene but ended, 'So now we're on our way . . . The guns are ready with live shell, the torpedoes fitted with warheads. I've read so many descriptions of the atmosphere before the last war. Well, now I know ours. Mild amusement, gentle interest and, otherwise, complete indifference. Certainly no excitement. We're just doing the job – and we're all in better spirits than I've ever known.'

As I wrote, HM ships from all over the world were converging on the Mediterranean. The Home Fleet was based at Gibraltar, reinforced by ships from the South African and West Indies Squadrons. From China and the East Indies, other light grey painted ships joined the Mediterranean Fleet in

Alexandria.

If the politicians had had the spirit of the Fleet, the first aggression of the dictators could have easily been stopped at the Suez Canal and World War II might never have happened. But the Italian troop ships went through unhindered, their passengers jeering at British soldiers on the passing banks. At either end of the Mediterranean lay the greatest concentration of Naval power that sea had ever known. The world would never see it again.

Chapter 4

DESTROYERS

In due course, my Junior Midshipman's time came, mercifully, to an end, and I and my Exmouth 'opposite number' in the *Achilles* gunroom were sent for destroyer training. For this, we joined an old 'V and W' destroyer and met a new Navy.

In 'the boats' one worked damned hard at sea and drank damned hard in harbour. Gin cost twopence for the first tot and a penny each for the next two. It seemed improvident to have just one drink and miss the next at half price. As in big ships, Officers' wine bills were officially limited to £5 a month but this regulation was largely ignored. The only inviolable rule was that the bar was never opened outside harbour. The normal drill was to spend the week doing day and night exercises at sea, during which the standard of professionalism was superb, and to return to harbour on Friday evening. The bar was then opened and serious drinking began. Saturday rounds of the messdecks were carried out punctiliously by the Captain and Saturday night saw a major thrash ashore. On Sunday forenoon the ship went to Divisions and Divine Service but it was not unknown for an Officer to be so drunk the night before that he was unfit to attend. After church the bar opened and hangovers were cured with Horse's Necks (brandy and ginger ale) until the drinker felt sufficiently recovered to start in on the gin. As destroyers were normally berthed alongside each other in Flotillas, there was much visiting between ships and, particularly in a Wardroom which had been visited by a strong team of friends from other destroyers, Sunday lunch often did not begin till well past tea time. This, in turn, meant that, by the time lunch was over, the bar was mercifully open for the evening session so that drinking was hardly interrupted and continued late into the night. But at 6 o'clock on Monday morning, the Flotillas sailed and it was inexcusable and indeed unheard of for an Officer to be affected by the weekend's alcoholic orgy. Pride in performance was far too high.

The world of destroyers was a fertile breeding ground for characters. I remember one CO who always wore a boiled shirt, even at sea. 'Soft shirts,' he said, 'are never worn by gentlemen.' Destroyers were handled with a skill and panache which were the envy of the other navies of the world. However, if there was a weakness in the individual, the destroyer Navy would lay it ruthlessly bare. Command of a ship, even of a destroyer, is total autocracy. In too many ships, when the Captain entered his wardroom all would stand with a sigh, knowing that an interminable session was in store in which their Captain would sit on the wardroom fender, self importantly telling stories and expressing views which all had heard over and over again through many boring hours before. It was unthinkable to interrupt or to start eating until he was ready and led the way to the table. But the best worked hard, drank hard, knew their job backwards and, during the long first year of war when the comparatively small peacetime Navy held the seas alone, underwent an almost superhuman strain until the RNVR and a new generation of young RN Officers came forward to share their burden.

My Captain was a ruthlessly efficient Officer with the normal capacity for gin and an advanced case of 'promotionitis'. But the half yearly promotion signal came and the Captain's name was not included. Six months of anxious waiting must pass before he could be selected. The whole ship sighed and, that night being a Saturday, alcohol ran riot as the Captain drowned his grief and the Wardroom sought strength.

We had had a particularly punishing week at sea and, with some prescience, Sunday Division had been cancelled for the next day. I had been ashore to the Universal, the best joint in Gibraltar, where beautiful Hungarian girls drank with the sailors from lunch time till eleven o'clock at night and then moved upstairs when the Officers' night club opened on the first floor.

My blonde had arrived in festive mood and by the time I got back on board and tottered into my bunk I had been feeling no pain.

At half past eight in the morning I was awakened by a frantic signalman. 'From Commander-in-Chief, Home Fleet, sir. I intend to walk round Divisions this morning.'

The First Lieutenant was unique in that he only drank sherry and beer. He was sick but just capable and he had gone to break the news to the ship's company who, well understanding the situation, had not wasted their Saturday evening run ashore either. Quick investigation showed the Captain, haggard with anxiety, cutting his face with his razor but, at least, upright. The Gunner had been Officer of the Day and was sober. But No. 2, Sub and Chief would obviously not be fit to greet their Commander-in-Chief in under an hour. My own 'oppo' was green but loyal to the cause.

At half past nine the Divisions were fallen in, their uniforms rough from the night before, their eyes glazed and dull. Sir Roger Backhouse, the new Commander-in-Chief, was greeted by the shrill of the pipes. He looked at the weather scarred Upper Deck, inadequately cleaned up on the Saturday, and the sagging ranks. Without a word he started his inspection. Behind his back, the Gunner and the two Midshipmen nipped down the blind side of the deck so that one of us was always there to report each Division as Divisional Officer. The Gunner reported for the stewards and cooks. I was apparently in charge of the stokers. The novelty was not lost on the Admiral. At last the dreadful charade came to an end and the Commander-in-Chief paused at the top of the gangway. He looked at the quailing figure before him and uttered his only words. 'Captain,' he said, 'I do not think much of your ship.'

Having started the day's routine, we mustered for Divine Service on the Mess Deck and gave the most unconvincing thanks that can ever have been offered. Then the bar opened.

Destroyer time based on Gibraltar was a wonderful experience for Midshipmen because we were treated as responsible Wardroom Officers. I used to hire a horse and ride over the border into Spain where miles of deserted sandy beaches could be galloped and it was because of this that I found myself invited to ride in the 'Naval Officers' Scurry', the annual high point of the Gibraltarian racing season. The horse allocated to me was owned by a Gibraltarian grocer and was normally ridden by a swarthy little Spaniard who, he assured me, was a 'gentleman jockey'. Horse and Midshipman were taken to the race course by this individual and I was briefed on how to ride the race.

'At this point, sah, do not be inside on the rails or the other jockeys will put their foot under yours and tip you over.'

'Steady on, old boy. These are Naval Officers riding . . .'

'Yes, sah, of course, sah. Ha, ha, sah! At this point, gentlemans, you must use your whip. Hit him hard, sah. He won't feel it but it makes him go. But watch, sah, because here all gentlemans uses whip not on horses but on noses of next door rider.'

'I say, I really don't think our race will be quite like that . . .!'

The day of the great race came and I weighed in. My owner insisted on leading his horse to the start and there he stood, still holding the reins so that my mount was almost staring over its shoulder, while he delivered his last minute instructions.

'Hold him back, sah. Stay right behind the field till a hundred yards from the post. Then you can let him go.'

'Yes, but look here, señor. The starter has the flag up. Please let go and get out of it.'

'Of course, sah. Ah, but you have a whip. Please give, sah, I could not bear to think of my so beautiful horse being beaten.' He snatched the whip from me as the flag went down and the horse, seeing its friends racing away, managed to free itself and gallop after them. Cursing the owner for losing me precious seconds, I made whipless, encouraging noises and, knowing the animal was a hot favourite, gave it its head.

Quickly we began to catch up and we were just forging ahead past the rear of the field when, like a car running out of petrol, I felt my beast begin to flag. At the same time there came a noise with which I was all too familiar when, returning to harbour in urgent need of fuelling, the remaining oil swilled from side to side in the tanks under my cabin.

We came in a long way last and, tense with anger, I sought out the owner.

'You watered him. You've filled him up like a bloody bucket. I'm going straight to the stewards . . .'

My owner uttered indignant denials and then decided to come clean. He had been worried about my weight. Of course, we should have won but we might not have and there was little enough money for a win while a place gave him nothing except top weight next week for a very financially rewarding race in which the gentleman jockey would be riding. If we came in last today then the horse would carry bottom weight the next week and could not fail to make it. I must understand this was not England. I could tell the stewards but they knew how Gibraltarian races were arranged and it would all be so embarrassing. Why did I, too, not share in the coming profits like a wise man?

Finally he talked me out of it and, the next week, all the Exmouths in Gibraltar raised every penny they could and, *en bloc*, we went to the races. The horse walked home and we collected the equivalent of about three months pay each.

'To La Linea,' went up the cry and, suitably refreshed, to La Linea we went. In one of the ubiquitous brothels of that insalubrious little town we watched our first Exhibition – two middle aged ladies lying naked on the floor lethargically transposing their stout bodies into what we were assured were all the known positions of love. Wearing our pork pie hats, in very British dogrobbers and large shoes, we watched with mild interest until the end of the performance when one of the artistes, finding it hard to believe that we had really evinced no excitement, ran round the half circle of Midshipmen checking quickly for herself. Professional umbrage and outraged disbelief. Madame called. The situation explained. A flood of enquiring Spanish then the dawn of understanding in Madame's eyes. A long pause while our two frustrated hostesses shambled out muttering angrily to themselves. Then Madame again, beaming with pride and triumph and leading in several sardonic small boys. Hastily we excused ourselves and made for the street pursued by an infuriated Spanish lady offering us, in language that even we could understand, the services of an ancient goat which happened to be passing.

We were really sorry when our destroyer time came to an end. A new battleship was about to be commissioned in Devonport and, to raise the manpower required, our Division of old V & Ws was sailed for home to be paid off into Reserve.

Arrived in Devonport, I went to Gieves. 'My friend and I are joining *Repulse* in Portsmouth in a fortnight. We are sharing a double cabin in our present ship and we haven't got enough luggage for the move. Can you fix it? We'd like someone to pack, mark any clothes that need it and wash and clean anything that's dirty.'

'Certainly, sir. Is there anything else that we can do to help?'

'Yes. Lend me five pounds to get home.'

They had never seen me before in that particular branch but the money was immediately forthcoming and we joined *Repulse* to find all our gear sorted, washed, marked and clean, waiting for us in the gunroom chest flat.

Such was Gieves.

Chapter 5

HMS REPULSE

R epulse, a battle cruiser of World War I vintage, was a truly beautiful ship.

Huge, menacing and impressive, she still managed to convey the lines of a yacht and the addition of hangar space and aircraft abaft her after funnel added to her sense of power. From the Midshipmen's point of view her greatest attraction was that, instead of the old brass-funnelled steam picket boats normally carried by capital ships, she had completely new three-engined fast power boats which could run white-waked rings round anything else in the Fleet.

We were to serve on the Mediterranean station, 'Up the Straits' as the sailors called it, and the Ship's Company viewed the prospect with little relish. They did not wish to leave home for two and a half years and they were fully aware that the high standards required in the Mediterranean fleet meant no let up in the drills, exercises and 'bull' of a big ship's routine. The younger, bachelor element of the Wardroom was delighted with both the ship and the prospects but the married Officers were not so happy. There were no marriage allowances for Naval Officers and no free passages for Naval wives in those days and, for those with only their pay, a foreign commission meant digging deeply into slender reserves or accepting the long period away from wives and young children.

The gunroom was prepared to enjoy life, particularly we Exmouths from *Achilles* who, no longer Junior Midshipmen, were hoping to be treated with rather more consideration. After the freedom and exuberance of life in destroyers, big ship 'flannel' and gunroom restrictions were rather a nuisance, but we knew the form and settled naturally into the familiar routine.

The day started at 0645 with PT on the Quarterdeck and then the forenoon was spent under instruction. The afternoons were usually occupied doing some form of practical training or having further instruction until evening quarters at 1600. The Dog Watches were passed in such constructive chores as writing up one's journal or, if in harbour and not under stoppage of leave, going ashore till 1915 (2300 once a week). The day ended with the usual full ceremonial dinner in Mess Undress or a riotous weekly Guest Night. At sea, Midshipmen kept watch on the bridge day and night. In harbour they kept watch on the Quarterdeck and ran the ship's boats from six in the morning till eight at night, being sent below during the hours of instruction.

It was a sound system in theory and worked extremely well in most ships where it was properly and imaginatively handled. Unfortunately, in *Repulse* it was not.

Our new Snotties' Nurse took little interest in the job and reckoned to have done his stuff if the Midshipmen were permanently employed doing something, no matter how pointless or repetitive. The Commander hated the gunroom and normally ignored us, except for intermittent periods when he became beastly on principle. The result was that we soon began to miss *Achilles* and realise how good the Navigator in that ship had been. In *Achilles* life had been hard, but there was a standard of perfection which never varied, which we could understand and accept. Justice was ruthless, perhaps, but at least it was fair and impartial. And we learned.

Repulse had all the weaknesses of *Achilles* but worse, far worse, was the fact that we never really knew where we stood. The Junior Midshipmen were allowed to get into Bad Habits without being checked and then, without warning, a pointless chasing would descend on the gunroom as a whole.

However, all this lay in the future when we sailed from Farewell Jetty in Portsmouth and if the real fighting worth, and the vulnerability, of World War I battle cruisers was to be demonstrated in a few years' time, we were hardly to know it. We were proud of our great ship, as well we might have been.

We had hardly arrived on the station when the Spanish Civil War broke out and *Repulse* was sent to Palma, Majorca, which, having declared for General Franco, was being bombed by Government forces and had been threatened with total destruction if the island was not surrendered at once. There were French, German and Italian warships there but all were involved to a greater or lesser extent in the politics if not the fighting of the war so it was left to the Royal Navy to do something constructive about evacuating the innocent foreign victims.

Majorca, in the thirties, had never heard of tourists. Instead, it was an idyllic haven for British 'remittance' men (and women) whose scandalous behaviour and dubious morals had caused their long suffering families to banish them overseas. Not as far as the colonies, perhaps, but far enough to have them safely out of sight and away from the prurient attentions of the Press at home. We spread the word ashore that any foreign nationals wishing to be evacuated should be on the jetty at two o'clock the next afternoon with not more than two suitcases apiece. Then we waited and watched Palma being bombed.

We had no idea how many refugees to expect. It would not be an easy decision for them to abandon house and home and all their worldly possessions at twenty-four hours notice. They could not expect to find much left when, and if, they ever returned. On the other hand, quite a lot of damage had already been done to the town and the Government ultimatum expired at 1900 – the usual time for the evening raid. In the event, the jetty began to fill from early in the morning.

All the afternoon, our boats ferried them out to the ship. Unseasonably, it began to rain and, to add to their misery, they were soaked to the skin. About five hundred came in all, mostly British but also French, American, German, Swedish, Norwegian, Danish and Swiss. Desultory bombing took place throughout the evacuation, which at least helped to speed it up, but it was a pretty miserable crowd which poured onto our immaculate Quarterdeck. We greeted them with our RM Band playing airs from Gilbert and Sullivan. The gunroom had been turned into a nursery/creche and all the officers gave up their cabins to the older ladies, but otherwise, we could only pack them on the Upper Deck and anywhere where there was shelter. Some were distraught, some simply bewildered, others drunk. One old woman was mad and, claiming to be the Duchess of Marlborough, demanded to see the Prince of Wales and be spared from her enemies the French until she was led, shrieking, to the Sick Bay.

We landed them all in Marseilles the next day and sailed at once for Valencia.

In Valencia, *Repulse* acted as receiving ship for refugees from all over southern and eastern Spain. We operated as a sort of floating transit camp, accommodating them as best we could till we could transfer them to the destroyers which ran a shuttle service to France. We rescued people of fourteen nationalities, ranging from the Vice President of a South American republic and his plump blonde mistress in a pink chiffon negligée, accompanied by a thug of a bodyguard with a veritable arsenal in his belt, to a small group of nuns who were particularly worried because they thought they would have to pay for their keep. Funny – it was always the foreigners who complained and the poor who tried to pay . . .

Valencia was, officially, Government controlled but in fact was in the hands of a mixed bunch of uncoordinated revolutionaries, communists and anarchists owing no allegiance to anyone but themselves. On one occasion we were given an 'officially' sponsored tour of the town during which we were proudly shown the charred bodies of a hundred priests and nuns burned alive in a church. They smelt of pork. (Years later, after the war, I mentioned this to a friend. 'Ah,' he said, 'those poor Jews in Hitler's extermination camps. It must have been the final irony . . .')

Another time, I went in with my boat to collect the ship's Intelligence Officer who had gone to see the Consul. He was not on the jetty so I went to find him and was quickly stopped by a barricade across the street. A terrible old man with what appeared to be an old fashioned blunderbus demanded to see my papers. Luckily I had in my wallet the guarantee for my cheap Ingersoll watch – an impressive looking document with a big red seal printed in the corner. It worked like a charm and I was ushered through by a delighted old monster whose ego had been beautifully massaged.

But I ran into real trouble when I got back to the boat. A Government Minister from Madrid had come to Valencia thinking that he would be welcome but had quickly realised that the questionable loyalties of the citizens meant that his actual life was in danger. As I stepped into the boat, he scuttled out of the crowd and, in broken English, begged to be taken on board *Repulse* forthwith. The watching crowd of heavily armed toughs on the jetty were pointing at him and muttering the Spanish equivalent of 'rhubarb, rhubarb'.

I wondered what on earth I should do. If I acceded to his request, the Ship's Officer would arrive on the jetty to find himself abandoned to an angry mob. Yet the Minister was becoming almost hysterical. 'They kill me,' he pleaded. 'They kill me.' Reaching a decision, I pointed to the White Ensign in the stern sheets. 'You are now under the protection of that flag,' I said rather pompously. 'You are quite safe.' I put him down in the cabin, out of sight, and prayed God the crowd would agree with me. Then I stood and glowered nonchalantly at the muttering thugs on the jetty. Perhaps it was the menacing presence of *Repulse* in the background but, luckily, they accepted the rules of the game. After a long ten minutes, the Officer arrived and we could thankfully scarper.

Finally, we left Valencia, sick to our stomachs with everything Spanish, greatly moved by the dignity and patience of British people in adversity and very proud to be members of the Royal Navy, a fighting service which had brought to the whole miserable business mercy, sympathy and kindliness in travail.

Going back to Malta was an anticlimax for us all but particularly for the Gunroom. Some of the more senior Officers had brought out their wives to join them and there was a swinging social scene ashore, particularly with the Fishing Fleet – young girls from home with speculatively matrimonial eyes on young Naval Officers. But no invitations were ever offered to Midshipmen. Neither was any attempt made to organise bathing picnics or even tours of the archaeological and historical treasures of the island.

With pay of £7 10s. a month and a mess bill of about £5, we could just afford the occasional run ashore to a cinema. Otherwise, even if our leave was not stopped, there was nothing for us to do but sit on board in the sweltering heat and yellow glare of Grand Harbour in summertime. It was not a very pleasant existence.

The sailors went 'down the Gut' – to Strada Stretta, that matelot's paradise of cheap beer and prostitutes. Every morning, running the early liberty boat, I would see dazed figures being brought down to the jetty by tired girls from the Egyptian Queen or one of the other night clubs for, if a sailor had a regular woman, she would never let him be robbed when drunk or remain absent over leave the morning after a debauch. Doing messdeck rounds during the night, one was struck by the numbers of unpromising men whose hammocks were provided with pillows beautifully and intricately embroidered with lace covers. The ladies of the Gut were, in some ways, much nicer than those of the Fishing Fleet. (How horrified those well brought up young women would have been at such a thought!)

Time passed. We paid a visit to Athens where the King of Greece visited the ship and was escorted in his barge by three of our fast power boats under my command. Then we did a cruise of the Greek islands, blissfully empty and primitive in those days. Finally, we returned to Malta and the ordeal of our examination for the rank of Sub Lieutenant.

In all the other ships, Senior Midshipmen were excused watchkeeping and boat running duties and allowed to concentrate on mugging up for the exam. Only in *Repulse* were we required to carry on as usual with the time we could have put to good use being pointlessly wasted doing the sort of basic seamanship we had learned at Dartmouth. But at least it was nearly over.

Home for Christmas leave, a stripe on my sleeve instead of white patches on my collar, Greenwich and the exotic delights of London. Then, the night before the exam, I was detailed like a Junior Midshipman to attend a Ball given by the Commander-in-Chief. Worse, as I was hiding morosely in a corner, I was spotted by the Flag Lieutenant who promptly lurked me to dance with some ghastly old harridan. It was too much. I went to the bar and had a whisky. And another. Gradually, the evening brightened. I had several more. I felt they were doing me good.

Finally, the time came to go. Admiral Sir Dudley Pound and Lady Pound stood at the top of the big marble staircase, seeing off their guests. Waveringly, I approached my hostess. 'Goodnight, Mishes Pound,' I said, 'and thank you sho much.' Then I stumbled down the stairs.

Next day, the great Snotties' Nurse in the sky handed me my retribution. Out of the blue had come a totally unexpected edict from Their Lordships. For the first time ever, Midshipmen were to take celestial navigation with their seamanship exam instead of as part of the Subs' navigation course. I was not ready for it and it was my weakest subject (which is saying a lot). Now, ground down by a sense of dreadful guilt and an even worse hangover, I faced this ghastly hurdle as the first paper. And I failed it.

It was only by one mark. Another Exmouth on the Station failed by two marks and one in the West Indies by five. None of us had expected this challenge.

In the West Indies, they laughed, told their Midshipman to do it again and pushed him through. In the Med, the two of us were told to give our reasons for failing in writing. The other lad had been on operations in Palestine so was allowed a rescrub. I explained that I had missed one cruise in *Achilles* after crashing with a horse and so lost four months' instruction. I added, quite truthfully, that I had been suffering from an abscess over a front tooth for a prolonged period but had had to accept the pain until our return to Malta and a dentist to extract it. All of which had not helped my studies.

But it was no good. Perhaps the C-in-C remembered that there could have been another reason for my failure. Anyhow, my friend passed his second shot and he and all the other Exmouths travelled home across Europe leaving me behind to wait four months for the next exam. I had achieved the impossible. For the first time for a century, a Midshipman had been passed over for promotion. Me.

Whistling sibilantly through the new gap in my front teeth, I celebrated, as the only Midshipman in the world over twenty and so entitled to drink gin, by getting horribly, tearfully drunk on Christmas Day. I was totally lonely and miserable.

We went to Tangier for New Year's Eve, taking with us the band of the Gordon Highlanders from Gib. Their pipers played in the gunroom after dinner – a hideous cacophony of howling horror reverberating inwards from the steel walls of the small compartment while we cowered in our chairs, appalled.

On New Year's Eve itself, we gave a cocktail party, inviting the Officers from the French and German warships in the harbour. It quickly became obvious that we had made a mistake. The French gathered at one end of our big Quarterdeck, the Germans at the other. Both lots scowled at each other, muttering. Between, keeping them apart, stood a carefully insouciant but unyielding line of *Repulse* officers. It worked until, after our party, everyone adjourned to a large hotel ashore to see in 1937.

Here the attention, particularly of the French, was temporarily diverted by Paquita – a beautiful and charming dancer from Gibraltar, greatly loved by British Naval Officers. But even her allure could not hide the obvious fact that the two hostile groups were getting ready for a punch-up. As Paquita's lovely body left the floor, they began to rise to their feet. Then, in the tense moment before all hell broke loose, there came a loud moan, followed by a shriek – and the pipe band of the Gordon Highlanders marched unexpectedly onto the dance floor. Kilts and sporrans swinging, great boots stamping, big drum thumping and pipes squealing, they marched stolidly round the little arena so recently graced by Paquita. The astonished French and Germans sank back into their seats. Midnight came and the pipes changed their tune to Auld Lang Syne. Delighted, the Brits made a circle, held hands and started to sing. Doubtfully, in ones and twos, the Germans and French came forward and joined in. Finally, a happy, laughing throng of international Naval Officers were toasting each other and slapping each other's backs. Diplomacy can take many forms . . .

After a spell on Spanish patrol, the ship went back to Malta, did another cruise of the Greek islands and returned to Gib for the Combined Exercises of the Home and Med Fleets.

For me, the four months had finally expired. I took the dread exam again and, thankfully, passed. At last my teens and Midshipman's days were officially over.

Perhaps I have over emphasised the hardships of those early years? In fact, looking back, they were happy and stimulating ones. Youth is resilient. I had visited a whole variety of places from the West Indies to the Middle East, including Casablanca, Madeira and the Azores. I had met strange people in foreign lands, seen war and death. Perhaps, most importantly, I had found myself tested, under stress, in a way that no civilian occupation could have offered. All this, I think, with hard training and discipline, produced young men who were tough, self reliant and self confident. Certainly, when I went home, I found my civilian contemporaries rather soft and vapid.

The System had turned me into probably a typical young Naval Officer. And, at last, I had my stripe. I was more than ready for the next chapter.

Chapter 6

COURSES

The object of Subs' courses was to give us a more thorough grounding in Gunnery, Navigation, Torpedoes and Signals than had been possible in our more general training in the Fleet. Before going on to the specialist schools in Portsmouth, we went to the Naval College at Greenwich to limber up our brains after the supposed mental stagnation of three years at sea.

Greenwich College is beautiful. Started by Henry VIII, and supposed to be the Palace where he composed 'Greensleeves', it was completed by Charles II. Later, it became the Navy's equivalent of Chelsea Barracks – a hospital and home for old sailors. Finally, it ended as the Navy's university.

In these lovely old buildings, we did French, Naval History, English, a sort of Junior Officers' Staff Course, designed to make us think – and Advanced Mathematics. They even tried to teach me calculus. They failed.

In the College, we had big comfortable cabins instead of hammocks. We fed well in the famous Painted Hall. But the greatest change was our new found freedom. Our wings, so long pinioned by the restrictions on Midshipmen's leave in the Fleet, were suddenly allowed to spread in all the glory of our adolescent display. London and the West End were just up the line. There was no restriction on the hours we spent ashore. After years of repression we were now offered the opposite extreme. Grabbing a bag of wild oats, we went sowing.

Greenwich, in short, was tremendous fun but, at the end of the course, a problem arose. I had celebrated my return home from *Repulse* by getting a dog – a tricoloured cocker spaniel which I named Brenda. Now my mother reckoned Brenda was too large and boisterous for her little Yorkshires and wanted me to dispose of her. As a last resort, a mere Acting Sub Lieutenant, I wrote to the Commander of the Gunnery School at Whale Island and, explaining my predicament, asked rather hopelessly if I could bring her with me. To my delighted astonishment, the Commander replied by return My dog would be welcome. Gunnery Officers, I realised, were truly gentlemen.

Brenda and I arrived at Whale Island in the late summer of 1937. We had a nice little cabin to ourselves in a long hut under trees with grass all round. Both of us were well satisfied. Perhaps sensing the very disciplined atmosphere, the dog quickly learned her place. She would sit at the edge of the Parade Ground while we drilled, then, watching carefully, join up in the rear as my squad doubled off to instruction. She spent the lectures at my feet or lying in the sun outside and probably learned as much gunnery as I did. (It was all horribly technical and thus, of course, largely above my head.)

Whale Island was bliss. Although I had missed going through courses with my own Exmouth Term, 'N' Group of twelve Sub Lieutenants, in which my dog and I found ourselves, was a small and friendly club which, in miniature, showed all the benefits of the Dartmouth system. One of us was publishing poetry in an erudite literary magazine, one was writing popular songs and a third was producing pictures for the dust covers of novels. A fourth, myself, was writing regularly for a monthly magazine. We may not have studied very hard but we were happy and, after all, had we not entered Dartmouth at the age of thirteen, it was most unlikely that this third of the Group concerned would ever have been in the Navy at all.

Whaley prided itself on its formidable bull and discipline on duty and its boisterous, friendly life in non working hours. One doubled everywhere, particularly on the Parade Ground which was dominated by the black gaiters, silver whistle and terrible voice of the Parade Gunner and his staff of Gunner's Mates. There was also a zoo, boasting two rather elderly lions, one of which was alleged to have escaped and been spotted by a Gunner's Mate making its way across to the Drill Shed.

'Sir,' said the shaken GI, 'There's a lion walking across the Parade Ground.'

'Tell it to double,' said the Parade Gunner simply.

We spent many hours drilling with rifles on the hot, sunny Parade Ground. Sometimes, if we were dozy in the summer heat, we would find ourselves doubling round the Island – a favourite remedy for idleness in the Gunnery School. But often the Gunnery Instructor himself would seem to go to sleep, rigidly at attention, thumbs at the seams of his trousers, swaying gently on his feet.

'N' Group of Sub Lieutenants discovered that, providing one kept up a suitable, chanting Gunnery noise, the sleeping GI would remain in his trance but the smallest hesitation or faltering in the drill provoked an automatic roar of displeasure and a furious Gunner's Mate, very wide awake. The secret lay in the noise and not the words. So I redrafted the Drill Book and we had a standing challenge which any Sub could take up by merging gently from the real drill into mine.

Funeral Drill. The squad with arms reversed. GI with eyes closed. Challenge offered. 'Upon the corpse appearing from the mortuary, deadhouse or other place of worship, the escort will assume an aspect mournful but subdued. At this point, the corpse will march through the ranks. For drill purposes only, I will represent the corpse . . . [A portentous slow march down the front rank.] Should the corpse become too heavy for the gun carriage crew, the mourners will advance at the rush and, removing the corpse, will lay him reverently in the gutter by the roadside. Under no circumstances must the corpse be allowed to interfere with the smart bearing and general appearance of the funeral cortege.'

If you got that far, 'N' Group of Subs owed you a pint each. If the GI was not really asleep and spotted that, though the sound was right, the words were wrong, then you would undoubtedly double round the Island and you would buy the group the beer.

Meanwhile, regular cheques were coming in for my writing so I was, at last, able to devote some serious attention to my sex life. Southsea provided the local equivalent of Malta's Fishing Fleet. Some were delightful, some very decorative indeed but, unless one's intentions were strictly honourable, which mine were not, their pursuit involved a lot of expenditure for a small return. Theirs was the circuit of five shilling dinner dances in tails at the Beach hotel to be, they thought, adequately rewarded at the end of an expensive evening by a chaste kiss. Moreover, in Southsea Society, everyone knew each other. Not only at the beach but wherever you went, be it the Hippodrome for variety shows, Handley's for Saturday morning coffee or one of the many cinemas (real 'Palaces of the Silver Screen'), you met the same familiar faces, watching who was with whom, gossiping, edging you nearer and nearer to a commitment.

But there was real fun to be had at the other end of the scale. The favourite pub was the Goat, presided over by a shatteringly sexy redhead who drew Naval Officers like flies to fly paper. There were others too and some of the lesser brethren met the ultimate Naval and social disaster by Marrying a Barmaid (though some made them damned good wives).

And there were the Assembly Rooms . . . The Assembly Rooms, known colloquially as the Arse and Belly, or simply the A and B, were situated on Clarence Pier. A huge dance hall with discreet sofas in dark little alcoves, their mothers ensured that the A and B was strictly Out of Bounds to the Southsea Society girls (another attribute in its favour if one was involved with any of them). But it attracted some devastatingly pretty and amenable 'popsies' from the shops and offices of the town and so, inevitably, young Naval Officers. These girls understood the financial resources of their partners and happily spent the evening on half pints of bitter giving, in return, stimulating companionship and often much else. I still have the most affectionate memories of the A and B and the very attractive girls I met there. I have much for which to be grateful to them.

After Whale Island, courses in other schools and establishments could only be an anticlimax. Moreover, nowhere else would take my dog. I found her a lovely home with another Sub who also loved her and whose people had a big estate in Scotland where she would be happy – but it was a sad parting.

After it, feeling rather forlorn, I went to the Navigation School to face my major hurdle. If I failed at Navhouse, I should lose my four months seniority for ever. If I passed the course as a whole I would, at least in theory, be back with the Exmouths.

Celestial navigation still defeated me but ship handling and Fleet exercises I understood. I could even follow the complicated evolutions of changing positions on the screen where the cry was always, 'And the speed must be one knot less than the maximum.'

The exams came and were dreadful. They culminated in a macabre exercise where we each represented the Plotting Room of a destroyer on the screen in an imaginary battle. The need was to keep a quick and accurate track chart of one's own movements and those of all the friendly and enemy forces involved. To make it difficult for us not to lose our heads, chits were issued unceasingly by the Directing Staff representing the orders, counter orders and stupid but time wasting questions of a panicking Captain on the bridge above.

Eventually, just as I lost control of the situation, I got a chit in great capital letters: 'One of our cruisers is steaming straight across the bows of the enemy battle fleet. What is she trying to do?'

I wrote back, 'One knot more than the maximum,' and gave it all up. But the Captain of Navhouse had a sense of humour and refused to fail the Sub who had given such an answer. I was safely through.

Of the torpedo course I remember little and of signals only that the Dartmouth cry of 'When You Get To Sea' was superseded by everything ending, 'But, of course, in wartime it's all different,' and then we paid attention because we knew that time was running out fast.

Chapter 7

HMS FORESTER

In the spring of 1938, I joined HMS *Forester* in the Sixth Destroyer Flotilla of the Home Fleet. She was a Portsmouth ship and so based on the Home Port which, after *Repulse* and Subs' courses, I had begun to feel was my home. And, at last, I was no longer under training but a full Wardroom Officer in my own right. Sub of the *Forester*. I was very proud of myself. She was a relatively new destroyer and the appointment was all I could have wished for.

The Captain was one of the finest Naval Officers I have ever known. Geoff Birley was a tall, slim, elegant aviator of dark good looks who handled his ship with a dashing perfection which was reflected in the pride and morale of the Ship's Company. We would all have followed him anywhere and, for years, I sought to emulate him until I realised that I would never be slim nor elegant and would have to plough a more substantial furrow of my own.

No.1 was a tubby little alcoholic and typical of the destroyer Navy of the day – a born seaman with an unlimited capacity for gin. No.2 was an extremely capable, rather quiet character whose brain was such that he could not bear to watch my incompetent efforts at analysing torpedo firings and so always snatched them away and did them properly himself, an arrangement which, as the ship's Torpedo Control Officer responsible for the dreadful things, suited me admirably. Then came myself and the Gunner.

Our Chief (Engineer Officer) was a two and a half striper nicknamed 'Bendy' Dawson from his habit, amongst other parlour tricks, of enlivening the late hours by bending his sword double. His main attribute was his habit of telling his seniors exactly what he thought about anything, including themselves, an asset which he balanced by being extremely kind to his juniors who loved him accordingly, myself included.

On one occasion, when friends had come over from another ship on a filthy night and we were roistering late, Bendy suddenly realised that the visitors' boat had come to fetch them and was lying off the stern, waiting. Knowing how uncomfortable this would be for the boat's crew, he ordered the boat to the boom and sent for the crew to come down to the wardroom for a warming glass. The crew came in – a Leading Seaman coxswain and Able Seaman bowman in glistening wet oilskins, and the stoker in his overalls. Even a strong tot of whisky failed to overcome their embarrassment so Bendy, determined to put them at their ease, reacted in the best way he knew. First he took the cover of *The Times*, set fire to it and stuffed it, burning, down the front of his trousers. He followed this with a jug of cold water because he believed that, if you did it quickly enough, the fire would not scorch anything that mattered and the water would not wet the trousers. (No amount of experience ever convinced him he was wrong.) He followed this *tour de force* by hanging upside down from a pipe running along the deckhead and bending his sword whilst simultaneously drinking a pint of beer from a glass held between his teeth. When he had emptied the glass, still hanging upside down, he ate it.

Throughout the astonishing performance no word was uttered. The boat's crew watched like rabbits stricken by a car's headlights and, at the end, muttered incoherently and ran from the mess. Their own Officers followed. Bendy looked after them, well satisfied. 'I think I managed to make them feel at home,' he murmured happily.

Meanwhile, the international situation was worsening. The Reserve Fleet was mobilised and came down to join the Home Fleet in Portland where we were inspected by HM the King. Then we went back to Portsmouth for summer leave at the end of which it was obvious that war was drawing ever nearer.

The night before we sailed, I thought I would have one last, mammoth run ashore so I repaired to the A and B for what might be the last time. There I met a most attractive and obviously totally immoral young woman who appeared to be ideally suited to the circumstances. A few dances in close embrace proved that I had, indeed, struck pay dirt – but there was a snag. She had already arranged to meet somebody else that evening and he was due at any minute.

Somebody Else turned out to be a Sub Lieutenant whom I knew vaguely and considered to be a drip. Fortified by several whiskies on board and a glass or so of the A and B's best bitter, I could not let him spoil such a promising evening so, with alcoholic inspiration, I suggested to my partner how we might deal with the situation. Laughing happily, she agreed.

The other Sub arrived and, when he saw me, his face fell but the girl, playing her part superbly, introduced me with the prettiest of apologies. I was, we explained, her dearest cousin. I had been involved in an unfortunate misunderstanding with the police in England as a result of which I had had to leave rather suddenly for South America. There I had made a good living as a smuggler and gun runner until one night, rather too full of whisky, I had piled my schooner up on some rocks and, being uninsured, had found myself flat broke. There were also difficulties, I hinted, with the father of a girl who had become unaccountably pregnant and, what with the police being after me again anyway, I had decided to risk coming home. I had only landed in Southampton that morning and here I was – and wasn't he going to buy us both a drink?

With a face like thunder he did so and the evening progressed well. I danced with the girl. He bought the drinks. Once, when he suggested that I might buy a round, I became truculently unpleasant and watched with glee the thoughts explicit on his face. 'I'm a Naval Officer . . . can't risk a scene with this ghastly fellow . . . probably has a knife . . . should go . . . but she is gorgeous . . . Oh, God, stick it out a little longer . . . but must be careful and humour him . . .'

At closing time, the girl suddenly suffered a burst of contrition, feeling she must give him some solace for his ruined evening. It seemed fair enough so, as the other Sub actually had a car, we arranged that he would drive us home but that I would say I wanted to walk to clear my head. He would drop me short of her house and take her on to the front door where anything might happen in the car. After he left, it would be my turn.

We went and he dropped me as arranged. There was a little churchyard from which I could watch them in the distance and see when he drove off. I went in, sat down, leant up against a convenient tombstone – and fell asleep. I awoke with a constabulary 'bull's eye' lantern shining in my face.

'Come on, then, what are we doing 'ere?'

'Waiting to say goodnight to my girl friend, Officer.'

As he considered what I realised was an unlikely explanation, I took a quick look down the road. The car, thank God, was still there.

'What would you say if I told you that the poor box in this church has been rifled recently?'

'Oh, Officer, do I look that poor?'

'Who are you then? Name? Address?'

I told him who I was and explained, truthfully, how I was waiting for somebody else to finish saying goodnight to my girl friend before she let me in to do it properly.

Another pause, then, 'Take off your raincoat.'

I took off my blue Naval burberry and handed it over. The lantern shone on the name tag.

'You say your name is Anderson. Why is this coat labelled Fairley?'

Consternation – till I remembered a Midshipman had joined us that afternoon and I had allowed him to use my cabin wardrobe. I must have taken his burberry by mistake.

The constable considered this latest explanation and decided to give me one last chance.

'If I took you to that there car, would they identify you as Sub Lootenant of the *Forester*?'

Still quite truthful. 'No, Officer. They'd probably tell you I was a South American gun runner.'

It was too much. I was nicked.

The Sergeant in the police station was an imperturbable man who had obviously dealt with young Naval Officers before. He listened patiently to us both and then, picking up a telephone, rang *Forester*.

'Officer of the Day, please.' A long pause while the Quartermaster walked aft and dug poor No.2 out of his pit. The Constable and I stood waiting in silence. Then No.2's voice on the phone. The Sergeant said, 'I'm sorry to turn you out, sir, but we have a young gentleman in custody who says he is your Sub Lieutenant. Could you help us to identify him?'

'Ask him his nickname,' said the phone.

'Ilackatooth,' I replied. (Shades of *Repulse* and Malta.)

'Ilackatooth,' said the Sergeant expressionlessly.

'He's ours,' said the phone. 'Would you send him back?'

They did – and in a police car which at least saved me the taxi fare. But I never lived it down in the ship . . .

We sailed for Rosyth a couple of hours after I got safely back on board but our programme was cancelled as soon as we arrived and we were ordered straight up to Scapa Flow. Here, in that vast anchorage, the Home Fleet lay ready for war. Once again the torpedoes were armed and live ammunition was brought up ready for the guns. Chamberlain paid one last visit to Hitler. In London, they started digging air raid trenches in the parks. At dinner, I looked at the Captain's First World War medals which I had never really thought about before. Now they took on a new significance. He knew what it was really like. He had been fired at. Had he been frightened? Would I be? I still had it all to come and I wondered how I would make out. This time, there were no singing crowds and emotion as there had been when we sailed for the Abyssinian crisis. This time it was serious and real and the shadow of Jutland lay over Scapa Flow. But only Munich happened and we returned to normal life.

The Home Fleet sailed for the Spring Cruise in early January and, after some truly appalling weather in the Bay of Biscay, the 6th Destroyer Flotilla paid a very successful, and bibulous, visit to Bordeaux. Then on to Gibraltar from where we operated until the Med Fleet joined us for the Combined Fleet exercises.

This was the climax of the year's training and was the occasion for two weeks' concentrated 'war games' at sea, culminating in a full scale action between the two great Fleets. All ships then returned to Gibraltar where the Staffs analysed and sorted out the lessons learned while the officers and seamen of the two Fleets renewed old friendships in a noisy, alcoholic thrash which must have been the nearest thing since Biblical days to splitting a Rock.

It was during this climacteric that a message flashed round the destroyers in the Pens that a notoriously stern and ascetic flotilla Padre had at last become drunk and was delivering a sermon, standing on his wardroom table, to the effect that, 'The weakness of the flesh is the fascination of the bloody stuff. Come on, chaps. Let's all go to the Universal . . .'

On that fell night, one famous destroyer Officer emerged from the bar in the Rock Hotel, looked down the long corridor, and saw the Commanders-in-Chief of the Home and Mediterranean Fleets in what seemed to him uncalled for pomposity of conversation outside the dining room. Reaching down, he picked up the end of the long strip of red carpet, and whether he pulled deliberately or merely fell backwards holding on to his only support will never be known. What is sure is that both C's-in-C were brought down and the culprit was whisked away by understanding friends before he could be identified. Appalled by what he had achieved, he then took to some serious drinking and, the next morning, turned the destroyer church parties and their band left instead of right and marched them back to the Pens, leaving an unsaluted Rear Admiral (Destroyer) standing alone on the dais outside the Cathedral.

Gibraltar, during the visit of the Combined Fleets, was a drunken, howling mayhem. The Main Street rocked to the noise of the bands and the packed bars. The patrols did their best. Provost Marshals uttered threats. But, just as good behaviour was expected in foreign ports, in Gibraltar there was an unwritten law that the Navy could enjoy itself in its own, uninhibited style. And it did.

Down in the harbour, in the early spring of 1939, the ships rested. Battleships, battlecruisers, aircraft carriers and cruiser flagships alongside the jetties. Destroyers in the Pens. Cruisers and destroyers unlucky enough not to find an alongside berth, at buoys. Light grey of the Mediterranean Fleet ships beside the dark grey of those from Home. All with the red, white and blue identification bands round 'B' turret called for by the needs of the Spanish Civil War

As the sun went down in a blaze of red glory over the hills of Spain, from bugles all over the harbour rang out the beautiful notes of 'Sunset' and the

White Ensigns came slowly down to be replaced by lights twinkling across the darkening water.

The great, concentrated might of British sea power lay there on the eve of war – and tragically unprepared.

The spirit was fine and the efficiency now beyond reproach. But Naval rearmament had started too late and, in any case, apart from the general obsolescence of the ships, we had still not built for the needs of the new war. With the Battle of the Atlantic only months ahead, the destroyers were intended to screen the Fleet and there was nothing to escort the convoys. Once again, the Combined Exercises had ended with torpedo attacks by the massed Flotillas of the two Fleets on the 'enemy' battle lines. Across the blue sea, over fifty destroyers raced against each other in a superb and unforgettable sight while the Commanders-in-Chief watched, delighted, from their Flagships' bridges. It was wonderful stuff. But it dated back to Jutland and 1916, not 1939.

Worst of all, we were entering a war in which air power would be supreme but we had pathetically little with which to counter it. In 1919, on dubious evidence, the Smuts Committee had decided to create the Royal Air Force. Jellicoe, as First Sea Lord, had argued that the Navy must maintain control of its own aviation but he was, by this time, so exhausted that even his handwriting had deteriorated. He made his case in such an unclear and muddled way that the First Lord minuted, 'Better not use this argument.' And so the RAF was born.

The result was that, in the few aircraft carriers we possessed, many pilots had been RAF instead of Naval Officers who understood the sea/air element. Now, too late, the Fleet Air Arm had become part of the Navy again but the aircraft were obsolete. How could a Royal Air Force, obsessed with a bombing mentality, be expected to divert valuable money and research effort into providing modern aircraft for the poor cousins at sea? Naval air power was symbolised by the 'Pusser's string bag', the old Swordfish, and a few obsolete fighters. Heart-breaking gallantry on the part of the pilots was not enough. The Navy was being sent to war almost naked to the air and, because the priorities were wrong and stayed wrong throughout the war with the RAF predominant in decision making, a great many brave men were to die needlessly and the war almost be lost in the Atlantic for the sake of bombing raids over Germany which had little comparative effect.

This, then, was the Navy which lay in Gibraltar harbour that spring evening in 1939. Tremendous in spirit, morale and skill but too small, wrongly designed and obsolescent in material for the test which lay before it.

Looking down from the battlements, though, one felt an almost emotional experience in the power, the pride, the sheer glory of the sight with the bugles of the two great Fleets combining in the lovely 'Sunset' call. The night was to come and we knew it. The night of darkness and struggle, of blood and death and closing waves overhead. But this was sunset, moving and beautiful. This was sunset of a day, a Navy and an Empire.

Chapter 8

HMS VERNON

Before the Spring Cruise I had volunteered for Motor Torpedo Boats of which the first flotilla had already been built. Now, on return to Portsmouth, I found, to my delight, my appointment to HMS *Vernon*, additional for MTBs.

On arrival, I found I was designated in command of MTB 21, one of four new 70-foot boats being built by Thorneycroft's and Vosper's. They were truly wonderful little ships, already a great advance on the original 60-foot Scott Paines. Bigger, faster, more seaworthy, better in every way, they had beautiful lines and their sinister black hulls raced through the water at over forty knots. I spent the summer watching her build.

Meanwhile, war was drawing close though, still, most people could not bring themselves to face up to the obvious. After Spain and Guernica, war, to civilians, meant instant and terrifying obliteration from the sky. The older people thought in terms of the carnage in the trenches. To them, only twenty years later, it was unthinkable that such folly should be allowed to happen again. Younger people, of my generation, had never known anything except peace and the unquestioned normality and security of their lives. They simply could not visualise nor accept the implications of war.

But the Dockyard was already blacked out with only dim blue lighting to stop people falling into the basins. Conscription was introduced for the first time in peace and the first 'militiamen', as they were called, appeared on the streets in their ill fitting khaki uniforms. Anti aircraft guns were being kept manned. On Southsea Common, little squads of recruits drilled uncertainly, watched by brightly dressed holidaymakers with a mixture of good natured derision, nervousness at the implications, or simple respect.

One morning in *Vernon*, I woke to the unexpected sight of a girl in my cabin. The old pensioner stewards had been called up and Wrens had taken over. We had never heard of them before except as odd, historic creatures with long skirts in old photographs of the Great War. Now we watched, amazed, as a whole squad of them, in cheerful summer frocks, drilled under an embarrassed

Gunner's Mate. Old and fat, young and beautiful, and everything in between, they tippy tuppied up and down the road in their high heels, meaning terribly well and trying so hard. Our hearts went out to them . . .

Then the whole country was blacked out and Air Raid Wardens patrolled the streets, pouncing on any errant gleam of light. Now nobody could fail to accept the inevitable. The mood of the country was one of infinite sadness and resignation, coupled with an astonishing resolve. There was no trace of World War I jingoism, no cheering crowds outside the Palace, no false emotions. Everybody knew well what we should be up against but knew too that the job must be done. There was no suggestion left of hanging back. The country understood that Hitler was evil and must be stopped. We had warned him that, if he invaded Poland, we would go to war. At 0445 on Friday 1 September, Hitler invaded Poland.

All that day, after the news had broken on the early morning radio bulletins, and all through the Saturday, the nation waited to hear of our declaration of war – but still no announcement came. The mood swung to one of anger and resentment. We were braced and ready. Surely there could not be the shame of another Munich . . .

On the Saturday evening, I went to the cinema, emerging to a terrific thunderstorm. The rain was pouring down, lightning was flashing and the thunder crashing just overhead. It was terrifyingly symbolic. At 1100 the next day, Sunday 3 September 1939, we listened to Chamberlain's tired, defeated voice on the wireless. 'I must therefore tell you, this country is at war with Germany.'

It had come at last.

And then, after everyone's fearful expectations, nothing happened. A couple of bombs were dropped in Scotland and killed a sheep and there was a false alarm in London. But nothing else. Life continued much as usual, except for the lonely and frightened city children who had suddenly found themselves with strangers in the countryside.

In *Vernon*, MTB 21 arrived and was commissioned. I took her proudly out and dashed round the Solent, putting her through her thrilling paces. It was bliss. Then, after a few weeks, I returned to harbour one day to be given the unbelievable news that 21 and 24 were to be sold to the Romanians. Apparently two urgently needed MTBs were worth less to us than the goodwill of a Balkan country. So I was appointed to MTB 100 in command.

MTB 100 was the training boat, one of the original 60-foot Scott Paines. Nothing like my warlike, impressive MTB 21, she was still great fun to take out daily, tearing round Spithead at high speed. But there was really very little worthwhile to do.

There was one excitement when the two remaining boats of what would have been the Thorneycroft/Vosper flotilla were ordered to go to Harwich and then cross the North Sea to torpedo the entrance to the big dry dock in Wilhelmshaven and so put it out of action. But they were soon back with the operation cancelled before it had barely begun. So we also learned what might be called Sod's Law of Hostilities – climax is always followed by anticlimax. (The very outbreak of war had been a case in point.)

In Felixstowe, the First Flotilla of the original Scott Paine boats were based in HMS *Beehive*, an ex RAF station adjacent to the little Felixstowe dock. They had come home from Malta, through the French canals, as soon as war was declared and now they waited for something to happen. In *Vernon* our few boats waited too as the Phoney War stretched pointlessly on through the winter.

The Battle of the River Plate was fought and *Graf Spee* scuttled herself in Montevideo. A good Naval victory was just what was wanted to bolster flagging civilian morale and show that, at least, someone was fighting somewhere.

In *Vernon*, we still sat in the small wardrooms of our boats, or in the Flotilla office, passing the hours till gin time playing 'Jutland' or gambling with Liar's Dice to see who would buy the drinks.

I shipped my second stripe on 16 January 1940, and, accordingly, was well satisfied with my new found dignity. At least, in *Vernon*, I could no longer be mistaken for a mere Acting Sub Lieutenant on courses – and my pay increased to £20 a month. The only snag was that my daily round still continued to lack anything much in the way of purpose. I was bored.

It seems to be inevitable that, when things are at their dullest and most secure, when you think that nothing is ever going to change or happen, life ups and banjaxes you. It happened to me.

I was wandering casually down the familiar corridor to the Flotilla Office when, happening to glance through a half open door, I saw a most attractive girl. In the Flotilla Office, I made enquiries. It appeared that her name was Pamela Miles, she was the Wren Personal Assistant cum secretary cum typist to Commander Maurice, our boss, and she had actually been there since war began but few of us had ever seen her because, with her door normally shut, she kept quietly to herself.

I went back to her office and asked her for a nonexistent Admiralty Fleet Order. She was so charmingly embarrassed at her inability to produce it that I had to help her look . . . By the time we gave up, the search had long ceased to matter and I knew I had found the nicest, kindest, most adorable girl in the whole wide, happy, wonderful world. My life had been transformed.

Meanwhile, other upheavals were taking place in life. MTBs were on the verge of their explosion into Coastal Forces. We would obviously need a proper, major base of our own. Many more boats were already being laid down and more officers were joining every day. The MTBs moved across the harbour and we established our own, custom built, base in HMS *Hornet* at the top of Haslar Creek.

The move had profound repercussions all round. Instead of being the only MTB Wren, Pam was now one of many. Cooks, stewards, stores assistants, telephonists, they came in all varieties and a Wren Officer in Vernon was appointed to keep an eye on them. Pam and Mam soon crossed swords. Mam wanted her in uniform instead of flowery frocks. The MTB officers wanted her to stay as she was. So did Pam. Whenever Mam came over to *Hornet*, Pam's uniform always seemed to be at the cleaners . . . Having picked up the old prewar destroyer expression which we used when ridding ourselves of an undesirable, Mam announced that Pam was 'a bad influence on the messdeck' and Pam was not recommended for Leading Rate.

Then the war hotted up. Our move to *Hornet* had jerked us out of our *Vernon* torpor. Now, on 9 April, Hitler invaded Norway and British forces were at last in serious action. But even this did not disrupt us too much. Every evening, I went ashore to Pam's flat in Queen's Gate and we fell more and more in love.

One evening, I was walking her home when the heel came off her shoe. Delighted with the opportunity, I swept her up and carried her down Osborne Road and up the stairs to her flat. As we opened the door the phone was ringing.

'*Hornet* here. Come back at once.'

Sadly, I left. At last, the sands were running out.

The next day I was on my way to Blyth. Two little Coastal Motor Boats of World War I design were to be sold to the Finns for their war against Soviet Russia. Now I was to commandeer them and bring them back to *Hornet* where they would form the nucleus of a new 10th MTB Flotilla to which I would be appointed in command.

I found them stowed as Upper Deck cargo on a merchant ship whose Master was most reluctant to unload them on my authority. However, eventually he did so in return for a rather scruffy receipt on a bit of a signal pad. Then we sailed – and an appalling trip it was.

I was used to boats with some form of bridge house, a messdeck for the sailors and a wardroom where the officers could sleep. Proper MTBs had heads and a galley where food could be cooked. They might be small but they were complete, self sufficient little ships. MTBs 67 and 68 were simply open 55-foot motor boats. They had a small forepeak abaft which was the engine room containing two large and noisy engines, the Motor Mechanic, the stoker, and a Telegraphist who could never hear his morse over the din of the engines on the rare occasions when the set had not gone off the board because of the vibration.

At the after end of the engines was a small platform on which stood myself, the Coxswain and an Able Seaman. There was just room for the three of us as we hung on, our feet in the engine room by the Telegraphist's ear but the upper part of our bodies vulnerable to the wind and spray which tore back into our faces over a small windscreen. Behind us lay two greasy torpedoes in troughs.

We carried no food nor water and even peeing had to be done over the side, an evolution requiring desperation, skill, two men to hold on to you as you stood with knees bent against the smacking down of the hull on the waves – and sublimation by a somewhat incongruous little trickle into the foaming water rushing past at your feet.

We had, of course, no chart table so that proper navigation would not have been possible even if our unswung compass had not been yawing 20 degrees either way. However, somehow I found my way to the Humber and we put in to Grimsby for the night of 10 May. Here, in a local hotel, we received devoted service because, spray soaked and bedraggled in our oldest uniforms, the management at once decided that we must be survivors from some heroic sinking. We ate a huge dinner, switched on the nine o'clock news – and heard of the invasion of Belgium, Holland and France.

We spent the next night in Dover and, on Saturday morning, I raced the final lap to Portsmouth.

MTB 67 went down to Portland to test fire our torpedoes and disaster struck. A very expensive noise from the engine room resulted in the discovery, in the gear box of one engine, of a lump of congealed brass filings the size of a fist. It was the precursor of many such incidents to come, leaving me with a permanent sense of insecurity and a fear that my boat might break down at any minute – hardly an encouraging state of mind later on when we were in hostile waters far across the North Sea.

Back in *Hornet*, repairs were put in hand and I met, with total disbelief, the remainder of my flotilla. It consisted of three boats, 104, 106 and 107. The first two were even smaller than 67 – a mere 45 feet with only one engine. The third was smaller still, only 40 feet, and could not even go astern so that there was no way of stopping it other than drifting to a halt. They were the product of the twisted mind of some insane theorist who had designed them to be carried on the upper decks of cruisers, which were apparently supposed to stop dead in the middle of a Fleet action so that the fragile little things could be lowered over the side into a flat calm sea to carry out the devastating attack available to them with their single torpedo. It was truly unbelievable but the war was going badly and this was, apparently, all we could raise in a hurry.

MTB67. Peeing was difficult . . .

Anyhow, what did I expect in the way of a command with my seniority? I was lucky not to be watchkeeping in a big ship. At least I was now V 10 – the CO of the 10th MTB Flotilla.

We had only a few days to get organised so Pam and I became engaged. Then, one day she appeared in her thick serge uniform. Mam had finally won. The war was serious now and the halcyon days were over. We had had just three months to meet and learn to love. Now the gentle time of courting had been brutally ended and, all of a sudden, our life turned upside down. The Army in France was in full retreat and Portsmouth was being bombed at last. The days, and particularly the nights, were noisy and menacing. The old, safe, familiar world had become strange and threatening.

Two days after I gave her the ring, I had to leave her. On 26 May, the Flotilla sailed to war.

Chapter 9

THE WOBBLY TENTH

L ooking back, it all happened so gradually. For years, Hitler's antics had
shown that war was obviously coming but, when it arrived, it was only
the Phoney War. Then, after seven months, we had the Norwegian campaign
to prove the war was real, but it was still distant and did not really impinge on
our daily lives. Even after the invasion of the Low Countries and the appalling
speed with which disaster struck, I was not really psychologically prepared
for the full implications when I suddenly met them.

We were fuelling in Dover on the way to *Beehive* and I stood on the jetty
next to an ambulance loading wounded. From inside, a voice was calling,
'Mummy, mummy.' It was the first time I had heard that most pathetic and
ubiquitous of battlefield cries. There were several soldiers standing around.
None seemed to be interested. They just stood, blank faces expressionless,
and I was vaguely shocked until I realised that, to them, I must have looked
just the same. Whatever we were all thinking, we kept our emotions to
ourselves.

This brought the reality of war home to me in a very personal way but
worse was about to come. Fuelling completed, I was sent for to be briefed for
an operation that very evening. Calais had fallen and a flotilla of the big,
powerfully armed German E-Boats was expected to go there under cover of
night. MTB 67 was to hide outside and, when they arrived and slowed down
to enter harbour, we were to get in amongst them and start firing. It was
appreciated that our pathetic pair of Lewis guns could do little damage but it
was hoped that the surprise would cause them, milling about in the darkness,
to panic and start firing at each other. When I had started an all German battle
I could scarper.

It was not a plan which filled me with enthusiasm. E-Boats had girt great
cannon and it would only need one tracer in the 2,000 gallons of high octane
petrol we carried to put an end to my war before it had even begun. It was
rather like telling a kitten to go and provoke a pack of pit bull terriers. I was,
I felt, too young to die, especially so soon.

Then, just before we were to sail, I was sent for again. Operation cancelled. Instead, we were to take three Belgian cabinet ministers, who had been having secret talks in London, back to their country. After dropping them off, we were to go on up the canal to Nieuport and collect the Belgian king.

The ministers turned up shortly afterwards, three charming middle aged men who made no complaint at being packed into our tiny cockpit but merely stood there, clutching their hats and getting soaked to the skin as we tore across the Channel to Belgium.

The trouble was, of course, that when we got there I had absolutely no idea where I was. We could just make out a low-lying coast and a sandy beach but no lights showed and there was no nautical way of fixing our position. Nicuport could be in either direction. My passengers stood, patiently waiting. Being civilians, they had a simple faith that ships, like trains, would arrive at their destination. They did not understand the 10th MTB Flotilla. Now they were my only hope.

In my best French, I asked whether they would be prepared to wade ashore, find a house, ask in which direction Nieuport lay and then come back and let me know so that I could go and collect their king. They took it magnificently. Removing their shoes and socks and rolling up their trousers, they paddled in to the beach. About half an hour later, just as I was getting anxious and wondering if they had forsaken me, one of them returned and shouted out to us the Belgian equivalent of 'It's thataway.' Perhaps wisely, he did not offer to re-embark and come with us. So, thanking each other profusely for services rendered, we went off in different directions and I eventually stumbled on the entrance.

As we crept in between the breakwaters, a figure appeared above us and shouted a question. Who were we?

'*Anglais,*' I replied.

'*Allez, allez,*' called back the man, agitatedly. '*Les Boches sont ici. Boches! Boches! Partout!*'

This was all we wanted to complete the night but I felt I could hardly use this warning as an excuse to abandon the king so, feeling rather as a rat must when it wonders if it is entering a trap, I crept on up the canal.

Suddenly, ahead, we saw torches and a group of people. As we looked, a vast royal car was pushed slowly over the edge of the wall to fall with a heavy splash into the canal.

Good for the king, we thought, but it was not His Majesty who awaited us but Admiral Sir Roger Keyes. He had been with Leopold trying to encourage him to fight on, but he had failed. Now he returned alone.

MTB 67 rejoined the rest of the Flotilla in *Beehive* the next day. Whatever the boats were like, the Officers and men were a magnificent lot. The sailors were all regular RN, thoroughly pleased to be out of big ships and prepared to enjoy their new life. 104 and 106 were commanded by two peacetime RNVR subs of the best sort who had been First Lieutenants in the First Flotilla. One, Richard 'Stinker' Smith was to become one of the best friends of my life. 107, as usual, was unique. As if to recompense me for being given such a ghastly little boat, it was commanded by Lieutenant John Cameron, RNVR, who at the ripe old age of forty, was known as Gran'pa to us all. He was a Scottish KC (later to become Scotland's most distinguished judge) who had the heart of a lion and the mind of a naughty boy. He was bliss.

However, affairs were moving too fast for me to get to know them then. A bare forty-eight hours after our arrival in Felixstowe, the Flotilla was ordered to land its torpedoes and return flat out to Dover. Wondering what on earth could be up now, we sailed and, at the entrance to the Thames estuary, met an astonishing sight. There, crossing our bows from one horizon to the other, was a long, disorganised procession of pleasure boats, yachts, paddle steamers and ferries. Used as we were to a deserted wartime sea, it seemed as if the world had gone mad in front of our eyes.

Alongside in Dover, we got the even more astonishing explanation. The Army was being evacuated from Dunkirk and everything that could float and move was needed there to help. The rest of the Flotilla were to go and lend a hand generally but I had special orders. I was to seek out Lord Gort, the Commander-in-Chief of the British Expeditionary Force and bring him safely home to Dover.

We managed to find Dunkirk because the pillars of smoke were visible miles out to sea. Close inshore, we cruised down the beaches of La Panne looking at the amazing scene. The sands were covered with khaki groups, straggling out to sea in long crocodile lines. To seaward, the bigger ships steamed slowly up and down, destroyers, sloops, paddle and pleasure steamers. Little yachts and anything else small enough to get into the shallow water off the shore were shuttling back and forth from the human crocodiles, taking the soldiers to the ships beyond. Enemy batteries further up the coast were firing in a desultory manner at both beaches and shipping and aircraft came over incessantly, bombing and strafing the troops and the ships. Over all the sun shone, the water was sparkling blue and the sands yellow. It was a perfect day to go to the seaside and, somehow, it made what was happening seem totally unreal.

I went alongside the Senior Officer's ship and, going inboard, reported my purpose and orders. He was in touch with Army HQ by radio and, in a short time, gave me the answer from Lord Gort – terse and to the point. The Commander-in-Chief would not even consider leaving his Army at such a time. He did not wish to hear from me again.

It seemed that Kings and Commanders-in-Chief were strangely reluctant to embark in MTB 67 but there were a lot of chaps around who would be only too pleased so we started in to evacuate.

We went back up the beach to the first crocodile. Weary, patient men up to their necks in water, they stood without complaint, waiting for rescue. We pulled them inboard and they lay collapsed on our tiny upper deck and in the torpedo troughs. One, his head covered with blood-soaked bandages, stood back. 'You seem rather full,' he said. 'I can wait.' We grabbed him as he stood, waveringly, in the water and gave him what little help we could. We shuttled back and forth from the beach to the ships, each time with about forty soaked, exhausted men. But the crocodiles never seemed to grow less nor did the crowds on the sands.

Finally, uncounted hours later, our fuel began to run low and we turned reluctantly for home, the whole boat crowded with a last mixed bag of wet, weary soldiers. It was an uncomfortable trip but at least a quick one. And they were too tired to care.

As we reached Dover, one engine broke down completely and the other one was suspect. From bitter experience by now, I knew we must have repairs. We staggered back to *Hornet* on the one unreliable engine. They took five buckets of sand out of the errant one and the other had to be stripped down completely. By the time we were ready again, Dunkirk was over. Gran'pa Cameron in MTB 107 had been the last to leave. He had been making circles in the harbour, unable to stop, scooping out soldiers by the light of the flames as he drifted past until the weight of machine gun fire had made him look up from his absorption to realise 107 was alone. Then, and not till then, with his boat full, he left.

When the 10th MTB Flotilla finally reassembled in HMS *Beehive*, I took stock of the situation. It was only about a week since we had originally sailed from *Hornet* – new, inexperienced, untried, even strangers to each other. Now we were veterans. We had been bombed, shelled and machine gunned. We had seen a broken Army in final defeat. We had run our boats and, indeed, ourselves to the limit, and beyond, of normal endurance. In fact, we had not really suffered much and far worse was to come – but we were not to know that at the time. The point was that we had been able to achieve in a few days what is beyond price in a fighting unit, that spirit of internal camaraderie and confidence felt by those who have been tested together and have come through. Nothing in peacetime can approach it and only those who have had the experience can really understand. We were a team. We had justified pride and confidence in ourselves and, with our pathetic little boats, we were prepared to take on Hitler and the whole might of the Nazi Reich. Our morale could not have been higher. Without my lifting a finger, I had been presented with a Flotilla with tremendous *esprit de corps*.

Beehive did take us seriously at first and thought we could be used as proper MTBs. The Germans now held the whole of the North Sea and Channel coastlines and, night after night, our boats crossed the North Sea seeking out enemy convoys. But what was possible for the First Flotilla with their seaworthy little ships was far beyond the capacity of the Tenth's small open motor boats. Even if we didn't break down, which someone always did, a sea state which the First Flotilla could take in its stride was far beyond our meagre capacity.

A night's patrol involved twelve to fourteen hours without food, rest or even a drink. The boats would rush across the sea with their planing bows crashing heavily into every trough between the waves, sheets of spray soaking us to the skin as soon as we left harbour. We stood, knees always bent against the merciless pounding motion, streaming eyes straining through the spray-soaked darkness to keep in touch with the others. When we returned the following morning we were so exhausted that it was physically difficult to climb from the boat to the jetty. It was a long way from the old forenoon spent dashing round a sunny Solent.

It quickly became obvious that the 10th Flotilla must be used for inshore work only. Luckily for our morale, there was an obvious job for us as a counter invasion patrol.

So now we spent our nights only a few miles off shore, waiting for the invasion barges to arrive. All the Dutch, Belgian and, particularly, the French ports were full of them – barges commandeered from the Rhine and all the major rivers of Europe. In England, the Army was regrouping, almost entirely lacking transport, artillery and armour, all of which had been left at Dunkirk. A wireless appeal by Anthony Eden produced overnight a new 'force' of old men and boys – the Home Guard, largely armed with shot guns and pikes and 'uniformed' only with brassards on their normal civilian clothing. 'We shall defend our island,' said Churchill, 'whatever the cost may be. We shall fight on the beaches, we shall fight on the landing grounds, we shall fight in the fields and in the streets, we shall fight in the hills. We shall never surrender.' The whole nation agreed and stood rock solid behind him. It was, indeed, our 'finest hour'.

I will always remember one particular night when the panic was at its height. MTB 67 lay a few miles off Lowestoft. Our engines were cut and we had gathered together in the cockpit for an illicit smoke. In the night and the dark and the circumstances, the inhibitions of rank and discipline fell away and we were just six young men discussing our innermost thoughts. We talked about the war, what might happen, how we came to be here in this little boat, waiting.

Obviously, when the Germans arrived, we would be very lucky if we survived our attack on their heavily defended convoys. Apart from our two dubious torpedoes, a couple of soldiers had more fire power than we had with our twin Lewis guns. On the other hand, we could broadcast the vital early warning and, given speed and determination, we could probably kill a damned sight more of them than there were of us. We sat in silence, considering what seemed the imminent prospect. The land was a faint streak along the horizon. I remember looking at it, thinking 'dear little island' and feeling somehow very privileged. Then the Coxswain summed it up for us all. Leading Seaman Brown was an enormous, ginger haired Cornish tin miner whose hobby was all-in wrestling. Normally rather dour and uncommunicative, his voice suddenly came from the darkness. 'I've got a wife and two kids,' he said. 'All I know is I want them to be free. And, if I have to die for that, it'll be worth it.' It may sound banal nowadays but it summed up what we felt. And banality can be moving . . .

In the meantime, the first stage of the invasion ('Operation Sealion') had begun with the Battle of Britain and the first stage of that was the bombing of ports and airfields. So now Pam was in the front line too.

We were planning to get married in early October when she would join me in Felixstowe. At the time, however threatening the war, this seemed to be a perfectly feasible plan. Then, one ghastly day, it all collapsed. Out of the blue came the totally unexpected news that, early in the New Year, the 10th Flotilla was to go to the Middle East. It meant the destruction of all our dreams and a parting almost as soon as we were married. Risking the wrath of the censor, I wrote a carefully worded letter explaining that the bottom was about to drop out of our world. I got her reply by return. 'Thank God you've heard at last. I've known for two months but couldn't tell you.'

The blitz worsened. Having failed to ground Fighter Command or close the ports, Goering switched his attack to London. Now the 10th Flotilla was given a new job. We went down to Sheerness and spent our time careering round the Thames estuary recovering the pilots, British or German, who had baled out over the sea. (The skill lay in guessing where a parachute high in the sky would eventually come down in the water and racing to the spot so that the dunking period was minimal. Perfection would be for the pilot to fall onto your deck – but nobody ever quite achieved that.) Meanwhile, the weeks passed and October drew near. We had planned to be married on the 7th when 67 was due for a much needed refit.

The day I should have left Sheerness, inevitably, it all had to be postponed. Operation 'Lucid' was designed to halt the invasion scare in one glorious, incendiary night. Some old merchant ships had been filled with a special chemical which, when it touched salt water, would set the sea on fire. The idea was to take them to Boulogne and Calais and scuttle them just outside the two harbours so that the flood tide would carry the flames in and burn out the whole fleet of invasion barges. (Straight from the Armada. Drake would have loved it.) At the last minute, someone had had a bright idea. Send the MTBs to follow the fireships and take off their crews as the scuttling charges went off. With luck, our speed would enable us to escape the conflagration.

Two nights running, for some unexplained reason, the operation was postponed – and I was in dead trouble. We had had to lift our torpedoes out of their troughs to make room for the scuttlers to sit on our decks and the dockyard crane driver had refused to do it until he had had his tea break. Our last minute inclusion meant there was no time to wait if we were to sail on time so we had done the job ourselves. Now the union was threatening to bring the whole Yard out on strike. Obviously we could not explain the need for our urgency to the dockyard maties and nothing would satisfy them other than my blood. I was thankful when we finally sailed.

The MTBs were taken in tow by destroyers to avoid the danger of our breaking down *en route* and we set off in high spirits. At last we were going to do something worthwhile. Then, after an hour or so, we heard the dull crump of an explosion ahead. A few minutes later, a dim blue light from the destroyer flashed us the message 'Operation cancelled'.

The leading destroyer had been blown up by the first use of an acoustic mine. Nobody knew then what it was but the Channel had been swept and all the ships degaussed against magnetic mines. It must therefore be something new and, if there were more and one of the fireships were to be sunk, the same flood tide on which we were counting would carry a burning sea into Dover and Folkestone. The risk could not be taken and the whole party was called off.

It would have been lovely if we'd done it – the invasion scare written off overnight, an electrifying effect on a nervous nation and a heroic bridegroom at the altar. But, once again, climax had been followed by anticlimax and, as it was, I just slunk thankfully away from Sheerness and its dockyard maties, put 67 on the slip in Felixstowe, and rushed down to Portsmouth and Pam.

The next morning, Monday 14 October, at eleven o'clock, we were married in the lovely little Garrison Church in Old Portsmouth. Within days, both the Garrison Church and the wedding photographer's shop were destroyed.

We only had time for a forty-eight hour honeymoon in a country hotel near Guildford where we stood in the garden in the evening watching the blitz over London. The next morning we set off for Felixstowe but the blitz we had watched had caused so much damage to the railway that no trains were running to London and we had to wait overnight in Guildford.

We tried again the following day and, as the train limped slowly into

Waterloo, I suddenly realised that I had been a total clot. It must be remembered that we were expecting the invasion at any minute, day or night. Even Naval Officers, therefore, carried big revolvers strapped round their waists at all times. I had taken mine off during the actual marriage service but it went on again immediately afterwards and, if I hadn't been able to wear a dinner jacket for dinner, at least, in uniform, I was properly dressed under the circumstances. But a large gun was an unusual appendage for a peacefully minded sailor on his honeymoon and, with so many nicer things on my mind, I had entirely forgotten it the morning we left Guildford. Now I suddenly realised that I had left a fully loaded Service revolver in the chest of drawers of our hotel bedroom.

We rushed into the nearest police station and I explained my predicament. They were very nice and understanding and, a few days later, a constable delivered it to me in *Beehive*, a major relief for which the Metropolitan Police charged me the princely sum of ninepence. (In the meantime, I had hidden the loss by carrying a spare gun filched from one of our boats which had been sunk.)

But the honeymoon really ended on Ipswich station. As we waited to change trains I saw, to my amazement, Ian Quarrie, the CO of MTB 106. He should have been down in Sheerness, recovering pilots. Now he stood in front of us, grinning. 'Hello, Mrs Anderson,' he greeted Pam cheerfully. 'I've been blown up on a mine and I find considerable difficulty in sitting down.' The acoustic mines which had caused the cancellation of 'Lucid' had become such a menace that they were using my poor Wobbly Tenth as human minesweepers until they could think of a better way of dealing with the problem. We were more expendable than merchant ships or destroyers.

We lived from day to day. The imminence of departure to the Middle East was always with us. The boats were still crossing the North Sea if the weather was calm or else mounting invasion patrols off the coast. One day, Pam and I went for a walk. A couple of Messerschmidts suddenly flew low overhead and machine-gunned us in passing. We had scarcely recovered when I saw a sailor on a bicycle coming up behind us. He was waving his arm and shouting. I was to return to *Beehive* at once.

Commandeering his bike, I pedalled furiously back to the Base. This could only mean that the invasion had started and, sure enough, as I arrived I heard the thunderous roar of all the boats as they warmed up their engines. There was a message for me to report to the Senior Officer immediately.

Accordingly, I trotted off to the Operations Room to get my orders, my mind in a turmoil. Dramatically wrenched from the side of my young bride, slightly out of breath, remembering the night off Lowestoft, determined that the Wobbly Tenth would justify its existence now that the hour had come, I was ready for anything.

The Boss was a tough Lieutenant Commander, Monty Donner, CO of the First Flotilla, a hard disciplinarian who demanded the highest standards at all times. He was standing staring at a chart of the North Sea, a pair of dividers in his hand. He looked at me, his face expressionless. I waited.

'V 10,' he said. 'This morning I saw two of your ratings walking along the jetty wearing overalls *and gym shoes*.' He was obviously genuinely appalled at the crime. Dammit, it was almost guff! I stared at him, suppressing a nervous inclination to giggle. Dartmouth and an outraged Cadet Captain rose in my mind. Forgetting emotion and idealism, I got the message. If Armageddon came, the professional Navy would still pipe 'Up Spirits' at the correct time. The standard was the standard and it would be maintained without bending or hysteria. If Hitler did come he would naturally be defeated even if it cost us our lives. Should it unfortunately do so, at least we should die correctly dressed.

We remained at immediate notice for some hours but no orders came through to sail. Something happened that day. There was talk of hundreds of burned bodies of German troops being washed ashore but, as far as we were concerned, it all fizzled out into just another false alarm.

Pam and I had a joint birthday party in our flat, her 21st and my 24th, then, as winter drew on, we moved to a bungalow in the town. By then, we knew that Pam was pregnant. I felt that, whatever was to come, I was leaving something behind me.

The invasion scare had diminished with the winter weather but there were no certainties. We sat together on the side of our bed and discussed what Pam should do if the Germans came after I had gone. Should I leave her my spare revolver to defend herself and our baby *in extremis* or would she be better advised to demand fair treatment as an officer's wife and trust that their rank consciousness would outweigh their brutality? The arguments seemed equally divided but we finally decided that to have a gun would certainly be asking for trouble whereas, without arms, she might be safe. I kept the weapon myself.

The Flotilla went for one final sweep of the Dutch coast and was accused, quite falsely, by German propaganda of machine-gunning lightships. At least, we felt, if they had bothered to invent such a story it meant that they had taken the threat of our presence more seriously than we might have expected.

In the first week of 1941, the boats were taken away to be freighted. I had to go to *Hornet* to make the final arrangements for our departure. Pam came too to make the most of our last few, precious days

As the train drew into the Town station, we looked out over the Guildhall square. Pompey had had its first full blitz the night before, though we had not known of it.

In the square, small queues waited at emergency soup wagons. As far as we could see, the city seemed totally devastated. We found a taxi which had to pick its way half round Southsea to do the short trip down to the ferry at the Hard.

The A and B had gone. The street where the Goat had stood could not even be identified through the ruins. Our favourite restaurant was lost somewhere in the wilderness of broken buildings. We drove through a wasteland, beyond speech, just clutching hands in stricken silence.

The Portsmouth which we had both known and loved had gone and somehow I knew my youth had gone with it. My father had met and married my mother after a short engagement and had then gone to the Middle East, never to return. Now history seemed to be repeating itself. But, this time, would even my wife and child be allowed to live?

Joining *Repulse*, Subs' courses and wild oats, *Forester*, *Vernon* and the Phoney War, falling in love and getting married – the end of it all seemed to be symbolised by the physical destruction of the stage on which it had all happened. It had been a short youth but a very merry one. Now I was being asked to pick up the tab. It was what I had been trained for so at least I was not having to sacrifice what my civilian contemporaries in uniform had to give. But, as we picked our way through the ruins, I thought wistfully of all that might have been.

The next day we set off. Pam was wearing a plain brown hat which I thought looked rather schoolgirlish and, whether my youth had been left behind or not, I was still young enough to feel it was unsuitable so, in London, we went to Oxford Street and I bought her a far more dashing one.

We caught the night train to Glasgow and, early in the morning, changed to a local train to Greenock. The carriage was packed with uncouth Scots shipyard workmen. Pam had to be horribly sick through the window. She collapsed weakly back on her seat, her face strained and white under the dashing little hat, and all the workmen cosied her with inarticulate sympathy. They were true gentlemen.

I went out to the troopship and found that married men were to be allowed to go back and sleep ashore for one night. Pam had stayed in case this happened. All the hotels were full but she had stopped a nice, comfortable Scots body in the street and sought her advice. We spent our last night together in a child's nursery with teddy bears and toys.

In the morning we said goodbye and I went out to the troopship across the tossing, grey waters of the Clyde.

The convoy sailed that evening.

Chapter 10

TROOPSHIP

There is something terribly final about sailing away in a ship. Leaving by road or rail at least you remain in the same familiar element. You even feel you could turn round and go back. But, in a ship, as the land drops away astern, you enter a new and entirely different world. All that has happened in your life up to that moment seems to have been left behind. It is something in the memory bank of a mental computer. Yesterday, last week, last year, are simply stored recollections, hardly more vivid in your mind than the events in a gripping novel you might be reading. Reality has become the vast, empty expanse of rolling ocean that encompasses you. It is a total translation from one life to another.

My new life was horrible. HM Transport *Salween* was a cargo liner which, in peacetime, ran to the Far East. Her holds had been transformed into dark, airless messdecks where daylight never reached and, because human beings weigh so much less than a full, well stowed cargo, she was hopelessly top heavy and rolled her guts out in the smallest swell. To make things worse, we met appalling January gales as we steered west halfway across the Atlantic to be clear of U-boats on the run south. Although she was a Naval trooper, most of the 'sailors' were young 'Hostilities Only' ratings who would have been seasick on wet grass. The Officers were not so badly off in the cabin accommodation but the suffering on the crowded messdecks was truly dreadful. If animals had been shipped under such conditions there would have been hell to pay.

The new Tenth Flotilla consisted of my own old MTBs 67 and 68 plus five more of the same 55-foot design, dredged up from the horrible Thorneycroft stable. They were to prove equally unreliable. However, being officially a bigger and better flotilla which would operate independently, it had been decided that V 10 should now be a Lieutenant Commander and I had been superseded by a chap called Peter Peake. The other officers were the best type of RNVR. Only half of them were to come home.

The Master of *Salween* was a silly old man who was terrified of the war.

He insisted on always having two Officers of the Watch (which meant they had to do 4 hours on 4 hours off and so were always exhausted) and he wanted his own Officers to be backed up by two Naval Officers. I evaded this tedious watchkeeping by volunteering to be the ship's censor, which meant that I spent much of my time wading through hundreds of letters home.

I soon learned that what most of the youngsters missed most of all was Dad taking them down to their local pub on a Saturday night, obviously an English institution of which I had been unaware. Other letters worried me. Too many, particularly among the married men, wrote home snivelling, whingeing letters full of self pity. They described the awful conditions on board, said how dreadfully they missed their wives so that they just couldn't stand life any longer and only wanted to die, and so on and so on. These writers (quite improperly) I sent for and spoke to firmly.

'Where do you live? Liverpool? How do you think your wife is feeling, facing up to the blitz and rationing alone? Don't you think she misses you just as much? Wouldn't it be nicer for her to get strong, loving letters of support from you? Can't you see you're only adding to her burden if she gets a miserable whine like this? For God's sake go away and write something cheerful which will help her to stick it out at her end.'

They all looked astonished then sheepish as the point struck home. None failed to take the advice.

I went back to my pile of letters and learned another lesson. We are truly an island race and, to us, the sea is something between Dover and Calais. Here was our ship going down the North Atlantic and the South Atlantic, round the Cape and all the way up East Africa, through the Red Sea to Egypt. Yet every one of these young landsmen wrote, 'When we get to the other side . . .'

We left the northern winter gales behind us, the sea became calm at last and the sky blue. We entered the tropics and put in to Freetown. No leave was given, but the palm fringed African shore looked exotic and exciting. There was a bum boat with the name 'Believe God' painted along its side whose occupant, an enormous naked negro in a top hat, would dive for coins thrown from the deck above. Wartime England seemed a long way off.

We sailed again and crossed the Equator with all the customary ceremony. Now our trouble was the merciless heat on the overcrowded messdecks. There was no air conditioning and the Master would not allow canvas swimming baths to be rigged in case the splashes of water damaged his (anti magnetic mine) degaussing cables. The fact that they had been swamped by half the North Atlantic meant nothing to him.

The hot, humid tropical days dragged by. In the Officers' Mess suggestion book someone wrote, 'To avoid monotony, can the ceiling fans rotate anti clockwise instead of clockwise?' The Committee replied, 'As we have crossed the Equator, this is, in fact, happening.'

We had a concert party and sang the *Salween* song:

> Send out the Army and the Air Force
> Send out the rank and file
> Send out the jolly Territorials
> They'll face the danger with a smile . . .
> Send out the boys of the Old Brigade
> Who made our England free
> Send out my brother, my sister and my mother,
> But for Chrissakes, don't send me . . .

Eventually, after nearly two months on board, we reached Durban and had a chance, at last, to stretch our legs ashore. But then came a bitter disappointment. It appeared that no leave would be given because we were not welcome in the town. However, this was immediately followed by another message. Of course we were welcome. They had thought we were Australians.

The Australians, it seemed, had drunkenly disgraced themselves in a previous convoy. They had swapped babies around in their prams and driven a horse drawn hearse at a flat gallop down the main street with the coffin bucketing about in the back. Australians, in Durban, were Bad News.

But not us. Our reception was unbelievable. The thousands of troops in the big convoy were simply adopted by the first people they met in the streets. It was World War 1 euphoria and we were the heroes off to the Front. Nothing was too good for us and lovely girls sat in their cars outside the dock gates waiting to pick up the lucky ones of their choice.

We had come from a wartime Britain with rationing, the blackout and the blitz. We had left Greenock in the snow. We had spent many long weeks at sea under appalling conditions. Now it was summer in South Africa. The lights blazed in the velvety darkness of the nights and the bathing beaches beckoned by day. At home, they would have been full of barbed wire and mines. Here they had only gorgeous girls and sun. Suddenly, we had been translated from the war to a peaceful paradise where beautiful angels loved us. We let ourselves go.

When all the troop ships had been coaled and made ready again for sea, it was decided that, before we left, we should thank this wonderful city by staging a march past the Lord Mayor of Durban. It was a major troop convoy and fifteen thousand soldiers, sailors and airmen turned out. *Salween*, being a Naval trooper, provided the leading contingent and I, being in charge of it, led the Navy. The band struck up and marched off. I followed. Behind me came the long parade, stretching back the whole length of the docks.

At first, all went well. The pavements were thronged, four or five deep, with cheering and clapping citizens. Our marching was good. We came to the dais. I gave the Lord Mayor a splendid 'Eyes right' and my best salute – and saw, to my horror, the band peel off, countermarch and stay beside the dais to play the marching troops past. Suddenly, I was all alone – except for the interminable cavalcade behind me.

It was easy to see where I should turn out of the square but, after that and with no music, the crowds thinned out and then disappeared. Which road should I take? Durban was still a strange town to me and I suddenly realised that I had no idea of how to find my way back to the docks from this unfamiliar street. Straight ahead? Turn right? Left? Wherever I went, fifteen thousand pairs of unquestioning boots would follow me. Out into the country – and a whole convoy of troops lost, never to be seen again? Pretend I was alone and just go for a much needed drink? I thought of the landlord's face if I should turn into the nearest pub . . .

We were coming to a big crossroads with streets leading off in all directions. Real panic began to rise until I heard a low moan from a police siren just behind me. The fuzz drew alongside and grinned. 'All right,' they said. 'Just follow us.' I was saved.

Our last night we were duty troopship and I had to stay on board. At about midnight, a call came from the Military Police. A group of drunken Australian deserters was smashing up a dockside pub. Could we send a patrol to help? I sent for Ginger Brown and explained the problem.

'Belt and gaiters, Coxswain,' I told him, 'and off you go. How many do you want?'

'I'll just take our own, sir,' he said. 'MTB 67 can deal with this.'

Later I heard what had happened from a fascinated Provost Marshal. Apparently the civil police were reluctant to go in and reckoned that they'd done enough when they'd cleared the street. The MPs had tried but been thrown out. So they had waited for reinforcements – us. Leading Seaman Brown had arrived with my stoker, Able Seaman and Telegraphist. He had sized up the situation, listened to the screams and whoops from the pub, then just nodded to the other three. They had marched slowly down the street with the typical matelot's roll, and in through the door. The noise inside rose to a crescendo, then there was a crash of breaking glass as an Australian came hurtling out through the window. Another crash and another Australian. Then dead silence. A minute later, out came my boat's crew, holding the arms of four more cowed Aussies. Ginger Brown had turned them over to the MPs, pointed back at the two bodies in the street, and then my four had just marched sedately and immaculately back to their truck. None of them had spoken a word. 'But,' said the Provost Marshal, 'they looked very happy.'

We went through the Suez Canal, arrived in Port Said, disembarked the boats and moved into a hotel. Home became distant again as we accustomed ourselves to the yellow glare of Egypt. The gallant merchant seamen in *Salween* had got into the hold and rifled the sailors' kit. There was a hell of a lot to do before, finally, everything was sorted out and we sailed the boats round to Alexandria.

Here, we met the war again. The Battle of Matapan had just been fought and British troops were being evacuated from Greece after our disastrous attempt to help when the Germans had reinforced the Italian invasion of that country. Now it was expected that Crete would be the next target so the 10th Flotilla were to be sent there. We sailed almost at once.

Chapter 11

CRETE

The Desert War involved a series of pendulum like advances and retreats on the part of the Eighth Army and the Afrika Korps. As each, in turn, drove the other back across the empty wastes, the victors were eventually left at the end of hopelessly extended lines of communications with food, fuel and ammunition impossible to provide in the bulk required. As a result, the advance had to stop. The vanquished, on the other hand, had been driven back close to their own base where replenishment was easy and plentiful. Like a spring put under compression, they simply replaced their losses and then shot forward again with their over-extended opponents now in retreat, and the whole process reversing itself.

Wavell had opened the game by advancing with the small force available to him and capturing virtually an entire Italian army. Hitler had replied by sending the Afrika Korps, under Rommel. Rommel had arrived, via Tunis, as Wavell was forced to denude his own strength by sending half his Eighth Army to help in Greece, so the Afrika Korps promptly advanced and Wavell retreated, leaving a garrison in Tobruk. Rommel bypassed Tobruk and it was not until his own advance had been halted that he turned his attention to capturing the small desert port which was such a thorn on his flank. To his amazement, Tobruk held – and the great siege started.

The 10th MTB Flotilla fuelled in Mersa Matruh and arrived in Tobruk under cover of darkness to fuel again for the last big hop to Crete. The long bay which formed the harbour was littered with wrecks and the port installations were under heavy air attack. We picked our way through the shambles by the light of the many fires and went alongside the battered jetty. We were used to fuelling quickly from a hose but here it all had to be poured in from leaky cans so the process took most of the night. Meanwhile the fires burned, bombs rained down and we could only hope that we weren't all about to go up in one almighty explosion. 'No smoking' signs seemed pretty pointless under the circumstances.

We were given a quick meal of corned beef and hard ship's biscuits and

82

were on our way again before dawn revealed us to the recce plane and the inevitable Stukas. The men on the jetty watched us go impassively. They were of Tobruk. This life of incessant air raids, siege, danger, shortage of food, divorce from all the normalities of daily existence, banded them into a tight clan from which we transients were excluded. Their faces were blank and they had nothing to say to the outsiders, no communication to pierce the invisible wall that stood between Them and Us.

The Flotilla set off rather wearily. It had already been a long journey and we had had no rest. But the worst part was to come. The boats had suffered quite a bashing too – and now the wind blew up and the sea became rough. The inevitable happened and they began to break down. Two boats, 68 and 215, were sent back to Matruh but then, after we had passed the point of no return, another started to give trouble. We left it behind and only heard what happened some time after our own arrival in Suda Bay.

The boat finally made the south coast of Crete and found the tiny fishing harbour of Spakhia. The locals thought it was a German E-Boat and came to surrender the village. The CO had spent his three months in *Salween* learning Greek. Now he tried to establish a dialogue with the crowd on the jetty but they only regarded him with blank incomprehension. Impasse. Then the First Lieutenant, who had done classical Greek at school, remembered a long forgotten phrase from those inky years. Hopefully he tried, 'Is there a soldier in the market place?' They understood him at once and, astonishingly, there was. A Private of the Royal Signals with a landline over the mountains to Suda Bay. And so, just as we were getting anxious, we heard the good news that the boat was safe. They limped into Suda the next day.

Our own arrival was not encouraging. Air raids were incessant. The wreck of the cruiser *York* lay in the harbour with her back broken and an ammunition ship blew up just after we had secured alongside. Of the four boats which had made the journey, only MTB 67 was fit for operations. Even the many facilities of *Beehive* had been stretched to keep these wretched little boats running. Here we had no base, no spare parts, no workshop facilities, nothing. There was little we could do in the way of repairs.

MTB 67 went out that night to patrol the Kithera Channel, just south of the Greek mainland. We saw nothing until we were nearly home when, just before dawn, I met, to my surprise, another MTB. Thinking one of the defective boats was being used for a local patrol, I cut engines, as was our practice, and hailed them. It was very dark, I could barely see the shape of the other boat, and I could make nothing of what they were shouting to me. When the other boat started its engines and made off, I did the same and entered Suda Bay. Later, I made enquiries. None of our MTBs had gone out. Suddenly, the penny dropped. I had been talking to a German E-Boat.

I met him again the next night – but, this time, I had firm orders. 'For God's sake, keep clear of that E-Boat,' I had been told. 'You're all we've got and we don't want you wasted by taking on one of them.' So now I reduced speed and crept off into the huge shadow of the mountain behind me. I still remember vividly the feeling of naked vulnerability. It was a warm night and I was wearing only a khaki shirt and shorts. Suddenly I began imagining the stream of incendiary cannon shells tearing into my unprotected back. Knees trembling, I risked a look astern. He was sidling off to seawards. He had obviously been told that he was there to bag a destroyer and not to risk action with an MTB. At least it was encouraging that they took poor little 67 so seriously.

The next afternoon, we were sent round to Canea to shorten the distance to our patrol area. It was a nice little town and, right beside the jetty, was an empty house which had been the German consulate. We broke open the door, took it over and I looked with lustful eyes at the consul's big double bed. Real sheets and a chance for a proper sleep . . .

However, before then, there was another night to spend in the Kithera Channel. The invasion was now expected at any time. Again we found nothing and returned to Canea in the early morning. I had heard that there was a small pension in the town where I could actually get a hot bath and I went straight to it as soon as we arrived in harbour.

I had just stripped and got in when the first bombs started falling on the town. Soon it was obvious that this was to be something much more serious than usual. I crouched in the hot water, too frightened to lie down and relax but determined to have a proper wash now that I'd got my clothes off for the first time since leaving Alexandria. As I crouched, the window was suddenly blown in and my cringing body was covered with broken glass. I leapt out and hurled on my shirt and shorts.

In the hallway, the proprietress peered anxiously from her front door. She was a most attractive Greek girl and she had also dressed in such a hurry that she had forgotten to put on a brassiere or button up her blouse. Normally I would have found much to stare at and appreciate but the look on her face distracted my attention and I followed her eyes and forgot everything else. Up beyond the roof tops across the road the sky was thick with parachutes and, hanging from each, was a man.

For a moment we both watched fascinated then, instinctively, I drew the pistol I had once taken on honeymoon in England and, cocking it, stepped out into the road. I heard a peal of laughter behind me and turned. The Greek girl pointed at the sky full of heavily armed paratroopers and then at my puny revolver. Her gesture expressed far more than words. She was still laughing as I ran down the street back to the boat.

We stood on the flat rooftop of the consulate and watched. One of the sailors had been into the ruins of a dockside bar hit by a bomb and was slightly drunk. He fired his rifle at an aircraft as it zoomed low overhead and the pilot must have seen us because, within minutes, three fighters swooped down machine gunning our roof. Miraculously, 67 was not hit but this was obviously no place for a petrol filled, wooden MTB. We dashed out and started up. As we left, an old woman ran down the jetty and thrust six new laid eggs into my hand.

Out at sea, we found a raft full of German survivors from what should have been the seaborne part of the invasion and rescued them. Then we went on to Suda Bay.

On arrival, I retired to a slit trench in the olive groves and tried to get some sleep. Bombing and gunfire were almost incessant, culminating in one enormous explosion which rocked the whole harbour area. The Germans had indeed dignified us with some nuisance value because fighters had been sent to deal with us. Firing incendiary bullets, they had roared low over the MTBs and boats, torpedoes, depth charges and high octane petrol had gone up in one almighty bang.

My dreadful little MTB 67 was no more. She had been to Dunkirk, Tobruk and now Crete, She had held so many vivid memories for me. I had often cursed her but I had loved her all the same. She had been the only boat of the whole Flotilla which never broke down in those final days and I was proud of her for that alone. At least she had met a fighting end and could go to infuriate some other unfortunate sailor in Valhalla but, on top of everything else, she was my last link with home and I felt bereft.

I looked down from the jetty and, in the clear water below, I saw her wreckage. Little was recognisable but I could see what must be the remains of the cockpit and the mast. I dived in and managed to salvage the little silver tiger which had been our mascot and the small commissioning pendant which had been my own, personal, symbol of command. They are beside me as I write.

We retreated to our olive grove but our movement through the trees must have been observed by the Luftwaffe because, almost at once, five Stukas arrived and began bombing us. They were in no hurry and they made it a practice exercise for their own amusement. There was not even a pretence of an RAF presence and they knew they had us pinned down. Round and round they circled over the trees and each, in turn, dived down and dropped one bomb at a time. Their machines had the screeching sirens on their wings designed to terrify their victims and they certainly terrified us. We had no slit trenches and no shelter. All we could do was to lie flat, clawing at the unyielding ground as the bombs burst, pulverising our senses as the splinters whistled round and branches fell on our quivering bodies.

That night we were all called down to the jetty. The Germans were advancing and we, as now useless mouths, were to be evacuated.

We stood in a long queue in the darkness. The bombing never ceased and I knew what the troops had felt like at Dunkirk. Around midnight, the destroyer *Jaguar* picked her way delicately in between the wrecks. A quick embarkation and we were off. Thank God, my friend the E-Boat missed us but the Stukas found *Jaguar* at dawn and bombed hell out of us. However, we were one of the lucky ones and we got back to Alex safely.

The thrashing of their Navy at Matapan ensured that the Italians would never have the heart to challenge us at sea again but the evacuation of our Army from Greece and, particularly, Crete had to be carried out entirely without air cover and this resulted in the Med Fleet being decimated from the sky.

Admiral Cunningham was faced with the most horrible of all duties for a Commander-in-Chief. There comes a time when success can only be achieved by a man great enough to disregard losses and, thank God, Cunningham rose to the occasion. 'This is not the time for destroyers to break down,' he said and also, 'It takes three years to build a battleship but three hundred to build a tradition. We go on.'

Ships returning to harbour in a state where they could reasonably expect repairs were sent straight back to sea. Ships were not even allowed time to complete ammunitioning. Back to the hell of bombers and dive bombers went the weary, unprotected cruisers and destroyers and day by day their losses mounted. But no enemy troops arrived in Crete by sea. From Greece, 51,000 of the Expeditionary Force were evacuated. 18,000 were taken out of Crete.

At the end of the operations the surviving ships returned to Alexandria infinitely weary. The cost to the Fleet had been two battleships, one aircraft carrier, six cruisers and seven destroyers severely damaged and three cruisers and six destroyers sunk. Only three battleships, three small cruisers (one with a temporary bow) and seventeen destroyers, in various states of effectiveness, were left. But the object had been achieved, the soldiers were safely back in Egypt and three hundred years of tradition had never shone more brightly. Black days lay ahead, tragic losses must still be born but the Italian fleet now knew its place and the Royal Navy knew truly that nothing was impossible.

Cunningham reported:

It is not easy to convey how heavy was the strain that men and ships sustained . . . More than once I felt that the stage had been reached when no more could be asked of Officers and men, physically and mentally exhausted . . . It is perhaps even now not realised how nearly the

Survivor. Returning from Crete.

breaking point was reached, but that these men struggled through is the measure of their achievement, and I trust it will not lightly be forgotten.

What might also be remembered is that these operations were carried out by what was, basically, the last of the old peace-time Mediterranean Fleet. These were the men who had originally gone 'Up the Straits' and 'Down the Gut', revelling in the Strade Stretta which was now no more. Guff, Ticks, leave stopped, no gymshoes with overalls – all this had gone to build their training and their spirit. I remembered the Navigator in *Achilles* . . . 'You will do your duty, to the limit of your ability and, if necessary, at the cost of your life.' It was just what the Mediterranean Fleet had done.

Chapter 12

AT SEA IN THE DESERT

A fter Crete, Peter Peake was blamed, I think unfairly, for the loss of our boats and was never seen again. I was put back in command of the sad survivors of the Wobbly Tenth (68 and 215) which had never even reached Crete and sent with them to Cyprus to await the invasion, now expected, of that island.

Cyprus was a welcome change. The two boats were based in the charming little north coast harbour of Kyrenia and the officers lived in the luxurious but empty Katsellis Dome Hotel just up the road. A solitary villa between the harbour and the hotel housed the sailors, whose meals were brought to them by waiters in tails carrying vast, covered, silver trays from the hotel kitchen. None of us had lived so well for a long time.

Today, what I remember as a small, deserted harbour is full of expensive yachts and the whole place has been ruined by modern tourism, with the Dome surrounded by a warren of mini tower blocks, but in early June 1941, the hotel stood by itself and Kyrenia was a lost, abandoned little paradise away from the war. Or almost . . .

In Iraq, Rashid Ali had staged a pro-German rebellion and British troops had moved in to protect the oil wells. Then, on 8 June, to pre-empt a German move down to our rear from the Balkans, British, Australian and Free French troops advanced into the Vichy French colonies of Lebanon and Syria. Unexpectedly, the advance was viciously contested by the French and a thoroughly unpleasant minor war developed.

Within a few days of the MTBs' arrival, therefore, we found that we had been sent to Kyrenia not just in case of a German assault, though this was still expected, but to blockade the Lebanon by stopping any seaborne traffic between North Cyprus and Turkey. In order to do so, two Swordfish aircraft were also allocated to my command.

It really was a remarkable setup. There were no troops closer than Nicosia, beyond the mountains and across the plain. The only other Naval authority in the island was a Commander in far off Famagusta. My aircraft operated from

Nicosia airfield but the aircrews lived in the Dome Hotel in Kyrenia. How we were to blockade the Lebanon was left entirely to me.

I started off by commandeering the best local bus to lift the aircrews and their ground staff between Kyrenia and Nicosia. The pilots came back with reports of a night club in the capital, full of untouchable beauties. They were untouchable because of the prewar system whereby all the night clubs around the Med had Hungarian hostesses. Hungarian girls were gorgeous but now Hitler had occupied their country and so, according to 8th Army Headquarters in Cairo, they were enemy aliens. However, they had not been interned and, indeed, the night club was still open for the locals' delectation – but, as enemy aliens, the girls were strictly out of bounds to the brutal and licentious soldiery and, as the RAF in Cyprus came under 8th Army command, to them too.

I did not come under the 8th Army and I had no such orders from C-in-C Med. (In fact, I had no orders from anyone at all.) So I reckoned that, for the Navy, the hostesses came under the heading of what was already becoming known as 'Rest and Recreation'. To the gratification of both ourselves and the girls (and the furious frustration of the other two Services), the Naval bus accordingly collected them on a Sunday forenoon and brought them to the Dome Hotel for lunch, an afternoon's bathing and an evening party. It was great fun.

The MTBs stopped and searched the odd caique and sank any found to be carrying contraband. The word spread quickly among those concerned and the traffic stopped abruptly. And the Swordfish aircraft really justified themselves by sinking a French destroyer found hiding in a Lebanese bay. She was a vessel we had wanted badly and the Swordfish pilot was determined to make sure he had the right target. Ignoring the gunfire, the old 'stringbag' waddled down her side while the observer shone an Aldis light to read her name, then they climbed, turned and torpedoed her. It cost them their aircraft but the pilot and observer were both saved to become prisoners-of-war.

On 22 June, after we had been in Kyrenia for three weeks, I was spending a quiet Sunday evening in the lounge of the Dome Hotel. The bus had just left with our 'Rest and Recreation' party. I switched on the radio for the news – and heard the dramatic announcement that Hitler had invaded Russia. I can still remember vividly my feelings as I sat alone in the big empty room. The news was totally unexpected because, till then, Stalin and Hitler had been allies. Now the entire strategic situation had altered. Hitler had made the same mistake as Napoleon. The Middle East would not have to bear the whole strength of the German onslaught any more and, best of all, Britain no longer stood alone. For the first time in a dreadful year, there seemed to be hope.

After Hitler had committed himself to this monumental folly, it was obvious that Cyprus could not still be under threat. With the seaborne traffic to the Lebanon halted, there was no further point in keeping the MTBs in Kyrenia and we were therefore sent to Haifa from where the boats could better help the Syrian campaign by operating off Beirut.

By the time the campaign in Syria ended, the boats needed urgent refitting. The Palestine Railways offered us the facilities of their workshops and our engineer officer dug up a short length of railway line from an abandoned siding and turned it up into a new propellor shaft. *Hornet* would have been amazed.

During the refit, I heard that Pam had produced a son, Bill, whose birth was duly celebrated. Then, when the boats were again operational as far as they could be without spare parts or proper base facilities, we were ready to move on. The move was to Mersa Matruh.

Matruh, in peacetime, had been a minor seaside resort for wealthy Alexandrians. It was the terminus for a single line rail track from Alex and it had a sheltered little harbour, with a wooden jetty, in a sort of lagoon protected by a rocky reef with one narrow entrance. As such, it was the railhead for everything which could be trucked westward to the Eighth Army along the desert road or sent by sea to Tobruk in craft small enough to pass through the gap in the reef. Though unimportant in every other way, it was therefore a vital logistical target and so was regularly and thoroughly plastered by the Luftwaffe.

Navy House, in what had been the village school, was clearly marked by our arrogantly flaunted White Ensign. Equidistant from the jetty and the rail terminus, it was the obvious aiming point for the bombers and, as an inevitable result, it was always just missed. We did have an Operations Room in a deep, heavily sandbagged dugout next door and the house was surrounded by slit trenches with lovely sandbagged lids but it was a point of honour that they were never used. Air raids, no matter how intimate, were simply ignored.

The MTBs were to be used to try and blockade Sollum and Bardia, 120 miles to the west. They did their gallant best but, apart from laying mines, were never lucky enough to find a target. In the meantime, I had been given an additional and much more fraught command – the Western Desert Lighter Force (WDLF) about which a word of explanation is necessary.

Tobruk, during the siege, was kept supplied by a remarkable variety of ships, all coming under the umbrella title of the Inshore Squadron. Destroyers ran from Alexandria, carrying food, stores and troop reinforcements. They did the trip at full speed, arriving after dark, unloading, embarking casualties or troops due for relief, and then racing off to be clear of the port and the Stukas before dawn left them naked to the skies. Even so, casualties were heavy.

Supporting the destroyers, a remarkable collection of small vessels ran from Matruh, personified by an astonishing character known as 'Pedlar' Palmer – an RNR lieutenant who made the run regularly in a little caique carrying a flock of sheep on its deck. And there was the Western Desert Lighter Force. The WDLF consisted of the very first Tank Landing Craft known, for some odd security reason, as A Lighters. They were the only vessels capable of carrying the guns and vehicles which were obviously so badly needed – but they were desperately slow and unseaworthy and, indeed, never meant for open sea work. They were only sailed, three at a time, in the moonless periods of the month but, even so, cumbrous and heavily laden, the journey took them thirty-six hours. With U-Boats, E-Boats and the ubiquitous Stukas during daylight hours, they were hideously vulnerable and never more than two, and sometimes only one, came back. Any Staff College will tell you that such a rate of attrition can not be maintained. It was.

These A Lighters were commanded by marvellous young RNVR officers who knew exactly what they were in for – and made light of it. They sang their own song, a parody of the popular tune 'Side by side'. It ended, 'Oh we don't mind the bombs or the weather, we're all right while we're still together, we'll travel along, singing our song, side by side.' And side by side they went to be slaughtered. When the moon shone over the desert and the slow weeks passed in waiting, I watched them in the Mess and wondered which ones I should send to their deaths next time. In a small way I came to understand the agony that Cunningham must have suffered when he sent the Fleet to be decimated during Crete. I still get a lump in my throat when a nostalgic radio programme plays 'Side by side'.

Sailors enjoyed playing soldiers in the desert because it was so different from our usual way of life but I did have one unexpected experience. Even though I was also responsible for running the tented Naval camp, my duties were not usually very onerous. It was therefore quite reasonable for the Naval Officer in Charge (NOIC) to interrupt my gentle siesta on the veranda of Navy House with the surprising news that I had just volunteered to be a lighthouse.

'The Fleet is going to bombard Bardia,' he said, 'and they want a final fix of their position before running in. You are to go to the spot marked on this chart and, in two days' time, flash the letter A to seawards for one minute every ten from 2200 to midnight.'

It seemed like a nice little jolly and the only obvious problem was how to get there. It had never occurred to Those Set in Authority Over Us that the Navy ashore might ever need wheels. After all, our rations were delivered to us and our duties lay essentially out at sea. It did not take long to walk down to the jetty and we had nowhere else to go. So I would have to hitch. Why not? The desert road ran interminably westward and there must be plenty of transport going that way . . .

I dug out my only luggage, a three and sixpenny cardboard suitcase from Marks and Spencer with a large hole in it from some long forgotten sailor's boathook, and I packed. A battery Aldis for the lighthouse, spare socks, two loaves of bread and two tins of corned beef. A water bottle. It should be enough . . .

I trudged off through the ruins of the little town and, by the time I reached the outskirts, I was sweating hard and the suitcase had become very heavy. Thank God there was a Military Police check point ahead. They would help . . .

I approached the two Red Cap lance corporals with all the happy confidence of an Officer with a clear conscience and I was genuinely shocked to find myself under arrest. One could see their point of view however. Here was an astonishing, bearded character on foot, in a strange uniform, travelling west and only able to account for himself with the unlikely explanation that he was a lighthouse. There was a big prisoner of war camp in the vicinity and the soldiers of both sides had a remarkable predilection for escaping and just walking across the desert back to their own lines. The MPs reckoned that they had nabbed an escaping Italian.

We carried no form of identification in those days and it was only my argument that no fugitive would slow himself down by carrying a heavy Aldis that finally convinced them that they might be wrong. A quick call on a landline to Navy House established my credentials and the attitude of the MPs became transformed. They still found it inconceivable that anyone could be fool enough to embark on such an enterprise with so little logistic support but the Navy was well known to be mad and at least they had broken their boredom with a story on which they could dine out in Red Cap messes for years. They stopped the first truck to come along and bundled me on board with a few quick explanations to the astonished driver.

And so Operation Bardia began. The Mediterranean Fleet, with all its pomp and circumstance, had sailed from Alexandria, bands playing and hands fallen in for leaving harbour. Their lighthouse started off from Mersa Matruh in a three ton truck, sitting on a load of badly stowed petrol cans.

Had it been a British Army truck there would have been an exchange of crashing salutes, the driver's mate would have climbed nimbly up into the back and the Officer would have travelled in relative comfort in the front seat. But they were Australians and so markedly lacking in rank consciousness. They were affably prepared to give me a lift but how I fared they did not give a damn. They ate their sandwich lunch without stopping whilst I, on a pile of shifting petrol cans, dared not open my suitcase and went hungry. Moreover, though petrol for the Afrika Korps was carried in the admirable receptacles known naturally as Jerry cans, the Eighth Army had theirs in rather fragile tins which tended to leak. We had just had to deal with some difficult scenes in Matruh when Libyan prisoners, unloading a petrol barge, became riotously drunk on the fumes. My truck, at least, was open which spared me the worst of the smell but the silver cans were highly reflective to the sun and made petrol vehicles an easily spotted and attractive target to aircraft. You win some and lose some. We were not spotted but glue sniffers should stick to their addiction. At the end of a long day's hungry drive, I was feeling awful and longing for a cigarette.

The truck finally dropped me by the roadside as the sun went down. A few hundred yards away across the desert was a tented encampment. Dinner, bed and breakfast? I started across the sand, lugging my suitcase and hoping. Halfway to my goal stood a rigid figure. Rifle, bayonet, white pipeclayed belt and turban. As I approached I saw that he was strategically placed between two lone stones, perfectly whitewashed – obviously the Indian Army and their main gate. Altering course, I passed carefully between the stones to be greeted by an almost inaudible sigh of relief and a tremendous butt salute. I had passed from one extreme of the military heap to the other.

The Indian Army was enchanted. Not for a long time in their isolated existence had such an apparition appeared out of the desert with such an intriguing explanation for its presence. Nothing was too good for this insane sailor. The only bottle of whisky in the mess, carefully preserved for some special occasion, was triumphantly unearthed and we celebrated with mutual esteem. A dug down tent was offered with clean, white sheets (far superior to my usual Matruh pit) and, after an excellent dinner, I slept well. The next morning, a batman woke me with a cup of tea and my scrofulous uniform neatly pressed. After a good breakfast, a 15 cwt was whistled up, we drove diagonally across the sand to pass between the whitewashed stones and the sentry and then turned west towards my destination. And now the real problems began . . .

The soldiers had looked at my chart with some incredulity. They had found it hard to interpret this large white sheet of paper with funny numbers all over the obviously empty sea and nothing but blankness on the land which should have been full of useful information. However, a rough correlation between their map and mine quickly showed that, although the precise positions of the forward patrols of both sides were uncertain, the site of my lighthouse was almost certain to be surrounded by ill disposed foreigners. In short, the Naval staff in Alex had omitted to phone Cairo and find out who was where before sending me on my way. The 15 cwt therefore dropped me well short of any possible danger and turned back for home. As he drove off, the driver gave me a beaming smile and said something in Urdu which might have been either an exhortation to Shiva to go easy on me or, perhaps, a doubtful hope that one day he might have the pleasure of seeing me again. Anyhow, I walked.

I walked all that day. The sun beat down. I learned Sod's Law of Aldis lamps – that their weight increases in exact proportion to the distance they are carried. I skipped lunch again. I had not the heart to stop and picnic in that hot, sandy wilderness and, anyway, I was far too nervous. However, by evening I had seen no signs of activity, friendly or hostile, and I thought that I must be in about the right place although I really had no idea where I was nor any means of translating what I could see of the little bays along the coast into an exact position on the chart. It occurred to me, in a fit of disloyalty, that it was a poor outlook for the Navy if the Fleet Navigating Officer, with all his skill and implements and the help of God with His multitude of stars, had to rely for his position on a navigational aid as lost and unreliable as myself. There was a huge boulder at the top of a cliff path. I put down my suitcase and sat leaning against it. I had never felt so alone and miserable in my life.

Cautious footsteps galvanised me out of my self pity. I jumped to my feet and drew my revolver. What did they do in adventure stories? Keep still. Keep quiet. Surprise is all. Let him be the one to walk into trouble. Pointing my gun at the corner of the rock, I shivered and waited for the sinister peaked cap of the Afrika Korps.

Instead, a pair of gentle blue eyes appeared over a hairy moustache which could have belonged to only one nation in the world. Now I had met the British Army. He looked at me kindly.

'Hello, old boy. What are you doing here? Do put that thing down.'

It was total anticlimax again.

He turned out to be a one man Beach Survey Unit. He thought that, yes, he was behind the lines. 'But if they're down that way today, old boy, they'll be back the other next week. I just don't worry. Nobody comes to the shoreline anyway and I'm well hidden. Someone in Cairo wanted to know what beaches along this coast were suitable for landings so I just swan up and down looking at them and letting the great big war pass me by.' He had a caravan down by the sea and he, too, had a last bottle of whisky – but, this time, it was more than a luxury.

He spotted where I should go at once and, after a good supper, he took me to the place himself. 'Useful little cave there, old boy. Jerry won't see your light.'

I flashed my A's as ordered but the night gave me no acknowledgement. Afterwards, I returned to the caravan and we finished the whisky. Again, I slept comfortably and well. The next day, with rather a hangover, I started for home. The trip back was a doddle and I returned smugly to Navy House. Apparently the Fleet had found and bombarded Bardia. I still had two stale loaves and two tins of corned beef.

On the whole, life in Matruh was quite enjoyable but by the time autumn had come, I couldn't stand just sitting on my backside sending out the A lighters any more. Moreover, the MTBs were achieving nothing, so I decided to move up to Tobruk and, wanting to show willing, sent the boats on ahead and sailed myself with the next A lighter run. It was fairly hairy but, thank God, we all got there safely and, at last, I felt I could look them in the face.

Tobruk was not pleasant. Navy House was a dominant, half smashed shell of a building on a low escarpment above the jetties. The whole harbour area was bombed almost incessantly, day and night, and there were also two big guns we called Bardia Bill and Sollum Sue which, from either side of the perimeter, lobbed heavy shells into the town at irregular intervals. Very off putting . . .

The harbour itself was full of wrecks, their top decks and upperworks sticking up out of the water. During the day it appeared deserted but at night, when the destroyers crept in under cover of darkness, everything came to life. Some ships managed to get alongside and discharge straight onto the ruined jetties, others went to the wrecks and, in a few frenzied hours' work, unloaded their stores onto them while Jerry, knowing perfectly well what was happening, rained down bombs in an effort to hinder the unloading and add to the wrecks. All ships tried to be well clear by dawn but, long after they had gone, Tobruk's famous harbour launch, *Eskimo Nell*, would still be creeping round the wrecks collecting the treasures which had been left there.

The night I arrived, I had hardly had time to report when the inevitable air raid started. Rushing prudently to the cellars, I was intercepted by a beaming character who thrust a Bren gun into my hand and cried, 'There you are. Follow me.' Here, it appeared, it was the custom for all officers to pour out of the front entrance when bombing started and, with whatever weapons they could lay their hands on, blast happily back at the Luftwaffe above. Once again, Navy House was the main aiming point for the bombers and, once again, the White Ensign was kept flying tauntingly above it throughout the siege.

As a result of this mentality, morale was sky high although our circumstances were grim. Food consisted of three identical meals, each consisting of two thin slices of corned beef (often melting in the heat), two rock hard ship's biscuits for those whose teeth were strong enough to bite them and, at lunch only, two vitamin pills. The water was so vile that you had to gulp it quickly (to avoid dehydration) and get as much down as possible before gagging on the awful taste and smell. We had a small bar but seldom any drink. However, it was known as the Bomb and Blast Inn. It had painted graffiti pictures on the walls of famous ships and personalities of the Tobruk run and it boasted what must have been the only armchair left in the ruined town. In it we used to seat our guests when a thoughtful destroyer provided the odd bottle of whisky and watch with interest to see how soon the clean, properly uniformed visitor from the outside world would start scratching. The chair was crawling with lice . . .

But at least the Navy was better off than the British, Australian and Polish troops manning the perimeter. This consisted of deep minefields behind which the infantry lived in fox holes. When Jerry made a serious assault, the tanks which got through the mines would overrun the infantry (who lay in their holes and let them do it) and then find themselves in an open 'box' where the guns, knowing the range to an inch, would destroy the tanks while the foxholes disgorged their occupants to kill the unprotected follow up Jerry infantry. It was a simple system but it worked well.

Meanwhile, the days and weeks passed, the bombs and shells fell on us, the Afrika Korps made their regular attempts to smash their way in, the destroyers and the other little ships of the Inshore Squadron were decimated – but the minimum supplies never failed to arrive, the soldiers hung on and Tobruk held.

Finally, on 8 December 1941, the Eighth Army advanced and the siege was lifted as the Afrika Korps were driven back. Typically, the Tobruk garrison did not wait to be relieved but broke out to meet their advancing friends.

A few nights later, MTBs 68 and 215 went out on patrol and somehow collided in the dark. Poor old 68 sank on the spot. 215 just managed to get back with a large hole in her bow. The base staff reckoned they could patch her up well enough to return to Alex. I said it couldn't be done because we should have to travel fast to lift the patch out of the water yet hitting a wave at speed would bash it in. However, I was overruled.

We spent the day visiting Bardia Bill and Sollum Sue which had made our lives such a misery. They were very big guns and we gazed at them with some awe. Then we peed on them.

The patch completed, 215 sailed at dawn and I took her myself. Jerry had mined the harbour during the night and we had to roar backwards and forwards the whole length of the long bay until it was obvious that there was a clear channel for the bigger ships. For some reason we did it singing at the tops of our voices but thankfully, unlike poor Ian Quarrie, we set off no mines. Then we started off for Alexandria.

I was quite right. We sank just off the coast at a place where, luckily, there were no longer any Germans. In fact, we were rescued by some charming New

Zealanders who dried, fed and watered us before sending us on our way.

In those days, the Med Station reckoned that a battleship lasted nine months, a cruiser six and a destroyer three. As far as the Wobbly Tenth was concerned, two of our COs were dead, we had suffered numerous other casualties and all the boats had been lost – for nothing really. Only five of my A lighters were left out of over a dozen but at least they had made a vital contribution to the siege.

However, the war had moved on, we survivors were back in an unbombed Matruh and it was Christmas. There was liquor and proper food. We celebrated it uproariously and 'Side by side' rang out again across our little harbour although so many of the voices had gone.

Somehow, for the time being we felt we had come safely home.

Chapter 13

TRANSFORMATION

After Crete, we were left with three battleships, three small cruisers and seventeen destroyers. Now, eight months later, the battleships were sunk or disabled and Malta convoys, the Tobruk run and other commitments had left us with only a couple of light cruisers and a handful of destroyers. Losses of submarines had been virtually 100%. The only consolation was that the Ities were so terrified of us that their powerful Navy refused to come out and face us on the open sea.

Morale in the pitiful remnant of the once proud Med Fleet was still high but there was another very different Navy in Alexandria. The whole city was full of Naval officers and ratings in barracks, transit camps and hotels. Most were base staff but many were idle, awaiting appointment. The Officers were essentially wartime call-ups, newly commissioned. Few had ever been in action and some were very odd, if not dubious, characters of uncertain background. Far from home, with little to do but womanise and drink, they were easy prey to defeatist rumours and lacked the experience to judge them. Morale ashore was very different from that in the seagoing ships.

Alex itself was an astonishing place. The fleshpots were unlimited. There was the Monseigneur, much patronised by expensive Greek businessmen and their ladies, the Union Club for serious minded misogynists, and a variety of nightclubs of which the Femina was the MTB Officers' favourite. There was also Pastroudi's for a good dinner or Mary's House, the officers' brothel in a discreet suburban villa. Mary's House was very well patronised, not so much for the charms of its delectable 'hostesses' as because Mary had the sense to produce the only straight whisky in Alex. When it suffered a direct hit, an understanding Naval staff informed the next-of-kin at home that their loved ones had been Killed in Action.

Alex was a prime target for the Luftwaffe and every evening trains departed with locals packed on the roofs and buffers of the carriages to avoid the bombing. Those who remained had a distressing habit of beating to death any solitary British they could find in the blackout. But in every other way Alex was a swinging city, offering wine, women and song of every variety and to suit every pocket. Its comforts and sophistication, its warm, if professional, welcome, were balm to the souls of tired, lonely, war-ravaged men returning for a brief spell from the desert or the sea. What Cairo was to the Army, Alex was to us. Alex was the Navy. The Navy of Matapan and Crete, but also of transit camp, idleness and debauchery.

Back from Tobruk to this salubrious place, we were happily looking forward to a period of glorious gluttony and disgusting behaviour, only to find a major surprise awaiting us. In our absence up the desert, a new, proper MTB base, HMS *Mosquito*, had been commissioned and, best of all, eight big, American built MTBs were about to be unloaded at Suez – and the survivors of the Wobbly Tenth were to form the nucleus of a new Tenth MTB Flotilla.

We went down to Port Tewfik and, when we saw them, we couldn't believe it was true. Enormous (to our eyes) beautiful 70-footers with messdeck, galley and a cabin each for the First Lieutenant and CO. No more living out of suitcases in hotels or desert ruins. Now we could live on board these lovely little ships in our own home.

I took MTB 261, the first to be ready, and set off up the Suez Canal. Standing on my real bridge, I beamed at the pilot.

'Right, Captain,' he said. 'Eight knots, please.'

We crept out, going as slowly as we could on one engine, and I expostulated.

'What speed did you want to go, Captain?'

'At least 40 knots,' I said and explained that, the higher the speed, the more the bow planed and so the less the wash. The pilot flinched but looked wistful. Finally he yielded and we raced up the Canal flat out, the banks and the odd feluccas flashing past. At one point, an Egyptian military policeman raced us on his motor bike along the bumpy road beside the Canal. I still have the movie I took showing him falling gradually behind.

In the Bitter Lakes, the second pilot was cross because we had arrived so much earlier than he had expected us. When I started off, he nearly had a fit. 'Eight knots,' he screamed over the noise of the engines. 'That's the Canal limit.'

I slowed down and explained again about the wash.

'What speed are we doing now, Captain?'

'About 20,' I said, 'but it would be easier a bit faster.' And I opened the throttles slightly.

'What speed now?'

'About 35 knots.'

'Who was your first pilot?'

I told him and suddenly he turned to me with a devilish grin on his face.

'Let her go,' he cried. And I did.

It transpired that there were three, thoroughly illegal, Suez Canal records – for the highest speed achieved, the fastest time between two stations, and the quickest overall transit. With the official limit of 8 knots, the pilots had little scope for cheating and rivalry was intense. No one had yet been able to exceed 9 knots or complete in under 8 hours. I clocked 47 knots, averaged 40 and did the journey in 2 hours and 18 minutes. The pilots shared the glory, the Suez Canal Company exploded in Gallic outrage and the rest of the Flotilla and all subsequent MTBs were restricted to 8 knots. I reckon my three records still stand today . . .

We did a quick workup in Alex and Haifa, and then we returned to Tobruk. The old familiar scene was the same yet different. Living conditions ashore had hardly improved but now the place was full of complacent, rear area types and the fighting troops had gone. No longer Them and Us.

The boats went out on patrol every night but, again, we found no targets. We would arrive back soon after dawn and hide alongside the wrecks. Almost at once, the first recce plane would fly overhead and then, when his photos had been studied, the bombers would appear and seek us out as the most attractive target. Although we still lacked any fighter protection, the horrible Stukas had moved on and these were conventional raids. We soon learned that Jerry would drop his load on the wrecks beside which we had been spotted lying so, as soon as the recce plane had gone, we shifted berth. After a time, Jerry learned this and plastered any wrecks other than the ones where we had been seen. So we stayed put and laughed again. It developed into a sort of Russian roulette with Jerry having to guess where we'd be and us guessing which wrecks he'd choose to hit. Thank God, we always won.

Ashore, there were still some soldiers who were anything but base staff. These were members of one of the Special Service outfits in which the desert war proliferated. Their speciality was to creep through Jerry's lines and do nasty things to him behind his back. They loved airfields where they could attach sticky bombs to unsuspecting aircraft and blow them up after they had safely withdrawn.

MTBs came to these characters like manna from heaven. 'Saves so much boring walking, old boy,' said my particular friend. 'You can land us and all we have to do is just skip up the beach.'

He was an impossibly blah Captain in the Scots Guards from one of the oldest and greatest families in Scotland. His batman was a truly villainous Glaswegian whose peacetime occupation had been as razor slasher in one of the vicious razor gangs for which that city was notorious. This apparently ill assorted couple lived in the ruins of a cellar in the town and the Captain quickly earned from us the nickname 'Gracious Living'. 'Gracious living' was all he lived for and, though he could hardly change for dinner, he insisted on his pretence of maintaining a suitable life style.

One day he sent me a message. 'My dear fellow, you must come and take luncheon with me. I have acquired a three piece suite and I can really offer you gracious living.'

Knowing Tobruk's rations, I had stuffed the cupboard under my bunk with gin and tins of NAAFI steak and kidney pie. I took a bottle and a tin, made my way to the cellar and was greeted with uncouth if genuine warmth by the razor slasher, doubling as butler. 'My dear old boy,' cried my host. 'Just look at this. Isn't it truly gracious living?' He had scrounged some old butter boxes and, with them, had created a rough table and two small seats. We had an excellent and bibulous lunch by Tobruk standards and I departed feeling suitably pampered and civilised.

A few nights later we landed the team miles behind Jerry's lines and, the next night, returned to the rendezvous to pick them up. Although the boats waited all night there was no sign of Gracious Living and his lethal batman.

I spent a miserable day thinking of the pathetic empty cellar and that night we went back in the forlorn hope that somehow they might be there. No sign. We were just about to give up when a lookout spotted something in the water. It was the razor slasher. He had waded out to avoid capture ashore and had stood there with the sea up to his neck for nearly twenty-four hours. In his arms he held the dead body of 'Gracious Living'.

When we hauled them inboard, he collapsed unconscious from cold and exhaustion. In Tobruk, he recovered as he was carried ashore on a stretcher. Someone muttered words of appreciation.

'Och,' he said, 'The Captain would have done the same for me.'

It was true. As I have mentioned before, the top and bottom of the community get on well together.

Time passed and, after another break in Alex, we set off once more for Mersa Matruh, intending to fuel and then return to Tobruk during the night. We passed through the narrow entrance, roared down the small lagoon and secured alongside the familiar wooden jetty at the end of the short road up to Navy House. Then we went there to find out the latest news.

The Eighth Army was retreating again after the advance which had relieved Tobruk and we expected to hear the usual tales of disaster which every retreat involved but we were quite unprepared for the general air of uncertainty and dismay which seemed to pervade Matruh. News was scrappy and the whole situation was obviously going badly wrong but, after all, this had often happened before. It was all part of desert life.

We fuelled the boats and had a quick supper in Navy House as dusk began to fall. By the time we were due to sail, the news was no better and nobody seemed to have a clear idea of what was happening but our programme was definite and I walked down to the jetty to warm up the engines before departure.

It was as I stepped on board that I heard from seawards the familiar throbbing drone of an MTB. The noise drew closer, turning into a powerful roar, and, a few minutes later we spotted the bow wave through the dark as the MTB swept round the last corner and up to the jetty. She seemed to have an unusual number of men on the upper deck. Looking up, I could see the tin hatted silhouettes against the starry sky but I still felt only mild surprise, wondering which boat she was and why she was coming into Matruh.

'What boat?' I shouted. 'What's going on?'

There was a pause, then a weary voice shouted back, 'Christ, haven't you heard here? Tobruk's fallen.'

It was totally unbelievable to us. The Army advanced and the Army retreated but Tobruk was Tobruk. Our Tobruk. It was more than a port – it was a symbol. If Tobruk had fallen this seemed to be truly the end of the desert campaign.

Later we were to learn that Naval losses had been so great during the siege that there were simply not available the little ships required to keep the fortress supplied were it to be cut off again. Knowing this, the defences had been allowed to decay. A new South African Division, unbloodied in battle, had been left behind a perimeter without the controlled defences of minefields and artillery required. The Germans had simply walked in, virtually unopposed, and the first the MTBs had known of their arrival had been when tanks appeared at the water's edge, opening fire at point blank range. Under cover of an MTB smoke screen, anything which could put to sea had gone with whatever troops and survivors they could embark. It was a total calamity.

Our sailing orders were cancelled and we spent a miserable night thinking of Tobruk in enemy hands. The next day the news became, impossibly, worse and we were faced with the realisation that, this time, we were probably going to lose even Matruh. A Naval Gunner arrived to blow up the few harbour installations and, out of disaster, a sort of febrile gaiety set in.

At the corner of Navy House there had been dug a three seater loo. Bumph consisted of unlimited pages from copies of World War 1 *Punch*. (God knows how they had turned up in the Western Desert.) When the old river gunboat, HMS *Ladybird*, had been sunk in Tobruk, my A Lighters had salvaged her Quarterdeck gangway sign and brought it home to Matruh. There it stood, outside our loo, a real relic of the peacetime Navy, highly varnished oak with blue shadowed gold leaf lettering proclaiming, in English and Chinese, 'OFFICERS ONLY'.

Soldiers, at our invitation, would travel miles across the sand to enjoy this fabled sanctuary which one described as 'the last outpost of civilisation west of Cairo'. The thought of leaving this to Jerry was too much and I sought out the Gunner and explained my needs. He was brief and to the point.

' I imagine their habits are much the same as ours,' he said. 'I'll set it to go up at 0900 in three days time. Crikey, their last thought will be to wonder what it was they ate . . .'

If the loss of Tobruk had hurt, that of Matruh was somehow even more personal. Matruh had been the railhead where one first met the desert. From its comparative safety had sailed the gallant little A Lighters on their dreadful journey to Tobruk. It had been our base and our home. We had spent Christmas there after the siege had been lifted, feeling we had returned to well loved familiar surroundings after ordeal by battle. Matruh was security in an uncertain world.

Now the soldiers, knowing what was coming, began to run. An army on the verge of collapse is not an inspiring sight. Suddenly, all trust and stability have disappeared. The whole, fundamental security of life has disintegrated. What was an inviolable, eternal strength has become a leaderless, disorganised rabble of selfish, rat-like individuals. Fear breeds fear, rumours proliferate and panic becomes uncontrollable. It is a horrible experience.

We witnessed enough to see what was happening and then we sailed ourselves, watching and hearing the explosions as the small jetty was blown up behind us. I felt it as a moment of immediate and tragic drama. Had I only known it then, I was to learn the end of the story in exactly twenty years time.

When we got back to Alex, the flap was already starting but all other news was overshadowed for me by the orders for my own future. I was to go home.

Home . . . Being with Pam again and seeing my son instead of two-month-old letters and snapshots. No more heat, sand and flies. No more being everlastingly bombed with no prospect of targets of our own to attack in return. It was a gloriously exhilarating thought and, in due course, I departed on air for HMS *Canopus 2*, the overflow transit barracks where I was to stay until my passage could be arranged.

That night came an unexpected call. I was to gather a working party of three sailors, all of us armed, and take Alexandria's entire outfit of Secret and Confidential books to Suez. A luggage van had been attached to a train leaving Alex at midnight, the books would be delivered to it and we were to remain in the van until the Suez working party opened the door at the other end. If anyone else tried to get into the van, we were to shoot them.

We spent a somewhat uncomfortable and depressing night but reached Port Tewfik the next day, turned over our van full of bags and then, having no other orders, returned to Alex, arriving in the early evening. As soon as the train pulled into the station, it was obvious that something was wrong. There were no RTOs on the platform, no white uniforms on the streets, none of the usual atmosphere of the town settling down for a night of revelry. No Naval truck awaited us and I got no answer when I rang for transport so we took a taxi, the driver eyeing us oddly and seeming strangely surly.

At *Canopus 2*, to my surprise, the sentry was in khaki with full equipment and tin hat instead of the usual whites of the gate guard. I went in, found the CO in the wardroom and quickly learned the incredible truth. Overnight, the shoreside Navy had simply run for it.

The rot had set in, as panic does, quite suddenly. With Rommel getting close and the Afrika Korps still in full advance, driving the stricken Eighth Army before them, the Fleet had wisely left Alex to base itself further east. But the movement of the ships had been taken as the signal for a general *sauve qui peut*. Plans were in existence for a controlled evacuation of Alexandria in emergency but these had gone by the board. From hotels, transit camps and barracks, the shoreside Navy had simply fled. If Matapan, Greece and Tobruk had been the Navy's zenith, this was certainly our nadir. But then, ABC was no longer Commander-in-Chief.

The CO, an elderly RN Commander, had found himself left behind with an incredible mixture of odds and sods who had gathered in *Canopus 2* for shelter. They included all the prisoners from the Detention Quarters, thieves, deserters, even murderers, and some men who were not in the Navy at all but had dressed in British Naval uniforms for security when the Germans arrived. With this odd bunch I was to serve as his First Lieutenant. Our first task would be to prepare for a last ditch stand in the dockyard.

The next morning I was called by my Egyptian servant and went down to the wash place to shave. When I got back, he had gone and so had all my money. In fact, the whole Egyptian staff had walked out after helping themselves to anything they could lay their hands on. We got breakfast somehow and fell in the hands on the parade ground in order to issue arms. They were captured Italian rifles but seemed serviceable enough. I gave the order to Slope Arms and a man on the left made a complete hash of the movement.

'What's the matter? Don't you know how to slope arms?'

He smiled at me ingratiatingly. 'No, sir. Never done it in me life. I'm a Merchant Service seaman, sir. Came in here for shelter, like.'

I looked down the ranks. There were certainly some awkward looking 'Naval ratings' but this was no time to be punctilious about the niceties. Merchant Service deserters could at least hump sandbags.

A team went down to the dockyard to establish positions for our defence of the harbour installations. Someone had decided that a few untrained Able Seamen with rifles could stand against the might and armour of a victorious

Afrika Korps. At least it showed a spirit of defiance which was obviously sadly needed but, as those most concerned, we were not sure that we felt that defiant.

However, we did the best we could and, the next day, tried some firing training on the range. The first detail lay down.

'Load.' Much fumbling with rifle bolts.

'Can't load, sir. The ammunition doesn't seem to fit.'

We had British ammunition for Italian rifles and indeed it did not fit.

The following afternoon the news from the desert was even more threatening and, while we were digesting it, an Officer came in who had been down in the dockyard. He told us that, beside each of our amateur efforts at making a strongpoint, the Egyptian Army had built a proper one – manned, dug down, fully sandbagged and armed with heavy machine guns. Each embrasure was sighted not up the road from whence Jerry might be expected to come but firmly onto our positions.

In the evening, I went over to the main barracks, *Canopus 1*. When the mass desertion took place it had been left, empty and unguarded, and, needless to say, the locals had been in. Silver, sheets, tobacco, liquor – all had been stolen. Now I saw something I could do other than just accept fate. With a few sailors to help, I smashed empty bottles inside all the ground floor windows so that the floor was covered with jagged slivers of glass. (Only the higher class Egyptians wore shoes.) Then I returned and walked round the sailors' messdecks. I picked the twelve largest, smartest Regular Service ratings I could find, explained my plan and sent them off to practise.

The next morning there was a crowd of several hundred Egyptians outside our main gate. They had not been valiant enough to take any overtly hostile action but it was obvious what they were there for and they exuded an air of sullen menace. The sentry, in his khaki and tin hat, was frankly terrified and asked permission to come inside. We had heard, during the night, that the end was only hours away and we must expect the Afrika Korps to enter Alexandria during the forenoon. The doctors had put on Red Cross brassards to make their non-combatant status clear, the rest of us had packed our suitcases in descending order of priority, not knowing how many we should be allowed to take with us. Outside the walls of *Canopus 2*, Alex with its familiar streets and night clubs was a strange, hostile city from another world. Inside, we sat and waited for the first signs of a field grey uniform to appear.

All except the twelve. At nine o'clock precisely, the gate swung open and a squad marched out. Their uniforms were virginally white, their belts and gaiters were blancoed to shame snow. With shouts and a stamping of feet which would have delighted even Whale Island, two ceremonial sentries were posted who promptly started marching up and down as if His Majesty himself was in residence. The khaki clad sentry vanished as if he had never been. The gate, remaining open, showed an equally smart gate guard inside. The Mediterranean Fleet, in all its peacetime glory, had never run to bull like this.

The watching crowd absorbed the transformation and, to them, the message was clear. Obviously the Germans were not coming as they had thought. The British were staying after all.

In twos and threes and then in big segments, they began to disperse. By lunch time they had all gone. In the afternoon, with almost symbolic timing, we heard that the Eighth Army had stopped running at last and believed that they could hold a line indefinitely at some place nobody had ever heard of called El Alamein. The doctors rather sheepishly took off their brassards, suitcases were unpacked and a visit to *Canopus 1* showed most satisfactory signs of naked feet bleeding all over the floor. Alexandria returned to normal.

But it could never be quite the same again. In *Mosquito* the CO had led the way and had last been heard of, it was thought, *en route* for Haifa. The boats had sailed with the Fleet and, leaderless, the very few base staff who had remained had acted on their own initiative and started demolitions. MTBs left on the slip had been smashed up. Newly arrived, vital equipment for which we had waited months had been wantonly destroyed. It hurt deeply. And it hurt more when we went ashore to our old haunts to find our uniform was now the target for angry taunts and jeers from the Army.

'Good God – Navy . . . I thought you buggers had all run for it.' Or worse, quoting *Cossack* and the *Altmark*, 'I say, the Navy's here. Must be quite safe now then . . .'

In so short a time had we come so far from Dunkirk, Greece and Crete.

At the height of the crisis, I had been stricken with dysentery, which pulls you down anyway. Add to this the shock and shame of the retreat and the rat race from Alex plus the cumulative effects of what had really been a fairly hairy eighteen months. Suddenly and unexpectedly I found myself thoroughly depressed.

I sailed for home with my own morale at a very low ebb and met the ultimate humiliation in Durban. This time, no beautiful girls and brass bands greeted us but a Provost Marshal demanding travel documents. Some Naval Officers, it seemed, had not even stopped running at Suez.

In Freetown 'Believe God' came out to us but he had added three new words and the slogan now read, 'Who Believe God silly sucker.'

I took his point. We had been told that we were expected to give a lavish tip to an idle and bloody minded steward who was making more money than I was. (Later I found that the cabin boy in the Holyhead mail boat, who washed up the dirty dishes in the galley and had never heard a shot fired in anger, earned £10 a month plus £10 'danger money'. Twenty pounds. Exactly what I had been paid as CO of an MTB Flotilla in Tobruk.)

Meanwhile, we heard on the ship's radio news of the bungled and disastrous raid on Tobruk and I guessed, all too correctly, that my old Tenth Flotilla must have taken heavy casualties.

When we got home, I found that nobody in England realised what had been happening in the Middle East and, worse still, nobody seemed to care.

It was wonderful being back with Pam and seeing my son for the first time but I was sour and morose and full of that peculiar resentment felt by those who have been where the fighting is tough for those who were not there. Them and Us again. The Middle East was full of bitter, disillusioned, battleweary men, quick and unreasonable in resentment. I was just a very small part of the whole.

Leave would help. But, after only ten days, I was recalled.

Chapter 14

OPERATION 'TORCH'

The appointment told me to report forthwith to Gourock, taking with me only 'a reduced steaming kit'. I had never heard of this requirement before and the wording sounded sinister. Whatever lay in store, it was obviously not a normal appointment if even Their Lordships of the Admiralty felt constrained to warn me to take the minimum of possessions. These were the days of crazy, suicide operations like the blocking of St Nazaire and such a hint must be taken seriously. Men are seldom at their most heroic when wrenched from their wives' bedsides and prefer gallant deeds to be something read about in the newspapers. I was quite prepared to die if I had to but, frankly, I didn't want to do it. Rather morosely, I set off back to war.

I arrived in Gourock to find myself one of a party of about eighty Lieutenants and Lieutenant Commanders all equally apprehensive about the new job. We were mustered for briefing in a big conference hall – and told the astonishing news. A great new American Army, supported by the British First Army, was to invade Algeria and Morocco. The Eighth Army was to advance from Alamein at the same time and the two mighty forces would eventually come together, cracking the Afrika Korps between them like a nut in pincers. We were to go in the troopships of the biggest convoy the world had ever seen to act as liaison officers to the British Merchant Service and the troops.

I joined the SS *Letitia* – a Scottish manned Western Ocean passenger/cargo liner running, in peacetime, from Glasgow to Canada. Now she was to carry several thousand American troops to Oran.

The Americans were an astonishing crowd. By British standards, their discipline was only notional. Half of them came on board carrying guitars and gambling schools promptly started all over the decks with heaped piles of pound notes, every one of which would have represented a week's pay to our men

Trouble started at once. *Letitia* being a British ship under UK transport control, the officers ate well in the passenger dining room whilst the troops, on the inevitably crowded mess decks, fared comparatively badly because they were on a lower scale of ration allowance. The troops complained bitterly at such inequality and the American officers felt guilty. The situation was made worse by the Scottish galley hands who promptly started a black market, selling night time feasts of bacon and eggs at grossly exorbitant prices.

When we sailed, there were even more problems. British troops are, of course, well known for their propensity to remain fallen in at attention while their troopship sinks under them. The Americans milled around at Boat Stations in a disorganised scrum. I quickly found that, if they understood the good reasoning behind an order, nobody could be more cooperative but orders they disliked or didn't understand were simply ignored.

The first morning out, a bitter signal came from the convoy Commodore complaining of the desecration of the blackout by the amount of smoking on deck. Obviously, something had to be done. I cut into the incessant music and spoke through the loudspeakers all over the ship. Pointing out, somewhat exaggeratedly, that a cigarette could be seen by a U-Boat five miles away, I suggested to these lads (half from the mid-West and total strangers to the sea) that they were now travelling in dangerous waters. 'I'm not saying that a man who disobeys smoking orders will be put in the brig,' I went on. 'I'm saying that, if you see your buddy light up and you want to go home again some day, thrown the stupid son of a bitch over the side and then you may have a chance.' Perhaps it was the limey accent but they loved it and, thereafter, at least in *Letitia*, the blackout was strictly maintained.

It occurred to me that boredom was the great enemy. The soldiers, moreover, would almost certainly have to go down scrambling nets to reach their landing craft. So I had some nets rigged aft above the well deck and asked the OC Troops to arrange for every man to get used to climbing up and down them in full equipment plus rifle. He saw the point and we started off with individual training, working up to team races. There were six elderly staff colonels on board and five of them insisted that it was their duty to start things off by going first. The sixth said that, in every ship he'd ever sailed in, they went down to boats by a goddamned staircase and he saw no reason why, war or no war, one could not be provided. But everyone else became quite expert and it gave them useful exercise to keep fit.

On the whole, I loved them and we established the friendliest of relationships. I particularly enjoyed their singing. Germans and Americans sing. Except for the Welsh, the British do not. Now I found that, if a few Americans got together, guitars would be produced and music would be made.

It happened that the day of the assault would be my birthday. The OC

Troops knew and he knew my views on their singing. The night before, I was working in my cabin when a message came asking me to go and see him in the lounge. When I got there, I found that they had arranged a special choral and musical evening for me as a birthday cum thank you treat.

I sat and listened to their old traditional melodies as the singers forgot momentarily their surroundings and thought of home. 'I'll be riding on the railroad', 'The old grey mare is not what she used to be' and, final and apposite, 'We're coming over . . . and we won't come back till it's over over there'.

The songs of a new Army and a new world filled the room. I thought of the heartbreak of Dunkirk and the threat of invasion, Crete, the hard, cruel slog of Tobruk and the desert war, Malta convoys, the long agony of the Mediterranean Fleet steadily decimated from the sky. Now the ship's radio was talking of a breakout from Alamein but this advance would not end with another retreat. It would end with a meeting. A meeting with a new, fresh Army from a new, fresh nation, limitless in its reserves of men and materials. Now, at last, I knew we were truly no longer alone.

I felt an enormous lump in my throat and I was very close to tears. It was wonderful and important to me because, at that moment, all my Middle East bitterness and malaise disappeared. It would take time but now I knew we were going to win this bloody war.

Afterwards, my particular friend, Captain Louis Bruce Scranton from New Orleans, came down to my cabin. I was still feeling very emotional. He was in the faintly exhalted mental state of a man who knows he is going into action the next day. He wanted to know what it felt like to be shot at. Would he be very frightened? How would he make out? I helped him as much as I could and we discussed the implications of our both being where we were. If we survived the war, what would peace bring? Certainly, we reckoned, Britain and America must never dissolve their present partnership.

We both had a young son of the same age and we both felt we wanted to leave them a thought from that moment. He produced a dollar and I a ten shilling note. On each we wrote the same message to the other's child. The dollar reads, 'To Courtney William Miles Anderson (Bill). Today is your inheritance from us. Keep it' and both our signatures.

Early the next morning, we started the assault. Disembarkation was difficult because the current kept swinging the ship against the wind and sea so that the landing craft had to keep changing sides, causing the anxiously waiting troops to be kept hanging about or chased back and forth across the deck. British soldiers would have been effing and blinding but, once they understood the reason, the Americans accepted it with stoical patience.

We landed them all with only one casualty – the sixth colonel who had refused to practise. He fell off the net and down into the boat below, stove in two ribs and broke an arm. When last heard of, he'd refused an ambulance and was standing by the road, hitching a lift into Oran. Spirit is spirit after all.

As I saw off the very last officer, he thrust an envelope into my hand. There was a note: 'Now we've gone, you can open the bar at last. Have a drink on us . . .' The rest was a wad of pound notes.

It had been a successful operation but it ended on a sour note. French resistance had been unexpectedly heavy and casualties much higher than anticipated. At 0200 an urgent signal came asking for blood plasma to be sent ashore at once. The plasma had been stowed underneath a lot of other stores due to be disembarked the next day and it would take a lot of effort to shift the cargo and get it up. To my shocked amazement, the Chief Officer of *Letitia* refused to turn his hands to and start the work until he had an authorisation to pay overtime. Only after a rather bitter altercation did he finally agree to go ahead on the strength of my signature guaranteeing payment. I was thinking of him with some contempt when another signal came from the Flagship saying that overtime was authorised. *Letitia* was not alone. Others in the convoy had refused blood to men dying ashore until our gallant merchant seamen were guaranteed their extra money for getting out of bed.

By the time we sailed for home, the U-Boats, which had failed to spot the enormous convoys from the USA and Britain, had had time to muster at the exit from the Straits. The first night, the ship ahead and the one astern of *Letitia* were both sunk by the same salvo of torpedoes. More interestingly, the one inside us also went from a fish which must have passed close by us. We were thirteen in the convoy. Lucky for some . . .

I went home to resume my interrupted leave. The Admiralty had told me that three years in MTBs was enough and it was time for me to return to the deep water Navy. So I watched the post daily till the brown envelope came. First Lieutenant of *Scarborough* in an Atlantic Escort Group. Early in 1943, I travelled up to Londonderry and entered a new kind of war.

Chapter 15

THE BATTLE OF THE ATLANTIC

Churchill once said that the only thing which had really frightened him during the whole war was that we might lose what he christened the Battle of the Atlantic. We damned nearly did.

In the twenties and thirties, the same sort of cretins who comprise today's CND had been mounting a similar campaign against rearmament and 'wasting public money on defence'. Many good young men were to die unnecessarily as a result and in no theatre of conflict did the resultant parsimony show so clearly as in our fight for the convoys. Most of our food, all our oil and petrol, all the raw materials needed for the vast war effort, had to come by sea. If the sea lanes could be cut, Britain would have been forced to surrender in about a fortnight. Yet it was here that our defences were weakest.

By the outbreak of war, in spite of left wing opposition, we had achieved a certain amount of rearmament but, for the Navy, it had been concentrated on making up the serious deficiencies in the Fleet. Apart from a few elderly sloops, there simply were no convoy escorts. A crash programme was started to build the primitive but tough little 'Flower' class corvettes – just big enough to carry basic Asdic and depth charges – but, when I joined the fray, the convoys were taking hideous losses and the situation was very much touch and go.

HMS *Scarborough* was a typical example of all that was wrong. She was a tired old sloop whose best days lay far behind her. Designed and built for showing the flag in peacetime on stations like the Persian Gulf, she boasted beautiful teak wooden decks and large square ports in the wardroom which even had a sort of glass 'French window' onto a Quarterdeck once immaculate but now covered with depth charges. Under any sort of pressure, from weather or the need for speed, bricks fell out of the boiler. At her best speed flat out in a calm sea with a following wind, she was two knots slower than a surfaced U-Boat. Apart from her Asdics, she carried a pathetic armament of two single Oerlikon guns against aircraft and a single 4" gun of World War 1 vintage which was jammed 5 degrees to starboard of the centre line. All in all, she was like an over-worked old horse on the verge of dropping dead yet flogged into carrying one last heavy load before it could do so.

Her Captain was a passed over Lieutenant Commander, 'Rastus' Carnduff. A big, burly, florid faced man, he got his nickname from his endless repertoire of stories concerning this apocryphal character from the Deep South. (Example – Rastus and Liza are copulating on the railroad track. A train appears and just manages to shudder to a halt, cowcatcher poking Rastus in the ribs. The driver leaps down and asks Rastus what the hell he thinks he's doing. Rastus: 'Waal, suh, boss, Ah was comin', Liza was comin' and the train was comin'. And yuh was the only one had brakes . . .')

Rastus had a fiancée who had been captured by the Japanese (and we already knew what that meant). He never took leave because he had nowhere to go and in harbour he stayed on board and drank. He was kindhearted, idealistic and naive and his only real fault was that he became hysterical under stress when he had a tendency to scream. I felt very protective towards him.

We lay in harbour for a few days with the rest of the tired, grubby, storm battered little ships along the Derry quayside. I spent the time learning about the tactics of the convoy war. It seemed that the U-Boats lay waiting in long, extended patrol lines across the convoy routes. When one sighted a convoy, he reported it to Doenitz in Lorient and then fell in astern, continuing to report the convoy's course and speed. Doenitz mobilised all his available forces who joined the shadower until a 'wolf pack' had been formed of anything up to thirty U-Boats. When concentration was complete, the pack would race up round the flanks, far out of sight of the convoy, and attack it from ahead that night.

The Escort Groups were lucky to have eight sloops and corvettes to cover a convoy probably consisting of about seventy merchant ships and spread out over a hundred square miles of sea. The surfaced U-Boats were faster than the escorts and many carried a heavy gun armament. In the darkness, they attacked on the surface and submerged to reload after firing their torpedoes.

On an average night, the Escort Group would probably have three escorts, miles apart, across the front of the convoy (which was formed in a rectangle of, say, ten lines of seven ships each), with two escorts on each flank and one astern to pick up survivors. All we could really do was to fire starshell to light up the sea and force the U-Boats to submerge, with luck, before they could fire. Then their speed would be reduced to three or four knots and the merchant ships might draw ahead safely. Even in contact with a U-Boat we could not wait to hunt. Once he was down and out of it, we had to get back to our station to wait for the next one.

Of course, the solution was simple. Aircraft with the convoy could keep

HMS Scarborough. One gun jammed on Green 05.

the U-Boats down so that the pack could not work its way round the sides to reach an attacking position ahead. But the escort carriers had yet to appear and the RAF, insanely convinced that they could win the war by bombing Germany, insisted on spending their money on buying more and more bombers instead of providing the maritime aircraft so desperately needed by Coastal Command. So, once again, we lacked the vital air support, the convoys suffered accordingly and we very nearly lost the whole war in the Atlantic.

The 39th Escort Group, three sloops and five corvettes, sailed on a cold, grey winter's morning. We passed down the narrow River Foyle, the wooded banks slipping by so close on either side that you felt you could almost touch them, and picked up our convoy off the north of Ireland. Then we turned west into the open Atlantic.

We knew nothing of 'Ultra' in those days nor of the Intelligence war which has since been so well documented. We only knew that the Admiralty forecasts of U-Boat movements were pretty accurate and that we could rely upon them. Sometimes they were encouraging, suggesting a clear run ahead and cheering us accordingly. On other occasions, we could see that there was trouble to come and we could only force on and pray . . .

For the first few days it blew hard. The wind shrieked through the rigging of the crazily twisting masthead. We stood our watches, feeling the great thumps as the bow reared up out of the sea to smack down hard in the next trough, ducking as the water crashed over the forecastle and swept in an icy sheet of spray over the open bridge. Every now and then, through the rain and away across the huge, grey, white-topped waves, we would get a brief glimpse of a blur on the horizon which was the nearest ship of the convoy on which we were trying to keep station. Beyond, somewhere, sixty-nine other ships laboured in their own private hells through the gale.

After four hours on the bridge, we went below to rest as best we could when just hanging on in the reeling wardroom required real physical effort and staying in one's heaving bunk was an art in itself. Anyhow, the wardroom at sea was dark and uninviting. The 'French window' to the Quarterdeck and the big ports were closed with steel doors and, as we tried to manage some sort of a meal, we heard the waves, intimate, terrifying, monstrous, smashing impotently on the deck outside.

On the fourth day, we were far south-west of Ireland in U-Boat waters and, sure enough, the evening signal from the Admiralty suggested that we had been sighted. The gale had blown itself out and the big waves had lost their fury, running in from the starboard bow in an interminable procession of great, sullen rollers.

I had a wall chart in my cabin with our route marked in white and the U-Boat dispositions reported by the Admiralty in red. The pin, which was the convoy, moved down the white line with heart-breaking slowness as we struggled south at a bare 8 knots and there seemed to be an awful lot of red dots around. Doenitz would have little trouble assembling his wolf pack for this run.

The second day of the threat saw an obvious movement of the red dots, all converging on our position, and the Admiralty warned us to expect attack.

The third day, and a week out of Derry, we realised it would come that night.

A large group of U-Boats had been assembled. The sea was calm. We stood on the bridge knowing that, over the horizon, the U-Boats were on the surface, forging ahead of us to take up their positions on either bow of the huge convoy as the ships steamed slowly along like patient animals plodding wearily to the slaughter house. What was the price to be this time?

The alarm bells rang for action stations at about 2200. Muffled figures came racing up on deck and the bridge filled with silent men peering out into the darkness. For some minutes, we stood in a shadowy group, the only sound the interminable measured ping, ping, ping coming out of the Asdic loudspeaker. Then, suddenly and hideously vivid in the blackness, a great gush of scarlet flame went bubbling up into the night as if a giant hand was pouring molten hell upwards from some enormous jug. Out across the sea, the ships of the convoy stood out in stark silhouette against the monstrous sight. Somebody on the bridge whispered very quietly, 'Oh, Jesus Christ,' and, at the same moment, we heard the sullen boom of the explosion. An ammunition ship had been torpedoed on the far side of the convoy.

God knew how many U-Boats had already got in among the merchant ships. Those that had would make a safe killing. All we could do was to turn outwards and light up the sea with starshells, having to swing the whole ship to do so because of our jammed gun. Then we would go for any U-Boats we spotted coming in, hoping to frustrate their firing long enough to prevent their attacking that night.

The fierce light of the ammunition ship was abruptly extinguished as she sank and now the only illumination came from the amber balls of the starshells hanging in the sky all round the horizon.

A radar contact. A glimpse of a tiny black spot away across the golden lake of the sea.

'Full speed ahead together.'

Scarborough's tired old engines beat us up to our full fifteen knots and we felt our bodies instinctively willing the old sloop forwards as we turned towards the enemy. Long before we got there, the U-Boat had submerged. A possible echo on the Asdic. We fired a depth charge pattern over the spot and, astern of us, the sea heaved up as the charges exploded far below. A series of mammoth thumps hit the ship's bottom and a few more bricks fell out of the boiler. No further contact on the Asdic but we must have been close. However, we could not wait. Back to our station on the convoy. The starshells were being extinguished as they fell into the sea and darkness came again on our sector of the screen. So we had to turn back slowly, firing, as we did so, the new pattern of starshell from our single, jammed gun.

In the Middle Watch, the attack died down. The U-Boats had fired their torpedoes, submerged to reload and fallen astern. Some had been driven off by the escorts and had failed to fire at all. All would be back for the next night's party. If only we had something in the air . . .

A cluster of tiny lights just visible in the darkness ahead. Survivors in the water. We stopped and put scrambling nets over the side. Out of the night came voices shouting, the cries and whimpers of pain. Slippery bodies covered with oil fuel, the dark, rich, ruby red of blood oozing through the slime. Half Lascars, half white. One of the Lascars lay on the quarterdeck moaning over and over again, 'Oh, oh. Plenty pain . . .'

The mercy of the needle and grey dawn breaking over the sea. Tired, white faces in duffle coats as *Scarborough* pounded after the convoy. Tonight it would all happen again.

The worst part of the journey was in the North Atlantic. As we progressed south, the danger from the U-Boats lessened, the sun grew hotter and the sky turned blue. We turned round in Freetown, oiling and storing in the sultry, tropical heat and then, with a heavily loaded northbound convoy, plodded slowly back to cold, rainy Ulster. We could hardly have had two less salubrious termini. One wag summed it up as going from the armpit of Europe to the arsehole of Africa.

Before we sailed, I had just had time to find a house in Derry. It was in a fairly mean little back street terrace, but at least it was a home and it seemed to be all that was available. When we got back from that first convoy, I was hoping to find Pam and Bill safely ensconced.

We arrived in Moville, at the entrance to the Foyle, and fuelled from the oiler. The Port War Signal Station had sent us a signal telling us of the parents and wives of our sailors who had been killed in the blitz while we had been away. In the Second World War it was not only the women at home who had to grieve at losing those they loved. It worked both ways and the women were vulnerable too. Now, a bottle of whisky on my cabin desk, I had the miserable task of sending for the sailors concerned and breaking the news.

We went back up the Foyle. Our young doctor had two bad habits. A surgeon manqué, he loved to lay out his horrible implements on the wardroom table at Action Stations and explain the purpose of each before he put them away. As his potential customers, we found this depressing. His other weakness was a futile ambition to celebrate each safe return by drinking a glass of brandy for every buoy we passed going up river. There being over thirty of them, this was a hopeless quest and the doc was always senseless by the time we secured. Now, stepping carefully over his paralysed legs, I rushed ashore to our little street, rang the bell – and Pam opened the door with Bill in her arms. It was a wonderful return from the sea.

Later, after a couple of runs (Freetown and back took about six weeks), we decided it was silly to pay rent we could ill afford for her to be left in these rather unpleasant surroundings whilst I was away. We therefore decided that she and Bill would be better off with my mother in Dublin.

I left her there and went back to sea. Convoy followed convoy. Sometimes nothing happened and the only enemy was the weather with the sheer physical misery and exhaustion of hanging on to your reeling world in the great North Atlantic storms. Sometimes we were clobbered and it was horrible. Apart from anything else, there is something infinitely sad to a sailor in watching a stricken ship rear her bows into the air and plunge backwards into the sea.

We had an arrangement with a Wren in the Derry Operations Room who would sent a telegram to Pam wishing her Many Happy Returns. It meant, 'Catch the next train from Dublin to Belfast and you'll just have time to get here before *Scarborough* arrives.' Then Pam would rush up to Derry and, while the ship boiler cleaned, we'd have a few precious days together in the ramshackle old Melville Hotel where the kindly Wren would have booked us a room. But the few days flashed by and, all too soon, it would be time for me to go back to sea.

In most ways, these six-weekly meetings were a wonderful break and relief but, somehow, in others they were demoralising. The contrast between the awfulness of the Atlantic war and the safety and comfort of a double bed in the Melville Hotel was too great. Just as I got used to the one, my life was transmogrified to the other. It was unsettling to both.

Early one morning, we said yet another goodbye. I need hardly describe these partings. On this occasion I left her, as usual, dry eyed but white faced with huge strained rings under her eyes. I left her standing in the middle of our room, looking after me. As I walked down the corridor, I knew I had to see her one last time. I ran back and opened the door. She was still standing there exactly as I had left her. She hadn't moved. We looked at each other speechlessly for a moment then I closed the door and went back to my ship. All these years later, I can still see her as she was at that moment.

In the late summer, *Scarborough* refitted at Harland and Wolff's yard in Belfast. Pam came up and we found a nice room in a private house. After a few lovely, peaceful weeks, the ship went out for sea trials. Just before we sailed, I looked over the side. A couple of dockyard workmen still had their welding torches going but we left on time. It never occurred to me that we wouldn't be back that evening but all went well and we were told to go straight on to Derry. We still had a few dockyard maties on board so we landed them at the end of Belfast Lough. I asked one of them if he could possibly ring Pam as soon as he got ashore and tell her what had happened.

On the way round the north-east corner of Ireland, water appeared in the starboard passageway coming from the wardroom wine store. I went in and found what the welders' last minute job had been. They had cut a hole in the ship's side and nicked all our booze. But my dockyard matey had not let me down. I got to the Melville just after midnight. Pam was there waiting for me.

And so the months passed. By the time we left Belfast, the Americans and British had cleared North Africa and the Mediterranean was, at last, open again. Now we ran to Gibraltar instead of Freetown and there, at least, we could have a really good thrash while we turned round.

In the late spring of 1944, everyone's thoughts were on the approach of D-Day and *Scarborough* was ordered south to Portsmouth. As the old chant has it, 'First the Nab and then the Warner, Outer Spit and Shithouse Corner.' Sure enough, we passed these familiar marks and found ourselves there – the dockyard's North West Wall, home of the little ships.

Having secured the ship, I ambled into the wardroom totally unprepared for the glorious surprise which awaited me. My relief had joined and I was to leave forthwith. Apparently, Rastus had reported on me favourably and, though junior for the job, I was to be given my own command.

I departed on air.

Chapter 16

HMS WIVERN

The command was HMS *Wivern*. She was one of the most famous of the grand old V & Ws in which I had done my Midshipman's destroyer time, and, for nearly a quarter of a century, she had been known to the Navy as 'The Tiddly Wiv'. I had been long enough in an Atlantic escort to have an almost unbearable envy of destroyers which could do double our speed and had no fewer than four real working guns. *Wivern* had all this, plus our outfit of torpedoes. I was moving to an infinitely better, faster, more strongly armed ship – a ship which really could take some offensive action. Having been helplessly on the receiving end for so long that was cause enough for jubilation. But this wonderful ship was to be mine. I was to be in command, and in wartime, which must be the zenith of any Naval Officer's ambition. Moreover, this was not just any ship – which would be honour enough. This was the Tiddly Wiv. Command of *Wivern* was more than an honour – it was a trust.

The trust lay alongside the Devonport dockyard wall looking anything but 'tiddly'. She had gone alongside a sinking Canadian corvette to rescue survivors and the corvette had sunk during the operation with the depth charges set to twenty-five feet. The resultant explosion would have finished off many new destroyers but the V & Ws were built to last. With a vast hole in her bottom and her engines lifted clear off their seatings, *Wivern* was towed some hundreds of miles back to Gibraltar and, eventually, to Devonport dockyard where they took the old ship in hand and made her seaworthy once again. There were snags, as we were to discover later, but they were not the ship's fault. In all the year I drove her we never once missed a convoy – though, on occasions, we had a stoker with a sledgehammer knocking wooden wedges back in when the steering engine tried to rattle itself loose from the bulkhead.

Meanwhile she lay alongside the wall looking as forlorn and derelict as ships do at the end of a major refit – dirty, unpainted, her upper deck covered with electric cables, unmentionable dockyard intimacies and lethargically squatting dockyard maties. Only a loving and knowledgeable eye could

121

visualise the splendid little ship which would eventually emerge from the grime and filth of it all.

D-day came and went and the rain poured down. Apart from the Engineer Officer, the whole Wardroom were as new to their jobs as I was to command. No. 1 was a very junior RN Lieutenant. No. 2 – the Navigator – was old enough to have been a schoolmaster in peacetime but had never navigated before. There were two Subs, one RN but both brand new, and a Gunner (T) whose thin stripe was equally virginal. Chief, on the other hand, was a real old reprobate of a Lieutenant Commander RNR – a man with years of sea time behind him who found himself in the difficult position of having to yield precedence in the Wardroom to a completely inexperienced RN First Lieutenant almost young enough to be his son. With a half stripe more than his Commanding Officer it was a classic formula for difficulties and it said a lot for Chief that there were none.

Some weeks after I joined, the ship commissioned. The rain had stopped at last and it was a sunny summer's evening in the dockyard. I stood on deck, looking down the jetty, waiting for the main bulk of the Ship's Company to arrive. A couple of three ton trucks turned up, full of bags and hammocks, and then, round the corner, they appeared – a long column of marching sailors.

It was a small drama the dockyard had known so many times before over so many years in peace and war. The dockyard maties did not even look round. A destroyer ship's company joining their destroyer was no great event in Devonport.

But to every marching sailor a new chapter in his life was about to begin. Good ship or bad? Home or abroad? Down past Drake's Island lay the open sea and the war to which they were about to return. What was this commission to hold for them? What were they taking on?

I looked at the strange yet familiar faces. Soon I should know every one and the character behind it. Most were even younger than the Wardroom but there were some obviously good Petty Officers among them. Already, by the very act of falling in and marching down to their ship together, the first fragile bond had been forged. They were no longer individuals in barracks belonging to no one in particular. Here, for the first of so many times, came the preparatory order, 'Ship's Company . . .' before they halted and turned left. Now they were looking at the ship with a frankly appraising stare, pointing things out to each other. What in particular? I realised a lot of eyes were looking at me. Why? Good God, I was 'the Skipper' of course. What this ship did or failed to do would be my responsibility and mine alone. When my boat was hailed with me in it, the Coxswain would reply, '*Wivern.*' In report, I should write not, '*Wivern* did this,' but, 'I did this.' The Officers stood up when I entered the wardroom. To the sailors I would be Ultimate Authority but, far more than that, the man on the bridge whose touch and skill would certainly regulate their living and possibly their dying too. This was command – and command in wartime at that. This was what all my past training was supposed to have prepared me for. Now, in *Wivern*, there was no one to go to for help. This ship and these men were mine. The whole weight of the Navy and England at war was behind me but, when it came to the crunch, I would be alone. Twenty-seven years old, two stripes on my sleeve, I went down to my cabin and sat there while the whole realisation flooded in on me. I felt totally humble and totally proud.

The next morning I addressed the ship's company for the first time. I told them something of our ship's history: how she had always been known as 'The Tiddly Wiv'; about the depth charges and how she had stood up to them; what we ourselves were now going to do. She might not be the newest and glossiest destroyer in the Fleet but our predecessors who had loved and served her for twenty-five years would look to us in her last commission, to honour their trust. Always remember, I concluded, an old violin 'plays the sweetest tune'. It was just what they wanted to hear and another bond was forged.

We sailed from Devonport for Harwich where we joined the Harwich Escort Force. Here, with a sluicing tide behind us and a vicious cross wind, I had to secure to head and stern buoys. By the time I had mastered that one, ship handling held no further fears.

We went out every night to patrol the off shore convoy route against E-Boats. As we passed Felixstowe Dock, we would see the MTBs and Motor Gun Boats emerging – great, powerful monsters compared with the old First Flotilla and the Wobbly Tenth of my day. Times had indeed changed.

One evening we were steaming up the swept channel off Lowestoft when we heard aircraft. My hackles still rose at the sound and I looked round anxiously to see a huge group of planes coming out from over the land. As I watched, the noise increased and I spotted more and more till the whole sky seemed to be full of them. Even in Crete I had seen nothing like this but even more were to come.

The droning became a roar till the very air above us seemed to be throbbing. Low over the sea and at all heights till they were mere specks above, from horizon to horizon, the whole world seemed full of aircraft. The ship's company had emerged onto the upper deck and we all stood in awe, faces turned up, looking at this limitless aerial armada, this sky literally saturated with aircraft. It was a thousand bomber raid on its way to Germany and anyone who had ever been on the receiving end could only feel horror stricken pity for the city which was to receive that load. How far we had come since the days of Dunkirk . . .

The beginning and the end. First Flotilla MTBs in foreground. HMS Wivern behind.

After we had operated from Harwich for a bit and shaken ourselves down into an efficient fighting unit, it was decided to combine all the small Hunt class destroyers to form the Harwich Force and concentrate the bigger V & Ws at Rosyth to escort East Coast convoys.

The job entailed taking some thirty or forty ships down the East Coast to the Thames and we soon learned that the bigger and better the merchant ships the greater the problems. We sailed from Methil early in the morning, formed up the main convoy in the middle of that night off Newcastle and the Hartlepools, and entered E-Boat Alley the following evening. This was the bulge of the East Anglian coast where the southbound route went to seawards of the dangerous sandbanks and shoals off Yarmouth and the northbound route passed up inside. The third night was spent in Sheerness, sailing the next morning with a northbound convoy and backing up its escort as far as the Humber, then returning the next night to Sheerness having reinforced the southbound. After this, we took the next day's northbound convoy the whole way back to the Forth and Rosyth.

The main problem was usually fog. The ships had to sail in two long lines and a big convoy was often ten or fifteen miles long by the time one had included stragglers. The lead escort was essentially a bellwether showing the way because the big ships came first and the deep sea Masters' coastal navigation was often primitive. The escort at the rear would be chasing up stragglers or running up and down the long line at twenty knots, keeping a general sheepdog eye open. Fog produced immediate shambles. Some ships forged hopefully on. Others hauled out of the channel and anchored. Others anchored on the spot – which raised difficulties if a 'forge on' man happened to be behind them. Close control and co-ordination was impossible.

Off the south-east corner of the Wash where the two swept channels split, there was one particularly narrow passage between the sandbanks, marked by two buoys. Deep sea Masters were liable to take a horrified look at the closeness of the two marks, lose their nerve and pull sideways like a frightened horse refusing a jump. This left a big merchant ship beam on to the channel and with inadequate room to manoeuvre even if the master possessed the skill to handle his ship in such confined waters. The tide moved fast, the remainder of the long convoy bore inexorably down, and the CO of the escort aged before his time.

The other indigenous danger was drunken merchant ship Masters. On one occasion, the Master of a large passenger ship was so drunk in the early morning that he could not be awoken when it was time to start from Methil. His Chief Officer said he was not paid to take the responsibility of command, and refused to sail, so the ship missed the convoy and remained behind at anchor.

Another, worse, example happened when a merchant ship suddenly veered out of our southbound convoy and crossed the vicious shoals off Yarmouth straight towards the northbound convoy in the inshore channel. It was a pitch dark night but, luckily, high tide. I followed, horribly conscious of the big, vulnerable propellors which must have been sweeping round literally inches above the sand. Morse lamp, a ten inch lighting up his bridge from almost alongside, blasts on the siren, none had any effect. Finally I opened fire with Oerlikon just ahead of his lifeless bridge and we brought him to a halt as he was about to ground on the inshore banks. Fortunately the northbound convoy was running late or there would have been a veritable motorway pile-up. As it was, I had to put my Navigator on board to take the ship into Sheerness because the Master and all his Officers were too drunk to understand what was happening. It was all in the day's work.

All through autumn and winter we flogged up and down the East Coast. Christmas came and went. (We sailed at 0400 on Christmas morning with our loudspeakers blaring 'Silent night, Holy night' across the quiet waters of the Forth.) Gales and fog gave way to gales and snow. Early in the New Year we actually met a freak calm. I saw the last of my convoy safely into Newcastle and increased speed for home. It was just after midnight and the sea was glassy. I stood on the bridge and peered ahead. Out on the starboard bow, the darkness of the night looking wrong. There seemed to be sort of white tinge to the blackness. 'Must be snow,' said someone idly and we went on to wonder if we were due for leave when we got in.

The wind hit us with a sudden, brutal force made all the worse by its total unexpectedness. One minute we had been gossiping peacefully in a still, quiet Middle Watch, the next the wind was howling and shrieking round our ears as if we had suddenly entered a typhoon.

Quickly the calm water became transformed into a mass of racing, tumbling waves and still the wind increased. After half an hour, the world was a terrifying, screaming hell. The seas were now mountainous and, with the comparatively shallow depth, infinitely more dangerous than those in the Atlantic.

In the wheelhouse the Coxswain took over. I stood on the bridge, peering over the windscreen, watching the forecastle buried in water one minute then lurching up, up, up the next as the bow lifted out of the water. The whole mad inferno had a certain dreadful exhilaration and I felt a crazy urge to shout back into the storm.

But after a while, I began to feel that something was wrong. At first I could not identify it. Then I realised that the bows were no longer lifting as they had been. Now she was putting her nose down but the forecastle no longer came surging buoyantly up; it stayed submerged and sluggish, as the great waves washed over.

Chief appeared on the bridge beside me. Putting his arm round my neck, he pulled my head down and screamed into my ear over the noise of the wind. He told me that the forward magazines were flooded. Devonport dockyard had earned great credit for the speed with which they had got *Wivern* back to sea but, to do it, they must have skimped on the welding. Now a weak bit had gone and we had tons of water where we desperately needed buoyancy. And the leak was beyond pumping.

All night the Coxswain wrestled with the wheel, trying to keep *Wivern*'s head into the sea. On the bridge, I hung grimly on, working the engines to help him. Down in the engine room exhausted men clutched their wheels, trying to give us the response we needed. The rest of the Ship's Company, wakeful and appalled, hung on in the shambles of their messdecks. Everyone knew that, if that waterlogged bow took charge, the end would come – terrifying and sudden.

I broke radio silence to send a storm warning down the coast of winds gusting Force 12 but the Commodore of the convoy behind us refused to believe it. 'Force 12?' he said. 'I doubt it.' He was quickly convinced. Even in the sheltered waters behind the sandbanks, he lost four ships. One was blown into the minefield, two ran aground and one was simply never heard of again. To the north of us, another destroyer lost bridge, funnel, mast and upper works but had the hull buoyancy to stay afloat. Happily, we did not know this at the time.

In *Wivern*, our world was our own staggering, stricken ship, the strained, overburdened bows trying desperately to lift to the great waves which thundered and crashed down onto the forecastle. Inside, flinching to every hideous blow, feeling the sluggishness, knowing of the water in the compartments beneath their feet, the sailors had nothing to do but listen, think and wait.

On the little, open bridge, peering out into the ghastly night, soaked to the skin and very frightened, I remembered the Naval Prayer – 'Oh Lord . . . preserve us from the dangers of the sea and the violence of the enemy . . .' For so long, I had thought only of the possibility of death coming from the Germans. Now, suddenly, it seemed very likely that it would be the sea which would kill me.

And so the long hours passed . . .

With the dawn, the wind decreased to Force 8 and we looked out to a tumultuous sea with thrashing, wild white waves but only of normal gale sized strength.

Slowly, I risked more speed. With dreadful reluctance she answered to the helm and we set course for the Firth of Forth. When we got to Rosyth, there was no question about leave. The ship entered the dockyard for repairs and we returned thankfully to homes we had never thought to see again. But one thing I knew, she was a wonderful little ship . . .

After our storm damage had been repaired, we did another convoy during which one of our ships, SS *Dalemoor*, was mined in E-Boat Alley. I went to her as she sank. Some of the crew, unfortunately led by the Master, had already jumped overboard into the sea and the presence of these swimmers in the water made getting alongside rather difficult but I managed it and eventually succeeded in saving everyone.

When they were all safely on board the errant Master came up onto the bridge. He turned out to be one of the famous characters who had run the Franco blockade during the Spanish Civil War when, apart from more strategic cargo, he had taken crates of Scotch to the Republicans. A suitably grateful General in the Republican forces had presented him with the Spanish King's own cigarette box which the General had appropriated from the royal desk whilst looting the palace. Now, the Master said, he would like to give it to me in thanks for their safe deliverance. I rather suspected this was a subtle way of asking me not to mention his unworthy conduct in my Report of Proceedings but whether it was or not I shall never know because I didn't anyhow. There seemed no point in crucifying this sad, shivering, frightened old man. He did send me the box a few weeks later.

We sailed again at 0800 on 14 March. We were running now on familiar tramlines. North of Newcastle, no problems. Newcastle to the Humber, routine navigational and convoy stuff. Humber to Sheerness, E-Boats, mines and generally stimulating nights. We knew just what to expect.

With this background in our minds, we picked up two merchant ships from Methil. As usual, we should be alone with the convoy until reinforced by the escort from the Humber for the run down E-Boat Alley.

It was a Sunday and one of those rare, sunny, early spring days that make one think, quite unjustifiably, that winter has gone at last. I wanted to get some sleep in the afternoon so that I would be reasonably fresh when, around midnight, I had to start assembling the darkened shapes of the unpredictable individualists who would come milling out from Newcastle. I had an early lunch, looked at the two merchant ships steaming placidly along behind and left the bridge for my sea cabin. The Officer of the Watch took over and the Asdic operator sat in his little office, listening with boredom to the ping, ping, ping in his headphones as he swept through the sea ahead. He had never heard a U-Boat's echo and, indeed, we had never even had the opportunity to exercise with one of our own submarines. U-Boats did not operate off the East Coast and, though we had the set and the operators, it had never occurred to anyone on board or to the Staffs ashore that we should ever need to use them seriously. The set had not even been modernised during our refit and the operators were out of practice and lacked experience.

To seawards, as I drifted off to sleep, Kapitanleutnant Hans Joachim Schwebke watched the scene through his periscope. He, too, had reason to be proud of his command. U714 was a brand new 770-ton, Type VII U-Boat which had just arrived for its first patrol between the Firth of Forth and Flamborough Head.

This, and the thinking behind his orders, became clear from post war studies of captured German Naval records. Doenitz, suffering heavy losses in the Atlantic, had reverted to his old trick of trying to find weak or unguarded points to attack and had guessed, correctly, that there might be easy pickings down our East Coast. Schwebke was therefore a guinea pig. If he was successful, his friends would all come crowding over for the easy kills. If our defences proved too strong – well, nothing had been lost except one U-Boat and Doenitz would try somewhere else.

Schwebke fired at 1400 on the Sunday afternoon and the old, familiar thump of the exploding torpedo shattered my sleep. Within seconds I was on the bridge looking back unbelievingly at the Norwegian *Magne*, the last ship in the line, already sinking fast.

Wivern turned in a beautiful circle of foaming water, white against the blue sea, and raced back to the sinking ship to use her as datum point for the search. Luckily, experience in the Atlantic had made correct action almost second nature. One did not even need to think before automatically starting the requisite search. As I did so, the lookout reported another ship approaching up the swept channel from the southward. It was the South African 'Loch' class frigate, *Natal*.

Never had I been so thankful to see another ship. Not only did the hunt require a minimum of two A/S vessels but I had a feeling in my bones that I knew where the U-Boat was, that it was in the other half of the search area which, by the book, I should not reach for some time. And here, *au moment critique*, was a beautiful, brand new anti-submarine frigate with all the latest Asdics and, even better, the new wonder weapon – an A/S mortar known as Squid which was supposed to be really lethal. I told *Natal* what had happened and gave her the position to start her search.

Natal altered course and, sure enough, gained almost immediate contact. A few minutes later we saw the Squid missiles arch through the sky and the sea reared up from the heavy underwater explosions.

There followed the short anxious wait to see what, if anything, came up. A large amount of wreckage or, best of all, bodies alive or dead were what we hoped for. A little oil or only some wreckage was no good. We had learned that such misleading debris could be ejected from a U-Boat as it escaped. More was required to be sure of a kill.

In fact, a little did appear but certainly not enough to prove success. The sea resumed its calm, untroubled blue and I prepared for a long hunt. There were two of us, one a superbly equipped ship, and I had no need to run after the convoy. We might well get him.

However, the South African had other ideas. He was only on his way to Scapa Flow to work up but, apparently, he thought it was more important to keep to his schedule than to help sink a U-Boat. Explaining his unusual idea of priorities, he wished me luck and just left *Wivern* to it.

Rosyth, in the meantime, was humming like a disturbed beehive. Every conceivable ship was ordered to sea forthwith to join the hunt for the intruder. This was one U-Boat which, on our very doorstop, must be destroyed. I continued the search without much hope. If we had both lost him after that first attack, *Wivern* alone was not likely to find him again and it would be hours before we got the support so urgently needed.

The long afternoon and evening passed and the light began to fade. We were ten miles away from the position of *Natal*'s attack and still searching. Then, as dark crept over the sea, we saw it – a long slick of diesel oil staining the calm water. Steaming slowly up, I investigated all round the source but never an echo could *Wivern*'s elderly Asdics pick up. However, the U-Boat must be there and its position was clearly marked. I hauled off and came back, steaming right up the centre of the slick. Getting to the end, I plastered the position with depth charges. And then I did it again. And again.

When we had spent all our twenty-five depth charges we had still brought up no wreckage but the oil was now coming up thick, sluggish and hard. It was obvious that the U-Boat would not be leaving. By now, all the available ships from Rosyth were just over the horizon and, with no depth charges left, it was time to think about rejoining my convoy. Fixing the position exactly on Berwick lighthouse, which had been clearly visible all day, I reported the situation and left.

On arrival in Sheerness, I got down to the detailed analysis of the action. A specialist A/S Officer from C-in-C, Nore's staff kindly came and helped and, between us, a few hours' work produced a text book Report of Proceedings, complete with sketch maps and a narrative of the operations of both ships. It was obvious that *Natal*'s attack had damaged the U-Boat though it had still managed to withdraw at about three knots and, left in peace, Schwebke would presumably have surfaced after dark and withdrawn to seawards and safety. However, the damage, though it produced no visible oil at the time, had eventually resulted in the telltale slick which had given away his hiding place ten miles from the original attack and thus offered us the chance which our primitive ping would have otherwise denied us. Although *Natal*'s subsequent sense of priorities may have been odd, his Squid had certainly handed *Wivern* the U-Boat on a plate.

We carried out the usual convoy cycle via the Humber, had an extremely successful brush with some E-Boats, and returned to Rosyth to find ourselves heroes. It tuned out that none of the ships sent out from the Forth had found anything. Darkness had fallen by the time they arrived on the scene and the oil slick had disappeared in the night. With equally old and useless Asdics, they had picked up no contact and, after searching all night, they had returned to harbour. With the lack of hard evidence, this left an obvious doubt in the minds of the Admiralty as to whether the U-Boat had been destroyed.

The experts in London were only too aware of how important it was to make sure that Doenitz was discouraged in this particular gambit. They guessed that success would produce a plague of U-Boat attacks on the East Coast which we were simply not geared up to meet. A Hunter Killer group had therefore been sent from Scapa Flow to investigate. These highly skilled specialists had no difficulty in finding the U-Boat in the exact position I had reported and, three days after *Wivern* had left, they had blasted the wreck open and gained all the evidence needed to prove destruction. Because no living U-Boat could remain submerged for three days, *Wivern* had been credited with the kill.

Messages of congratulation poured in. Our gin bills quintupled overnight. Nobody, ourselves included, could get over the fact that an old V & W from Rosyth had sunk a U-Boat. It was rather as if a pedestrian had run over a car.

We sailed for another convoy, came back – and found that we had been sold down the river. It appeared, unbelievably, that the First Sea Lord didn't like South Africans and his staff thought it would not only be politically desirable but useful with their master if the story could read that a South African frigate, unworked up, had casually destroyed a U-Boat in passing. *Natal* had put in no proper records because she had lacked the bridge organisation to do so. Mine, so comprehensive and carefully produced, had been suppressed and replaced by an imaginative if inaccurate 'narrative' concocted in Rosyth. All the signals and letters of congratulation from C-in-C downwards were forgotten and *Natal* was given sole credit for the kill.

As a result, Roskill's *War at Sea*, based on Admiralty records, and the post war Confidential Book listing all U-Boat actions and the ships which were present at the scene, show U714 as being sunk by *Natal* alone with no other ships in company.

Under the circumstances, it is not remarkable that *Natal* collected two DSCs, two DSMs and five Mentions in Despatches. What is, perhaps, surprising is that *Wivern* actually earned three Mentions in Despatches for her success in an action in which, officially, she never took part.

It was very demoralising to find Authority behaving like this but, by now, events in the war were moving so fast that the vast canvas of Germany's defeat began to fill our minds to the exclusion of all else.

Then came VE Day and our role changed. With East Coast convoys no longer necessary, the Rosyth Escort Force was redeployed to run a shuttle service to liberated Norway.

Wivern went first to Stavanger taking, as passengers, two members of the Central Leadership of the Milorg (Norwegian Underground) who had been forced to escape to London, via Sweden, when the Gestapo were hot on their heels. Through them, I was introduced to the local Milorg leaders in each of the ports we visited and, as a result, a close and fascinating liaison developed between *Wivern* and the Norwegian Underground.

Apart from this, we quickly found that, wherever we went, children came up, smiled shyly, took our hands and walked beside us. I explored the town with two kids each side of me and met all my sailors, hands equally gripped by enchanting little blond boys and girls of five or six years old. A Norwegian friend explained.

'Ever since they can remember, they have heard of Father Christmas who will bring them presents and the English who will bring them freedom. You just happened to turn up first. Now you know what would happen to Father Christmas if he ever came to town.'

It was greatly humbling and very moving. Our sweet ration quickly disappeared.

We sailed for Kristiansand, which was being run entirely by the Milorg under one of the most famous of the Underground leaders, a huge man called Robstadt, and here the *Wivern*/Milorg friendship became even stronger.

Robstadt had taken over the old Gestapo headquarters, a pretty little villa in a pine wood on the outskirts of the town. In the cells below, the entire Gestapo team were locked up. A Milorg member showed me his wrist, the scars plainly visible where a device had been clamped on it which, tightened a turn every few hours, produced excruciating agony and a hand which gradually swelled up like a throbbing balloon. The Gestapo torturer who had done this to him was locked up below but the Norwegian had never even gone and kicked his backside.

They showed me their Gestapo captives. Blond, blue eyed, good-looking Aryans and dark, sulky young men, sitting in a cell with all their washing strung up on a line. Germans are very clean. As the door opened, the Gestapo men sprang up and stood rigidly to attention. They considered themselves 'soldiers' and this was the correct way to behave.

The Norwegians closed the door and smiled ruefully. 'It is most interesting for us,' said one, 'to see now how professionals should behave in defeat. We were only amateurs and never understood the rules. I am afraid we must have disappointed our victors dreadfully.'

I was invited to sit in on the Gestapo chief's interrogation by a government representative from Oslo. The Gestapo chief, Koener, was a short, squat, apelike man whose muscles bulged obscenely through his tightly fitting uniform. He came into the room, handcuffed, and bowed to me correctly on his way to face his interrogator. Sitting on a stool, words spilt out in a flood of denunciation of his ex-colleagues. Nothing had ever been his fault. He did not know what his men were doing. He was a soldier. He had only carried out orders.

The Norwegian interrogator listened and encouraged the damaging confidences. (Amongst other things, the German Naval liaison officer was denounced as a Gestapo agent. I had him arrested the next day.) At the end, I was given the little leather cat o' nine tails which Koener had used, when he was the interrogator, on the faces of his victims. He had christened it 'Wotan' and the name was carved on the wooden handle.

We went on to Oslo, where we finally landed our Milorg leaders, and then we spent the next few weeks on the Rosyth, Stavanger, Kristiansand, Oslo run, but time for *Wivern* was running out. The end of the European war meant a concentration in the Pacific and there was no call for elderly V & Ws in that theatre.

On our last trip, I discovered that the Army mails were taking three weeks to reach home so I offered to take all they could give me, letters and parcels, and have the whole lot within the UK postal system in forty-eight hours. This offer was rapturously received and a convoy of 3-ton trucks turned up loaded with mail – and crates of the good champagne the Germans had looted from France and our troops had 'liberated' from the Germans. As a result, at a time when champagne had been unavailable in the UK for years, every one of my sailors was able to take a free bottle in his kitbag to celebrate his homecoming.

But, even with this and the end of the war, there was a remarkable atmosphere of subdued sadness on board because, on our return to Rosyth, we must turn over our much loved old ship to the knacker's yard. It had been a wonderfully successful and happy last commission and it really hurt to think that the end had come – and particularly such an end as this.

Our thoughts and feelings must have been obvious to the Norwegians. We were due to leave Kristiansand early in the morning. Just before we sailed, a deputation from the Milorg marched down the jetty carrying a huge wreath, embellished with the message, 'Goodbye, good luck, *Wivern*.'

We crossed the North Sea, destored the ship and stripped her of her bell, name plates and badges. With them went her personality and the 'tiddly' from 'Wiv'. I said goodbye to my Ship's Company and my thoughts were with that opening talk by the wall in Devonport Dockyard which now seemed so long ago. I looked down at the faces around me, the familiar, well known characters. They had been a splendid Ship's Company and they had maintained our trust. We all knew it and we all knew that, with the death of this small, stricken hull on which we stood for the last time, something precious and a corner of our hearts would have left our lives for ever.

She was towed away down the grey waters of the Forth like a tired old dog, its collar removed, going slowly off to be put down. But on her final journey, where my commissioning pendant had once flown, she wore at her mast head our own last Honour – 'Goodbye, good luck, *Wivern*.'

Chapter 17

EAST INDIES

A fter paying off *Wivern*, I went on leave and was happily and constructively employed when, one morning, I collected the newspaper from the front door and read the astonishing news of the atom bomb being dropped on Japan. Nobody, of course, had even suspected the possibility of such a weapon and, after the first amazement had worn off, Pam and I sat down and analysed the implications for ourselves.

Obviously Japan must now surrender. With the whole war finally over, demobilisation would start immediately but there was going to be a tremendous job to be done in the Far East for which ships would be needed more than ever – so it was even more obvious where my next job would be. But doing what? If I must go, I wanted to be in command of my own ship. Others would want the same . . .

I have always believed it pays to volunteer for what you know to be inevitable so I went up to the Admiralty and did so. The offer and the apparent keenness were well received. Was I ready to go at short notice? Choking back my real feelings, I smiled brightly and assured them that I was. The next morning, a telegram came. I was to report to the Naval Officer-in-Charge, Greenock, the following day.

I did some hurried packing and, once again, Pam came north with me on the night train to Glasgow. I reported to the NOIC and was told to take immediate command of HMS *Loch Killisport*, sailing for Singapore in forty-eight hours time. Farewell again – and so soon.

The ship was the newest and latest of the big Loch Class A/S frigates – a wonderful command and a far cry indeed from poor old *Scarborough*. As Captain, I had a large, comfortable cabin with a private bathroom *en suite* but even this unheard of luxury failed to make up for the awful imminence of another long parting – and one, moreover, of unknown duration. Pam came on board and admired it all but it was pretty pointless trying to hide our real feelings. It seemed to have come so suddenly and it was horrible.

I was relieving an RNVR officer, due for early demob. The First Lieutenant,

135

also RNVR, had just rung up to say he felt unwell and would not be able to rejoin in time to sail. (His relief joined by pilot boat as I went down the Clyde.) There was only one Petty Officer on board who was surly and mutinous, reflecting the feelings of the Hostilities Only (HO) Ship's Company who were thoroughly bloody minded at being sent to the Far East when the war was over and they reckoned they should be sent home. The whole atmosphere was very different from *Wivern* and I wished I'd never volunteered. We hit a full gale in the Irish Sea and all the young sailors were seasick – which added to their misery.

In Gibraltar, the Army were in a state of open mutiny, demonstrating outside the Governor's Residence. Against all the regulations, I managed to put my rotten Petty Officer ashore, plus several other obvious troublemakers, and then, in Malta, I filled the Petty Officers' mess and all my other empty billets from the Fleet Drafting Pool. It made up my numbers but it produced an even more sullen bunch who had expected to go home and were furious at being sent in the wrong direction.

In Port Said, all the libertymen broke their leave and then, going down the Red Sea, we suffered in the summer heat. The wind was behind us so that even scoops in the scuttles failed to move the still, steamy air. Fresh from England, on top of the inevitable troubles from sunburn, the miseries of prickly heat appeared.

In Aden, the RAF had mutinied. All personnel on the RAF station fell in, without their Officers, and, led by NCOs, marched into the town to protest not to the Air Officer Commanding but, again, to the Governor. Here I cleared the last of my rubbish by leaving a sub lieutenant behind. (Looking back, I am amazed that I got away with such a ruthless solution to my troubles but I did, it worked and I was rid of my ullage.)

As far as *Loch Killisport* was concerned, thirty Motor Fishing Vessels had to be escorted to Cochin. So, instead of being able to press on, we had to proceed at a rate of about five knots, spending our days and nights going back to broken down stragglers and towing them back to the main body while repairs were carried out. Now the Ship's Company got really fed up and the new First Lieutenant warned me that, after the examples they had seen from the other Services, they too intended to mutiny when we finally reached Colombo.

We dropped the MFVs in Cochin, steamed round the tip of India and berthed in Colombo harbour. I gathered the hands as soon as we had secured.

The Ship's Company meant no harm. They were just young HO ratings who simply wanted out. Everyone else seemed to be 'going on strike' and, now the war was over, they could see no reason why they should not too. After all, it was the inalienable right of the British working man to down tools if he felt he had a grievance and they did not consider themselves real Navy anyhow.

Standing on a grating, I looked at the unhappy faces around me. The line to take seemed fairly obvious. I pointed out that the Age and Service Group system for demob guaranteed that no one, wherever in the world he might be, would leave the Navy a day earlier or later than his due date. In the meantime, they were lucky that, instead of hanging around awaiting their turn in cold winter waters at home, they were now going to enjoy some sunshine, excitement and an experience they would remember for the rest of their lives. Instead of dreary wartime Defence Watches there was a new and very different job to be done but one just as vital. The British had come back to the Far East where our reputation was now in tatters. We must rebuild our prestige. Building our prestige abroad was something at which the Royal Navy had always been pretty good. Now they would join in and see how it was done. The ship must shine like a yacht. The ceremonial guard must be perfect. Meanwhile, I wanted to leave them with one very important thought. All our Naval wars and battles had been won by young landsmen like themselves, whether gathered by press gang or call up notice. Their like had built our Naval heritage and they were as much part of a victorious Service as any regular. So let us never hear the term 'HO' in the ship again. We were all part of one company with a really important job to do. Then, sensing their response to these thoughts, I risked a little more taurocrapology as a peroration. 'You will soon find,' I promised them, 'what that White Ensign there means and, when you do, you will feel proud . . . But, at this moment, have a look at the jetty behind you and then go away and think.'

While I had been talking, tenders had landed some ex prisoners of war. Gaunt and emaciated scarecrows, some hobbling on sticks, most clad only in the remains of khaki shorts and the pitiful wreckage of boots, they fell in somehow on the road. A military band had been provided and it played the music of the Horse Guards Parade as it led the ghastly little procession from the quay. The Ship's Company watched in dead silence and, as they went forward, nobody spoke. But, from that moment, there was no more talk of mutiny and a spirit began to grow in the ship.

The white man might have come back to re-establish his position but it soon became apparent that he was going about it pretty badly. After a few days recuperating from the long journey east, *Loch Killisport* sailed for Singapore and the Forward Area. Admiral Mountbatten, understanding the need for 'face', had hoped to re-occupy Malaya by means of dramatic assault landings which would clearly show the British taking back their own by force of arms. The dropping of the Bomb and the sudden collapse of the war had robbed us of this impact on the local population but the plans were so far advanced that it was too late to change them so we had simply gone ahead hoping to gain what bonus we could. What, perhaps, we had forgotten was that our prestige in the East depended not only on our ruling position but on our total incorruptibility. In a part of the world where venality was as normal as childbirth, the scrupulous standards of the British Civil Servant and Colonial policeman established for him a formidable position of untainted authority. We may not always have been liked but, at least, we could be completely trusted.

Now a vast, civilian minded Army was unleashed on the reoccupied territories with a morality which used the euphemism 'liberating' for straightforward theft and which considered every form of shoddy self enrichment to be the fair perks of victory.

In the Dutch East Indies, the Japanese had interned all the Dutch residents and treated them appallingly but all their personal possessions had been clearly labelled with their names, inventoried, and scrupulously kept in store. The liberating British had taken everything and the Dutch lost their belongings to their allies within forty-eight hours. Cameras and watches were particularly desirable acquisitions and a brisk black market started up. The British traded their loot with the locals who sold it back to other British for medical supplies. M & B tablets were in particular demand. An empty M & B bottle, which could be filled with aspirin, bought an expensive camera. The locals were delighted. This was a morality they understood. But Britain's pre-war position and 'face' in the East could never be regained.

Loch Killisport stayed only briefly in Singapore and then sailed for Java where major trouble had broken out. We went alongside in Tanjong Priok, the port of Batavia, which lay a few miles inland.

During the war, the Japanese had encouraged the Indonesians to believe that, with peace, they would be given their independence from Holland. The abrupt cessation of fighting left a void. The Dutch were still interned and the British, who had expected to have to fight their way back, were not ready to move straight in. The Japanese were quick to make the most of the delay. 'Look,' said the Japanese. 'The British and the Dutch have not beaten us. They don't even have enough soldiers to come here. It's only because of the American Bomb that we have had to give up and nobody can use that on you. Here are our arms. Take them and declare your independence. There's nothing to stop you!' And, in that moment, the Dutch lost their East Indian empire.

When *Loch Killisport* arrived the situation was confused. The British had nominal control of the bigger coastal towns like Batavia, Sourabaya and Semarang. Some Dutch soldiers had been released and there was a strong element of Dutch Navy in Tanjong Priok but the Dutch forces were being kept well out of the situation. As far as the Indonesians were concerned, they had declared their Independence and Soekarno was their President. There were, therefore, in Batavia a British Military Administration, a number of Dutch officials and an Indonesian 'government' all co-existing. The interior was almost entirely in rebel hands and an already complicated problem was made even worse by the fact that the Dutch women and children were still in their prison camps throughout the island. If the British troops officially engaged in shooting at Indonesians, there was a serious risk of a dreadful massacre of the innocents.

I borrowed a Jeep and went ashore with two of my Officers. We found one of the women's camps and drove in. It was like a minor council housing estate of small, identical bungalows. Fifteen or twenty women and children lived in each tiny room and holes had been knocked in all the walls to serve as extra doorways to the outside. There would have been no room to walk through the houses.

The Jeep was at once surrounded by small children and the scenes from Norway were repeated but, this time, on a tragically greater scale. These kids had never lived a normal life nor seen a motor vehicle nor a white man. We drove slowly round the camp, the Jeep covered like corn on the cob with excited children. Then we returned to the gate and took on another load. Hours later we managed to stop, get out and walk. They hung on to both hands, three or four children at a time. One rode on our shoulders. Another wore the Naval cap. They did it all in complete silence and a small queue formed round each of us, waiting its turn for hand, shoulders or cap. At intervals, by some dreadful, unspoken camp discipline, they changed places and the queue moved up. One small five-year-old boy took my cap. I just had time to see, as he put it on, that his head was covered with festering sores. I made to snatch it back, revolted, but, thank God, checked myself before it was too late. Sick with shame at my civilised reaction I trudged on.

We invited them all, escorted by six mothers, to a children's party on board the next day and then we set off back to the ship. Driving through a street in Batavia, packed as usual with pedestrians, we heard a woman scream. We found her seconds later – an attractive young Dutch girl. A kris had sliced her right hand off at the wrist and her assailant had already vanished in the crowd which hemmed us in, silent and hostile. On a wall behind was painted the slogan, 'We fight for the right of 70,000,000 people to be free.'

The next afternoon we sent a convoy of three-ton trucks to the camp. There was a long straight stretch of road between Batavia and Tanjong Priok where the Indonesians sometimes hid on the overhead branches of the trees or in the bushes alongside and fired on transport with everything from guns to bows and arrows and poisoned spears. The loaded, open trucks roared down this bit, a sailor armed with a machine gun at each corner, the children singing.

We had swings, seesaws, chutes, swimming pools and pirates. Never had a ship given such a party and never had a party been such a success. They ate a huge tea and eventually it was time to leave. The canteen had been cleared of sweets and a big sack stood at the gangway.

The first child to go down into the boats was given a bar of chocolate. She looked at it, knowing already what it was although she had never tasted it till that afternoon. Then she handed it back, gave a small curtsey and said something in Dutch. A mother was called to translate. We all waited. The mother gave us one of the most dreadful, bright smiles I have ever seen and explained. 'She says it is very nice but it won't go far in her room. Could she change it for half a loaf of bread?'

They went down and filled the boats. As well as sweets they had all our bread. The Sick Berth attendant had had an inspiration and had handed out his own small present as each child went over the side. Now the motor boat drew away, towing the whaler. Amid shrill cheers, a forest of inflated balloons of unmistakable shape waved back to us. The six mothers were laughing as the tears poured down their faces. Jack had indeed given his all.

We left Batavia and went to Semarang. Here the local Brigadier had dealt with his problem in exemplary fashion. 'If you've given your arms to the Indos,' he said to the Japs, 'you can damn well get them back.'

The Japanese did. Attacking with bare fists and sticks they overran the Indonesian 'army', took back all their weapons and were now being employed at our side to keep the peace.

Some distance inland, at Ambarawa, there was a big RAPWI (Repatriate Allied Prisoners of War and Internees) camp, full of Dutch women and children. The town was under siege by the Indonesians and was being held by a small force of Indian Army who had called for help.

It was decided to run a convoy of empty trucks to evacuate the Rapwis and I offered to unscrew my Oerlikon guns and mount them in the vehicles for added, heavier protection. The offer was gratefully accepted by the Army and we had a fascinating run through the interior of Java, luckily meeting no resistance from the kampongs through which we passed.

We arrived only just in time. Indonesian infiltrators had managed to get into the local hospital and had massacred horribly the women and children they found in the wards. We loaded our trucks quickly while Indian artillery kept up a covering barrage round the town, then, with the guns behind us, we raced for the coast. As we finally withdrew, they had already started burning the deserted town.

On arrival, the Rapwis were lodged in tumbledown old godowns at the waterside. There was no other accommodation available and there were no plans to evacuate them further. After four years of hell and on the edge of safety they were still unwanted. The mothers were the same age as Pam, any of the little boys could have been Bill, now safe at home. Undernourished, with only the clothes they stood up in as their worldly possessions, infinitely brave and patient, even dockside sheds offered at least security after years of Japanese oppression and weeks of wondering whether every day would bring the ghastliness of watching their children cut up by the kris in front of their eyes before their own turn came for something worse. *Loch Killisport* was under orders to return to Singapore and I could not sail with an empty ship leaving this human tragedy behind. I offered to take a hundred.

One hundred and eleven actually arrived on board but we fitted them in. All the Officers' cabins and the big seamen's messdeck were turned over to them. Camp habits prevailed and, before they came on board, they had already elected their own committee to take charge of their affairs.

I looked into my cabin. The floor space was neatly allocated and a young mother with her two children occupied the bunk which I more than filled alone. Before I could speak she looked at me with glistening eyes. 'Clean sheets,' she said. 'And, oh, it is so soft and good.'

On the bathroom door I found a long notice and asked, curiously, what it said. This was the translation:

By the extraordinary kindness and hospitality of the Captain and the crew of this ship, who gave up all their comfort and personal freedom, even their own cabins, in order to fetch us away out of very unpleasant circumstances in Semarang and Ambarawa, we have the unexpected chance to go to our husbands and relations after waiting for four years.

Show our hosts as much as possible, whether you speak English or not, how thankful you are for this privilege.

Evacuating women on a warship is not a usual event, so no demands can be made. Please put your camp experience into practice!

Remember, in rainy weather, that the Captain himself and all the Officers will become as wet as yourselves.

We trust that, even in this curious situation, you will keep the cabins and bathroom as clean as possible.

Be British!!!!!

At least they did not have to get wet and, during daytime, the awning covered decks became a nursery for enchanting little blond children. My Night Order Book the first night contained the warning:

Attention is called to the nuisance value of small boys, several of whom

141

have already proved their worth, particularly The Teuton Terror (crew cut, blond, 5 years old, khaki shorts with blue spotted braces, plays mouth organ incessantly).

But it was no good. Nobody had the heart to frustrate the activities of the small, stocky, squareheaded little saboteur. All corners of the ship suffered from his depredations and his particular joy was to follow the torpedomen who tested the circuits every evening, breaking all the switches they had just checked as made.

The trip was not uneventful. Running short of food with our unexpected numbers we closed another frigate, met on passage, and sent over a whaler for urgently needed provisions. Next morning we passed through a small group of islands and found Sarutu Island lighthouse flying a distress signal. Rumours swept the ship. 'All the keepers have been killed by natives.' 'They have smallpox.' 'They need a fourth for bridge.' Amid great Rapwi excitement, the armed platoon was sent ashore complete with doctor and stretcher. But the call was only for food, paraffin and medical supplies.

In spite of language difficulties, fraternisation bloomed. By day, the upper deck was one long, non stop children's party. At night, after the children had been put to bed, the mothers gathered on the Quarterdeck and sang. Shyly till they saw how they were received, the Ship's Company joined them. A piano accordion and a guitar appeared and a mixed voice choir was formed. Maybe it was not always a very good one but I could stand on the bridge, hearing the quiet swish of our progress through the water, looking at the great canopy of the tropical stars overhead and savouring the singing as it floated up, mellowed by the vastness of the sea and the night.

Meanwhile the Rapwis had read in the ship's newspaper – *The Dog Watch* – about the Teuton Terror. On the last forenoon, as Singapore appeared out of the hazy skyline, a small boy, mouth organ carefully confiscated, was brought up to the bridge by the committee. In his hand was a scroll (of pusser's foolscap) decorated with a large bow of the Dutch colours. It showed Java with Ambarawa, surrounded by firing guns, making SOS, SOS, SOS in morse. In the top right hand corner was *Loch Killisport*'s crest making, again in morse, 'We will come and save you.' The map continued up to Singapore and Malaya in the top left hand corner with our route marked, showing the various incidents on passage interspersed with the hundred and eleven signatures of every Rapwi on board. The whole was framed in the morse message, 'Thank you for what you have done for us. We will never forget.'

The artist was the Teuton Terror's mother who, in turn, received with every evidence of maternal pride the relevant page of my Night Order Book suitably autographed, to be handed to the Terror (whose name was Pim) when he was old enough to appreciate it.

We landed them that evening and, the next day, I was officially rebuked for what I had done. British policy was apparently to leave them where they were because political opinion in Australia, where they might have been sent, was on the side of the Indonesians and the Dutch were not welcome.

Neither could they be received in Malaya because we were afraid that to take them there would inflame Malayan opinion and the Malays would turn away from us and towards their Indonesian brothers. And we certainly did not want another Indonesia starting up in our own Federated Malay States. So I had had no business to take such an initiative without requesting permission which would certainly have been refused.

I returned on board thinking of those women and children still in their camps in Java. A Dutchman had said to me, 'What would you think if the Japanese had conquered India and we, your allies, had reoccupied it and refused your Army its weapons back and kept your women and children in their camps in case they annoyed Indian rebels?' I had had no answer then and now I had even less.

I went up to my cabin and got stuck into a bottle. My cabin steward came in. He messed about a bit and obviously had something on his mind. 'What is it?' I asked.

He looked sheepish. 'You remember, sir, in Colombo you said we'd come to understand the significance of the flag, like? Well, I thought you'd like to know – the lads are saying they see now what it was you meant.'

I thought back to the fierce blast I had received and was very glad that I had earned it.

The months slipped by. Much water had passed under our propellers since that first arrival in Ceylon when we finally sailed back to Trincomalee for what turned out to be the last time, and we were a very different ship and company from what we had been when I gave that talk in Colombo. However, I now had the sadness of seeing it all wasted. *Loch Killisport* was to go home and pay off. Moreover, although my lads had indeed had all I had promised them in the way of interest and adventure, the end of their Far East story only concluded an episode in mine. Next door lay HMS *Loch Achray*. Her Captain was RNVR and due to go home for demob. C-in-C did the obvious thing. The two *Lochs* swapped COs and he took my *Killisport* back to the UK whilst I took over his *Achray*. She was a good, efficient ship but *Wivern* had always been special and *Loch Killisport* had started from the bottom and been hauled up into the successful and happy ship she had eventually become. Both would always occupy a corner of my heart which *Loch Achray* could never fill in the same way. Meanwhile, my new Ship's Company were as strange to me as I was to them. The first thing to do was obviously to make my mark.

I was cogitating about this problem when we left Trinco for the Forward Area once more, stopping off to visit the Andaman Islands on the way. We went to the capital, Port Blair, where the new Chief Commissioner had just arrived and this seemed to offer a good opportunity to impress on the natives the returned might of the British Raj and to exercise a Ceremonial Guard. We had heard that, in the neighbouring Nicobars, a party landing from one of HM Ships had been greeted from the trees by a shower of poisoned spears and arrows but our lot seemed friendly enough and a flotilla of small canoes came out to watch the fun as HE was received on board by the ship's DIY bugler and the ten gratified sailors who had shown themselves most proficient at handling their unaccustomed rifles.

The official call went well. The Chief Commissioner was pleased because he was new to the job and this was the first time he had had the fun of being treated to such courtesies. The Guard and I were pleased because nothing had gone wrong – which I think surprised us all. That afternoon I decided to celebrate by going ashore and stretching my legs. There was a small, wooded island just astern of our anchorage which seemed to be uninhabited and so unlikely to produce a greeting of unwelcome missiles and, in my innocence, I foresaw no other dangers. I took the motor boat, told the Cox'n to come back in an hour and landed.

The sun was hot and I was in no hurry. I sat on the beach for a while and allowed myself the childish pleasure of throwing pebbles into the sea. Problems seemed a long way away. Finally, I rose to my feet and started to amble slowly round the shore line of the island. I had gone about halfway when, from the other side of a little promontory, I heard a girl's voice singing.

Perhaps I hastened my steps but nothing prepared me for what I saw when I turned the corner. A small stream ran down between the trees and, in it, two totally naked and very beautiful girls were doing their laundry. I must have jumped back in my surprise because the movement caught the singer's attention and she looked up. As I gazed, entranced, she got slowly to her feet. There was no sign of the charming confusion or maidenly embarrassment I might have expected as she found herself in such circumstances confronting A Man. Instead, she stretched herself slowly just long enough for me to see that she had no need of a brassiere, then, still singing her pretty song, she advanced purposefully towards me.

Suddenly there came to my mind that old hurricane warning about an 'indescribable feeling that all is not well'. There seemed something sinister about her meaningful advance and her song – and her friend was standing up as well. Yet here was I – alone on a desert island with two lovely and obviously eager naked girls. It was like a matelot's dream but . . . I took one further look at the beautiful, idyllic scene – then I turned and ran like a rigger.

Behind me, I heard two delighted shrieks. Abandoning their clothes to the stream, the two nude lovelies joined my game and came sprinting after me. Along the sandy beach I tore and the devil on my left shoulder kept muttering, 'What are you running for, you fool?' while the Guardian Angel on my right urged, 'Let's get the hell out of here.' Which might have won eventually I shall never know because the matter was clinched by the sight of a few huts up among the trees. Jinking like a rugger three-quarter, I made for them, bleating pathetically for help as I lost my last breath. 'People,' I thought. 'Help is at hand.'

How wrong can you be? Like some scene from an awful nightmare, they came bursting out from the doorways. More and more women, all naked or nearly so, all howling with primitive joy as they joined the macabre hunt. It was action which might have delighted the producer of a blue movie but I have never been so terrified in my life.

Tearing through the trees, some instinctive sixth Naval sense took me finally back to the little jetty where I had landed and, thank God, the motor boat was there. I took one leap and landed in the sternsheets on all fours. 'Shove off, Cox'n,' I pleaded. 'Back to the ship, quick.'

All along the shoreline, naked women jumped up and down, screaming. No pop star ever knew anything like it. Shouting, singing and posturing, they called me back. The Cox'n blew three blasts on his whistle and, as we went astern, regarded the remarkable scene, his face quite expressionless. Finally he turned to me and said simply, 'My God, sir, you don't do things by halves, do you?'

I knew then that, as far as the Ship's Company would be concerned, I had made my mark.

(I found out later that they were Japanese Army 'comfort girls', mostly very attractive Eurasians, who had been rounded up from all over the whole area and put on this remote island till they could be repatriated. It seemed that they did, indeed, miss the male company to which they had been accustomed but most suffered from the inevitable unpleasant affliction. I moved the ship that evening. The island had been within swimming distance and Jolly Jack would not have been as pusillanimous as me . . .).

We went on to Rangoon where, once again, I passed up an opportunity. The Governor General was away and, in his absence, one of his staff invited me to dinner in Government House. We drank a lot of whisky and actually ate in a restaurant in the city where Chinese waitresses sat on our laps, one arm around our necks while the other fed us with titbits on chopsticks. Between courses, they split sunflower seeds with their long nails and popped these into our mouths in case we got hungry. The meal ended with hot towels on our faces and pretty farewells from our smiling hostesses.

We returned to Government House for what the my host described as 'the only thing to follow a good dinner'. But he was not thinking of brandy and cigars. His Excellency's own Rolls Royce drove up to a side door of the Residency and from it emerged, in a peacock flutter of vividly coloured silks, two Burmese temple dancers. They were lissome, highly recommended and very willing but their faces were painted green and a green faced paramour, no matter how skilful, was something up with which I did not want to put. I returned to the ship and my monastic bunk and was told, the next day, that my host had dealt more than adequately with both of them. But, whatever his sexual powers, I could not help wondering how many Burmese knew of this little Government House routine and how much damage it did to our already battered 'face'.

From Rangoon, *Loch Achray* was recalled to Trincomalee where our treatment, on arrival, horrified us. We were banished to a remote anchorage at the far end of the huge harbour where a terse signal ordered that under no circumstances was anybody to leave the ship nor was anyone to be allowed on board. The day we had left, bubonic plague had broken out in Rangoon and we were in strict quarantine. Not only were the implications rather frightening but it was really rather horrible suddenly finding ourselves totally cut off from the rest of humanity as something like lepers of old, untouchable and unclean. Fortunately, we had no cases although the ship had been alongside and, coming back from my Government House evening, I had run over a huge rat in my Jeep.

However, it was with considerable relief that we returned to the Forward Area and on to Java where, this time, we went to Sourabaya. Here the Indonesians had murdered the British Brigadier outside his office and turned on our troops, scattered thinly throughout the town. There was now quite a little war going on.

We had only been there a couple of days when 5 Indian Div's Intelligence officer called on me. He was a delightful Major called John Taylor who was unhappy because Indonesian rebels were infiltrating a small town just down the river where the Chief of Police had been a loyal and valuable ally. Major Taylor could not bear the thought of what would happen to the Chief of Police if the Indos captured him and felt he owed his friend at least some attempt at a rescue. Would I help?

It seemed that his own authorities just didn't want to know nor, I soon found, did mine. Both would turn a blind eye to any unofficial operation we laid on but God help us both if anything went wrong or if we caused a Major Incident with the Indonesian 'Government' in Batavia. As John Taylor kindly pointed out, nothing much could happen to him because he was shortly due for demob but, as a regular, I might well feel that there was little future in it for me so, if I refused, he would quite understand. In fact, apart from the challenge, I was so fed up with what I considered the cowardly and supine attitude of our bosses that I agreed.

John Taylor's plan was to sneak off down the river in my motor boat, make a clandestine landing at the town's small quay and then creep, alone, through the streets to find the Chief of Police and bring him back. He set off about midnight and I stood on the bridge, thinking the whole thing was like some crazy adventure story in the *Boy's Own Paper*. I wasn't quite sure what I could do if things went wrong but I had steam up, the cable was ready to slip and I had my armed platoon standing by to land.

Suddenly, from far away down river, a light started winking morse. 'A-M-L-A-N-D-I-N . . .' Then darkness again.

Obviously something had indeed gone wrong. Whatever the reason, he had been unable to complete his message. Caught in the act? If so, God help him. The Indos liked to slice people to death with the kris or else flay them alive. And my boat's crew?

I slipped my cable, raced down river, landed the platoon with orders to capture and hold the quay till further orders and then, in order to create pandemonium and panic ashore, through which I hoped John Taylor could escape if he were still alive, I opened fire with starshell over the town. It would be very alarming to the Indos but would cause no casualties.

At the height of the noise and the brouhaha, I suddenly saw my boats returning. As usual, excitement, farce and tragedy had all been mixed together. The signal had stopped so dramatically because John Taylor had dropped his torch in the water. He had landed, crept through a godown, heard someone following him, breathing heavily in the dark, attacked the intruder only to find it was a goat and then, somewhat shaken, gone on into the town. The Chief of Police had already been killed messily but the Major had found his wife and daughter and at least brought them safely on board. My starshell had cleared the streets and given him light enough for all three to race back to the jetty where they were thankful to find my platoon. Altogether it was a funny old way to spend a night.

When we finally returned to Singapore we had to escort some landing craft full of troops. Well on our way, diphtheria developed in the convoy. I signalled Singapore for medical assistance but the RAF were again 'on strike'. However, the mutineers allowed a flying boat to come out to our aid so that nobody actually died.

Arrived back in Johore, I went confidently into the dockyard to scrounge a Jeep as I had everywhere on the station so far. But no dice. Nasty little dockyard officials had come out from the UK and taken over. A plump, pallid young man, appalled at my presumption, put me firmly in my place. As I withdrew, defeated, I spotted a small Japanese inscription on a door.

'Look, if I can't have a Jeep, would you let me have that?'

Pause while he tried to think of a reason to refuse me. Then, finding none, 'Oh, well, I suppose so.'

Thanking him profusely, I fished out my knife and unscrewed the little piece of wood. He watched suspiciously.

'Do you speak Japanese then? What does it say?'

I looked at him seriously. 'Didn't you know? It says, "Celestial sanctuary of honourable fulfilment and serene repose".'

As I left, I heard his plaintive bleat, 'I say, chaps, do you know what it said on our shithouse door?' (Actually, translated later, I found it merely read 'Paymasters only.')

It seemed that everything was turning sour in South East Asia and, when *Loch Achray* was ordered to return to the UK, I was thankful to go with her. It had all been tremendously interesting, exciting and colourful but there had been an obverse to the bright coin. I was tired of corruption and the East, of being yellow with mepacrine, of skin ulcers, humidity and prickly heat. I wanted to experience Peace; to be back with my wife and child, walking in an English countryside, savouring foggy autumn evenings when the leaves turned golden before blowing down in a cold wintry wind. I thought of women in furs, of red double decker buses and snow.

John Taylor was finally due for demob so I offered him a passage home. He turned out to be tremendous fun and it was the start of a lifelong friendship.

We finally sailed from Trincomalee with a long paying off pennant streaming from our masthead and an aircraft carrier's band playing the traditional 'Rolling Home to Merrie England' as we steamed out of harbour.

We crossed the Indian Ocean in the monsoon, went up the Red Sea, transited the Canal and met the dry, golden sunshine of the Mediterranean. We left Gib behind and savoured the cold, salty Atlantic. We passed the Nab and then the Warner, Outer Spit and – as we steamed up the Channel past the Southsea Naval war memorial I could see a waving figure in a well remembered red coat with a small boy jumping up and down beside her.

I was home.

Chapter 18

NAVAL INTELLIGENCE

It was lovely to have some real leave in the house we had bought in Southsea but, professionally, the prospects seemed bleak. With the numbers of ships rapidly declining there was no prospect of another command. I might have to go as No.1 of the sort of ship I had been driving or, worse, end up watchkeeping in a big ship but, just as I was feeling thoroughly depressed at the thought, Their Lordships suddenly produced a real humdinger for me – Assistant Chief of Naval Intelligence in Occupied Germany.

The appointment was totally unexpected. I knew nothing of Intelligence except what I had read in spy thrillers but I was thoroughly prepared to enjoy my new clandestine world.

The initiation was fun in itself. I was sent to Scotland Yard where they trained me in a wide range of skills including safe blowing, lock picking, forgery, housebreaking, security and interrogation techniques. Then I went to work for a time with Special Branch and ended finally with MI6 (the Secret Intelligence Service or SIS). The mornings were spent learning the technique of the spy's trade, the communications and hardware, how to run a reseau with cutouts etc. In the afternoons there was practical stuff. Using dead letter boxes. How to shadow. How to spot and evade your own shadowers. And, finally, to show the strain under which a real agent lives, the surprisingly frightening experience, even in my own capital city, where I suddenly realised everything had gone wrong and the police arrested me.

Eventually, I went to Germany just before Christmas 1946 and, early in the New Year, was offered a house if Pam could join me in a fortnight. She managed to let ours and find homes for our dog and a litter of eight puppies, arriving triumphantly on the fourteenth day.

That winter was hell. The snow lay thick and the cold was bitter. It was bad enough for the British but, for the Germans, living in the cellars and the rubble of their ruined city on a nominal 1,000 calories a day, even basic survival was difficult. Not that we cared very much. After all, they had murdered eleven million Jews and ravaged most of Europe. Dachau and

Belsen were in the British Zone, their ghastly revelations fresh in our minds. If the Germans were suffering now, it seemed only justice.

Actually, although the port was wrecked and the industrial outskirts flattened, the city centre round the Alster lakes was largely unscathed and, in the residential area where we lived, there was little sign of damage. Our requisitioned house was small but delightfully situated beside a pretty little canal. It was modern, well furnished and attractive and we even had Hans, an ex-steward from the Hamburg-Amerika line, as our general factotum.

I soon found that the corruption in Germany was infinitely greater even than that in the Far East. The Control Commission (Germany), the ubiquitous CCG, was largely staffed by the worst type of little bureaucrat and 'temporary gentleman' from the war years who found the prospect of demob and starting again in Civvy Street to be too challenging. Better by far to hang on to their little authority in the Military Government. The Reichmark was worthless. Everything, and I mean everything, could be had for a few cigarettes which were the recognised currency, though food, razor blades and chocolate were welcome too. Encouraged by the example of the very top, the Brits set about enjoying and enriching themselves.

On the Intelligence side, we kept a careful finger on the German pulse watching for any signs of potential trouble but, already, our eyes were looking Eastwards. Even in 1946 the Cold War had begun in the Intelligence world and, in the next few years, it became very icy indeed. The Zone was full of scientists and technicians whose brains and services were urgently wanted by Britain, America and Russia. I found a leading expert on floating docks working on a farm and living, thankfully, in a pig sty in return. We did not want him because we are rather good at floating docks but he would have been very useful to the Russians. He was provided with a room, given some homework to do in the way of writing reports and allowed a ration card which kept him above starvation level and unlikely to be tempted East. Others, better qualified, found they could name their own price, particularly to the Americans.

The Germans concerned quickly latched on to the existence of this quiet background battle and the news spread to less desirable sections of the community. A number of ex-generals in the British Zone organised an underground movement and approached the Military Government.

Briefly, they suggested that war with Russia was obviously imminent. When the Russians moved in we should certainly be thrown out but they were in a position to offer us a large, powerful and organised underground movement consisting of patriotic Germans who would work on our behalf after we had left and without whose help our eventual return would be most unlikely. If we refused their offer, they added, they would not only offer their services to the

Russians instead but they would guarantee that their activities would be enough to make it unlikely that we could even stay in Germany long enough to await the Russian arrival. However, they were sure that such threats were unnecessary. The only mistake had been that our two countries had ever fought each other. Germany and Britain should dominate Europe between them, militarily and financially. Only thus could Russia be contained and our two great countries prosper as they should. France was decadent, defeated and ineffectual. The Yanks would soon go home. With Hitler and the Nazis removed there was now no longer any barrier to a friendship between the two great Nordic races to their mutual glorification and strength. Meanwhile their price was that we should cease all further denazification and demilitarisation, free those already detained and guarantee the worthless Reichmark with the pound sterling before establishing a new German Government consisting of their nominees.

Intelligence had this organisation well penetrated and, when we were ready, we intended to round up the lot. But unfortunately the *Daily Express* got onto the story and, naturally, broke it with banner headlines.

Nothing could have been more unwelcome. Ernie Bevin was due to attend a Foreign Ministers' conference in Moscow in the very near future and to have gone there with the existence of such an organisation public knowledge, and with the British authorities apparently having taken no action, would have rendered his position too vulnerable. The Intelligence services were told to make the arrests as soon as possible, accepting the fact that, as a result, some of the plotters might escape.

For Intelligence as a whole this was truly exasperating because a most promising operation must now be laid on at half cock. For the Naval element, however, the order was potentially disastrous. We were onto much bigger game which had actually come to us first from a Press source.

Brian Connell, later to become a TV personality, was working as a correspondent for the *Daily Mail* and he had stumbled across three East German scientists who, behind the main organisation in our Zone, were threatening to destroy the United Kingdom by germ warfare. The scientists intended to do this by loosing their bugs over a period of three days – the first in London theatres, cinemas and main railway termini, the second in the House of Commons and the third in newspaper offices and the BBC. Three weeks later an unexplained plague would break out simultaneously all over the country to be followed the next day by the dramatic demise of Parliament and, the day after, by the extermination of all news media. Brian Connell, who had served in Naval Intelligence during the war, realised that this was far too dangerous a piece of information to be treated merely as a scoop and, appalled by what he had learned, came to his old colleagues and told us the whole story.

We had succeeded in contacting the scientists and were actually negotiating with them when the orders came to round up the whole underground organisation in the Zone. This might be possible for the main operation but our birds were over the border under Russian protection and were proving extremely wary, suspicious and difficult to tempt over to our side. Apart from anything else, the fact that Attlee was Prime Minister of a new Labour Government meant nothing to them. Like so many Germans, they considered that Winston Churchill represented England and only with him were they prepared to deal. We had to find an intermediary.

We had, in our office, a young member of the Secret Service who called himself the Staff Officer (Security) and, as cover, dressed as a Lieutenant RNVR. Son of a Turkish Jew who had fought for Britain in World War 1, he had been living in Holland with his Dutch mother when the Nazis invaded. The mother had escaped to Britain, leaving the boy behind, and he had spent an eventful war deceiving the Germans and operating very successfully for the Dutch Resistance. He was a very pleasant, willing, fresh faced youngster who would pass as English and his particular qualification for his position on the clandestine side of the Naval Intelligence staff was the fact that even then, he was showing his potential to become one of the most brilliant professional spies that any country has yet produced. His name was George Blake.

The leading East German scientist was accordingly told that, by a remarkable coincidence we had, in our very office, a young Officer who actually happened to be a relation of Winston Churchill and who could communicate with the great man on the family net. The Herr Doktor bit and he and his two assistants came to Hamburg to meet George Blake.

What happened next we watched from our office window through telescopes because, by a real coincidence, the Germans had chosen to lodge with a genuine relation who happened to live in a block of flats right beside our Headquarters. We saw them arrive and we saw three four by fours drive up immediately afterwards carrying Churchill's 'relation' and two other Officers. The Germans were told that they had been invited to lunch with the Military Governor of Hamburg and, for such distinguished Doktors, one car each was protocol. Happily they climbed in. Obviously everything was going to be all right, they thought, and they were still in the same mellow, defenceless mood when the doors of Fuhlsbuttel gaol clanged shut and, before the full dreadful realisation had burst upon them, they found themselves split up and each facing not a Military Governor host but a hard faced interrogator.

It transpired that they had far too high an opinion of their own capacity and that we had nothing to learn nor fear from them. The main organisation was rounded up that night. We did not get as many as we could have but those we missed lost heart and caused us no further trouble.

The next day all the newspapers carried the press release with the dramatic news of the mass arrests. The *Express* naturally claimed all the credit for first revealing the plot. The *Mail* covered the basic story in a few paragraphs but their headlines and their front page went to town on the germ threat to the United Kingdom. It was probably the biggest scoop of the post war decade and Brian Connell deserved it.

George Blake carved a new notch in his espionage dagger. In due course, he would be betrayed by other traitors and sentenced to forty-two years imprisonment – the longest sentence ever given by a British court – from which he saved himself by his dramatic escape. He has since claimed that he turned his coat in Hamburg but I cannot believe it of the eager young man I knew. I think he was turned after Seoul. Idealism is always vulnerable.

In the summer of 1947, our second son was born and the small Naval Intelligence unit moved down to Minden.

The move was essentially designed to bring us closer to the Headquarters of the other Intelligence agencies – CCG, SIS, Army and Air Force, who were all in the vicinity – but a side effect was to produce a big change in an already pleasant standard of living. We were administered by the CCG who worked with titles rather than ranks so, although only a very junior Lieutenant Commander, I was Assistant Chief of Naval Intelligence and, in CCG terms, the Assistant Chief of a department or division was big stuff. Pam and I were therefore given a beautiful house surrounded by a large garden. Our staff consisted of cook, housemaid, nanny, gardener, driver and, after I acquired a horse, a groom. It really was Gracious Living . . .

The work continued to be fascinating. A trickle of Russian Naval deserters was coming through and these I kept in a local 'safe house' for interrogation. I was also compiling a book giving details of all the Russian occupied Baltic ports which we found it fairly easy to penetrate. Pam typed it and was paid with sausages and tinned meats – officially kept for rewarding German informers but a welcome addition to our own rather meagre rations. These were also supplemented from our three local shoots which gave us splendid sport on Saturday afternoons.

What was really fun though was owning my own horse. I don't remember exactly how it happened but it was essentially the work of a German groom called Spiess. This cheerful rogue had been working for a Colonel Hildebrand in a nearby Army unit but he spoke little English and the words he knew he had learned from the soldiers. The result was inevitable. He respectfully greeted the Colonel's lady, 'Ah, f.....g Mrs Hildebrand,' after which, again in his own words, it was, 'Spiess in hoosegow. Spiess piss off.' Anyhow, he came to me. His wages, the rent of a stable and the horse's fodder came to under £3 a month. It was the equivalent of a bottle of German gin or a few cigarettes and I could afford it.

The horse, which came with him, was a lovely black animal of indeterminate age which had been taken over from the German Army by the British and renamed Guinness. His Wehrmacht record showed that he had served mostly on the Russian front so he must have suffered a dreadful war but, apart from an unsurprising nervousness when faced with the unexpected, he was a gentle creature whose only desire was to please. I loved him dearly and, having found a safe home at last, he seemed to enjoy the association too. I hacked him daily and, having got used to the saddle again, I even started learning to jump.

It was one day when horse and rider had triumphantly navigated the minor obstacles which constituted our jumping ring that Spiess put forward his great idea. My German and his English provided only a tenuous means of communication but I gathered that the 7th Armoured Division were holding some form of horse show in which there was to be a jumping competition for novices. '*Eine kleine hop, hop, hop,*' as Spiess engagingly described it. He thought we should enter.

I rang the military accordingly and said that I understood that they were holding a bit of a bash and could the Navy join in? I was, I assured them, not much good but keen to have a go if the jumps were not too high. The Army were delighted and assured me of the warmest welcome. What colours did I ride in? This floored me momentarily. My riding breeches dated from gunroom days and, in spite of a massive gusset in the back, would not quite button across my stomach (a failure hidden by a wide leather belt) and the rest of my equine wardrobe was of the same standard. But I had an old white shirt . . . 'White,' I said firmly.

Our small Ship's Company were delighted by the challenge. To enhance my virginal appearance, one sailor produced a pair of white seaboot stockings which, with white gym shoes, replaced the German jackboots I usually wore. To make a horsebox, a couple of spars were lashed fore and aft in a 3-ton truck and carefully padded with hammocks to ensure Guinness's comfort. I drove my battered old prewar Mercedes which, with carefully crumpled mudguards and German civilian number plates, I used for my more furtive undercover work. Horse, sailors' cheering party, rider and rider's wife set off in fine fettle.

It was a long drive to Sennelager. As we finally drew near, we noticed Army signpointing to '7th Armoured Division Point-to-Point'. Obviously my Novice's jumping competition was to be some form of sideshow to a much more important event.

We pressed on happily till we were stopped by a large Military Policeman who regarded my squalid vehicle with outraged eye. Meekly, I explained my presence. His face remained professionally impassive but I thought I spotted a look of glee as, with a crashing salute, he waved me into the car park. The Merc slunk in and hid between the gleaming Staff cars.

I left Pam and set off to join Guinness. Almost at once, I was stopped by an indignant Colonel. Who was I? Where did I think I was going? Again I explained. Again the flare of outrage. Where was my hard jockey cap? I hadn't got one. 'Sar' Major!' 'Sah!' Another crashing salute. 'Sar' Major, get this [gulp] "rider" some proper headgear and put a white cover on it. Then take him to weigh in.' But the weighing in Sergeant took one look at my stout frame and laughed. 'I don't think you need get on the scales, sir. You'll be top weight anyhow.'

I was beginning to realise that something was terribly wrong when finally the heavens fell in. Pam was approaching and she looked very pale. In her hand was the Race Programme. There was no Novice's competition. I had been entered in the Open Race for horses which had not been 'regularly hunted' with the cavalry's own Warman Hunt. It was an euphemism for the crack riders from other units all over Germany. But worse was to come. A friendly soldier had briefed her on the unexpected enormity of my undertaking. It appeared that this was an international course which the prewar cavalry had considered to be the most challenging in Europe. The jumps were, quite simply, murder. Two horses and one rider had been killed the year before. Entries for the Open were limited because so many expert horsemen were not prepared to risk themselves or their horses in such a hazardous affair. Pragmatic even on the verge of hysteria, Pam issued her instructions. 'Stuff Guinness back in that truck,' she said, 'and let's get out of here.'

I was appalled. I had told them my status. 'A bit of a bash . . . not much good but keen to have a go if the jumps aren't too high . . .' Now I realised that, of course, in Armyspeak, this had meant, 'Stand from under, mate, I'm an expert.' But what to do? God help me, I was really so ignorant and inexperienced that I was more afraid of chickening out than of carrying on. How could I explain to Spiess and the sailors who had come all this way to cheer me on? What could I say to them as I returned their hammocks? 'Nonsense,' I replied firmly and, quaking with terror, rode Guinness into the ring.

The odds up to that moment had been firmly behind us. An unknown horse called Guinness, ridden by the Navy at number thirteen, had appealed strongly to the soldiers as a sporting outside bet. Now they saw the field. The finest, mettlesome hunters ridden by the top riders of the British Zone. Several Hussars. Others from the Very Best Regiments. One in mere 'Hunting Kit', the others in their own private racing colours except, at the back, 'Guinness-

White-Royal Navy'. As the horse trudged round under my weight, I became conscious that the gusset in the back of my breeches was of a slightly different colour. Guinness, too, seemed to realise that, as a combination, we were Socially Inferior. Like mine, his ears drooped. We crept apologetically round behind Our Betters and the odds leapt skywards.

The race began with a long, sandy, upwards slope. Guinness tore up it and we had an exhilarating gallop. It was a mistake because, by the time we reached the top, he was already flagging. Before us was the first jump. It seemed reasonable, only about three feet high, though there was a pine edging along the top that meant you had to clear it or else . . . I was just wondering why I could no longer see the other riders who were already well ahead when we became airborne and I made the mistake of looking down. Behind the jump there was a sunken road. In it, lying very still, were the Rifle Brigade's best rider and his horse. The other side was a hedge and, after that, a steep drop to the field beyond.

When we had recovered from our shock, Guinness and I slowed down till I realised that Hunting Kit was trotting just in front of us and, with an insane burst of hubris, urged the horse to overtake so that, at least, we would not be last. The effect of this challenge was unexpected. Courteously, Hunting Kit swept off his top hat, wished me luck and turned back for home. In the distance, I could hear the siren of an ambulance coming for the Rifle Brigade.

It would be tedious to describe the horrors of all those ghastly jumps. I just hung grimly on and somehow Guinness kept going. Halfway round there was a small coppice with a red course marking flag beyond it. A steward came galloping over to see that we went round this buoy. By this time we were not even in radar contact with the rest of the field but I was still foolishly determined to finish the course. So, obviously, was Guinness.

I reduced the revs again and we floundered on till we came to a big water jump. The steward was there again – laughing. With a last despairing effort, Guinness took off. Over we went – and found there was water on the other side too. Guinness stumbled and I went over his neck. Lying in the cold water, I realised that it was time to admit defeat but, at that vital moment, I caught the horse's reproachful eye. Guinness hadn't given up. I suddenly had an awful thought that he was going to kneel like a camel to help me climb back on board but I think he was too tired to do so. Anyhow, he just stood there, gasping, while I got back into the saddle. After that, we walked for a bit. I believe we were both sobbing.

At long last, the final jump appeared. Designed primarily for show rather than blow, just to make a dramatic looking finish, it was relatively easy and hid no unexpected horrors. Calling on Heaven knows what ultimate reserve, somehow Guinness made it and we staggered over the line. We had done it.

Riding in white . . . Guinness takes the last fence.

Pam had spent the race sitting in a car. Her helpful soldier had stood on the roof, promising to let her know when we went down. 'Don't watch,' he had exhorted her, 'For God's sake, don't watch.' Now, miraculously preserved from premature widowhood, she came running to receive me back, squelching, into her life. She had heard an exchange between two cavalrymen.

'How did you get on, old boy?'

'Beaten by a damned sailor. And a fat damned sailor at that.'

Spiess was grinning all over his face. The sailors were cheering. Guinness and I were heroes. I couldn't understand it till a kindly official explained. The rest of the field had all come in together, a glamorous crescendo of colour and hooves – but only three of them had completed the whole course. Not only Hunting Kit but most of the others had known when it was too much for their expensive thoroughbreds and had saved them from undue stress by turning short of the coppice or skirting that dreadful water jump. Hence the watchful steward for me.

All the other horses had been living comfortably in the green shires of England while Guinness had been slaving across the wartorn Russian steppes. Their riders knew the course, their mounts were in perfect training and at the peak of their corn fed fitness. Guinness subsisted on the poor German fodder which was all I could get in Minden and was hacked once a day. Now he ranked with the flower of the British cavalry. Through the pig ignorance of his rider and his own sheer guts he had completed Europe's premier point-to-point course and we had been placed fourth.

I sent him back to the remount depot to be put out to grass and given a well earned rest. His fame went before him and he was received by the Army grooms with affection and respect. Nothing, they promised, would be too good for him.

A few days later, the phone rang. It was the CO of the remount depot telling me that Guinness had died in the night. His great heart had just given out.

We had a long talk and he understood my feelings but refused to let me grieve.

'Look at it this way,' he said. 'That horse must have had a rotten life. He wasn't all that young and what had he to look forward to? Passed on from hand to hand as an old hack until he was finally worked out. As it is, he's had his moment of glory and quit while he was ahead. Wouldn't we all like to go like that?'

Of course, he was right. And I knew that, although Guinness had gone and my days would be miserable and empty, the spirit of that wonderful horse would live on in my heart. It has. Here I am, fifty years later, still recalling his last, epic race with laughter and pride but still, too, with humbleness and shame at my own ineptitude. I asked too much of him and he gave me all.

By the New Year (of 1949) the time was coming close for the birth of our third child. My interpreter, John Hartman, had a delightful red-headed wife who was also heavily pregnant. (The German drivers were betting on which would deliver first.) It was another cold, snowy winter and, to get to the RAF hospital, Rinteln, where the births would take place, involved crossing a range of hills where driving conditions were dicey. Hartman and I therefore decided that, whenever the time came for either, day or night, we would ring each other up and I would drive the mother in my comfortable but mechanically unreliable Merc while he would follow in his big, military 4x4 in case of accident or breakdown. Inevitably, the time came for Pam in the middle of the night. Our organisation worked and, when we got to the hospital, John Hartman came in too.

The night sister was sitting in a dark room with just a pool of light from a standard lamp on her desk. Pam advanced to report in. John Hartman and I, in raincoats and trilby hats, stood together in the doorway and watched from the shadows. It was a ploy we had often used when going to question a German and it had always worked. Two large, silent men standing in a doorway, just watching you, can be unnerving. Now, though we had adopted the pose quite innocently, it certainly unnerved the sister. Gradually, her brisk, efficient questioning wavered till, finally, she could stand it no longer.

'Mrs Anderson,' she said, 'which of these two gentlemen is the father?'

It was too much for Pam who, naturally, was also anxious. She gave a nervous giggle and said, 'I'm not sure so I brought them both.'

It was a reply she never lived down.

After a long delay, our third son was finally born safely and the following August, after two and a half years in Germany, we returned home and came down to earth with a bump. But at least we now had three sons instead of one. We hadn't wasted our time.

Chapter 19

HMS CONTEST

A fter a job of absorbing interest in Germany I returned home hoping to have a chance to live in the house we had bought in Southsea at the end of the war. This meant a Portsmouth based ship and, since dreaming is cheap, I dreamed of command again, preferably of one of the CO class destroyers which, to my mind, rank with the wartime Town class cruisers as the most beautiful ships we have ever built. Tentatively I made my hopes known to the Appointers . . .

Some weeks later the family came downstairs to breakfast and saw, inside the letter-box, the vital buff envelope which held our fate for the next eighteen months or two years. The Far East or the Mediterranean? Goodbye again? A battleship or an aircraft carrier? Another shore job? For better or for worse the hopes and optimism were over. Now I should know. I opened the envelope and the familiar words of the appointment leapt out. I was 'hereby appointed Lieutenant Commander of His Majesty's ship *Contest* in command' and directed 'to repair on board' in Portsmouth in a few days' time. There was one CO class destroyer in the Portsmouth Local Flotilla, her command had become available at the vital moment and they had given it to me. Bless their marvellous Admiralty hearts!

It was wonderful being back at sea again with my own ship though, in an odd sort of way, there was a sense of anticlimax. Here was this beautiful great modern Fleet destroyer, the old surge of excitement as we left the jetty and drew out to sea with the shoreline slipping away behind us and the open horizon ahead – but no enemy to be met and challenged, no convoys, no tropical islands and excitement, just the old routine exercising with a submarine or the gunnery shoot at nothing more dangerous than a drogue target towed by a bored aeroplane.

Across the world, the Fleet was still at war. In Korea, the Navy was producing an epic of endurance and efficiency which was never fully appreciated at home but, for me, in a Portsmouth local destroyer, the main interest lay in seeing the beginnings of the modern Service the years of peace were to bring.

The exciting new construction of the next few years still lay ahead and the greatest and most obvious difference was in the men. Before the war, the drafting of Ordinary Seamen to destroyers had been considered a dangerously retrograde step. An Able Seaman could be immediately sent to a big ship by use of the magic phrase, 'A bad influence on the Messdeck.' Now, in *Contest*, I had a big Boys' Division and almost all the rest of the ship's company were Ordinary rates. Our few Able Seamen, youngsters in their early twenties, were rare jewels. But the calibre of these kids was beyond praise. Although National Service was still in force and, for the Army, would remain a vital asset for some years, the Navy took few NS sailors and my ship's company were virtually all volunteers. Not only were they volunteers, moreover, they were enthusiasts. None had had to join to avoid unemployment like the majority of pre-war ratings. These lads' England offered plenty of well paid jobs. They had entered because they believed that serving in the Royal Navy was a worthwhile way of spending their lives and their spirit and morale were a joy to lead. They would take on anything they were asked to and the more difficult the challenge the more they enjoyed it.

Our seagoing programme was pretty drab – day running from Portsmouth interspersed with trips up to the Clyde where, based on Rothesay, we exercised with submarines. In actual fact, we were almost continuously at sea and could not even fit in the time to give long leave in two watches but there was certainly none of the 'travel and adventure' these young sailors had joined to enjoy. We spent one weekend in Londonderry and the Ship's Company hit the beach as if it was really a foreign land.

I stood on the old, familiar jetty the first night and closed my eyes. In the darkness I could feel, all round me, the ghosts of the battered, camouflaged little corvettes and sloops which had come in for rest from the Atlantic battle. But, when I opened my eyes, they had gone and the comparatively huge bulk of *Contest* towered up beside me, her bright lights reflected in the still waters of the Foyle, her immaculate light grey paint shining out of the darkness. If only we had had such ships then . . .

We did get one chance to visit a real foreign port, taking the Army Staff College to Cherbourg for a Battlefield tour. They arrived on board at about eleven o'clock on a windy, black night with the rain pouring down. It was really a disgraceful way to make them travel because, of course, we had no accommodation for some seventy Army Officers and, realising this, they prepared to accept the miseries of a night crossing sitting in damp huddles on the bare, rainswept iron deck. My sailors were appalled at the situation and, unbeknownst to me, they went round collecting the military and leading them below to the warm shelter of their messdecks. My chaps slept under the messtables and on settees and Army Captains slept in the sailors' hammocks.

HMS Contest. The loveliest ships we ever built . . . .

Neither service seemed to see anything untoward in the arrangement.

I found the General sitting in my cabin which I had turned over to him. He was laughing delightedly and, as I entered, he waved a small brown OHMS envelope in his hand. 'My God,' he said, 'I really hand it to the Navy. You're marvellous!'

It turned out that my Leading Sick Berth Attendant had learned with horror that soldiers abroad were not issued, like sailors, with the real necessities of life. Accordingly (shades of *Loch Killisport!*) he had stationed himself at the head of the gangway and, with the matelot's sublime disregard of Army rank, particularly for soldiers who must indeed be pretty low level to be shipped in this way, he had issued out his envelopes to the figures stumbling down the gangplank. The Commandant, unrecognisable as any different from the rest in the rainy darkness, had arrived on board to be greeted by an arm round his shoulders and the cry of, "Ere y'are, lad. All you need in France.' With a military instinct born of years of wartime evacuations by the Navy, he had meekly accepted the envelope containing, presumably, some vital orders, had opened it in my cabin – and found inside one French letter for each of the five nights the Staff College were to spend on their battlefield tour. 'I take it,' said the General, 'not only as a charming tribute to my virility but as a gesture of superb optimism. Where we're going, I doubt if even soldiers will find the opportunity to use them.'

The only problem in *Contest* was our Commander D. Stocky, red faced with white, almost crew cut hair; his wife had left him in despair and he lived in his *Boxer*, a great, ungainly, converted merchant ship covered with aerials and odd shaped appendages for her very secret role as an experimental radar vessel. Being a real destroyer man, D hated driving this unwieldy thing and spent most of his days and nights popping up in the destroyers and sloops of his Flotilla. The expression, 'I couldn't care less,' sent him through the roof. His mottoes were, 'Of course it can be done,' and 'An evolution of everything all the time.'

He would accept no excuse for storm damage, which could only be the result of bad ship handling. Every day in every ship, a young officer and a young rating had to do something together which frightened them. For instance, they might jump from the wing of one bridge to the wing of the ship next door when the two ships concerned were just too far apart for it to be safe. He would accept, he said, a broken limb and a broken collar bone a month. Successful training for war required peacetime casualties. Life must be lived dangerously.

He was always sneaking on board, trying to catch us out, and, even at sea, we were not safe from his depredations. We would be exercising placidly far out in the Channel when a harmless looking fishing vessel would call us up by Aldis and order us to stop. The next thing we knew, D would be on board exercising fire parties, damage control or a breakdown in steering. Then the ship would have to return up harbour with only the Captain allowed to remain on the bridge in case of ultimate disaster but, otherwise, all the Officers locked in the wardroom, the Coxswain 'in command' and Petty Officers in charge of all stations. 'You don't know who'll be left alive after an action. Give 'em practice now.'

Finally, I decided it was time to give this dreadful man his comeuppance. I was drinking, late one night, with an old RNVR friend and describing to him the awfulness of life under such a boss. By 0200, we were both full of whisky and The Idea came to me. D was always waffling on about the need for good security and how, even asleep, a good Destroyer Officer had antennae which would warn him of imminent danger. 'No good Officer is ever caught out. He'll always wake up, alert, thirty seconds before anything goes wrong and you can stop your ship in that time . . .'

My friend had a car. We drove down to the dockyard. In *Boxer*, the Quartermaster was about to start his Middle Watch rounds. I crept on board and followed him. As he unlocked and checked each highly secret compartment, I sneaked in behind him and wrote on the white paint in red chalk – BOMB. When he had finished and gone off to brew up a cup of tea, I took *Boxer*'s log and wrote in it: 'Security in this ship is poor. The Bomber.'

Then I remembered I had brought along my darkroom clock, also clearly labelled BOMB. What to do with it? Snidely, the whisky told me. There could be only one target . . .

I crept up to D's cabin. Heavy breathing inside. I slid through the curtain and stood there in the dark. Surely the breathing was a trap? This terrible man must be now wideawake and about to switch on his light and catch me redhanded. Suddenly I felt very sober and very frightened – but it was too late to turn back. Swiftly I slid across the cabin, slipped the clock under his pillow and fled.

The next morning, when his steward called him, D demanded, 'What's that ticking noise?'

'I don't know, sir. It seems to be coming from under your pillow.'

'Nonsense. How could it?'

The pillow was wrenched up and there it was – BOMB.

God help me, I thought D would actually appreciate the spirit of the thing and admit the biter had been bit. How wrong can you be? All hell broke loose and *Boxer* suffered greatly but he could never prove who had done it though he might suspect. He roared on board *Contest* and told me furiously what had happened, watching for my reaction.

I smiled blandly and said, 'Well, sir, whoever did it must have known you have a sense of humour and would take it in the right spirit.'

Officially, that was the end of it. The more humourless a man, the more he is afraid of being accused of lacking a sense of humour. But, of course, the whole Flotilla knew and I was given the dubious accolade by one of my fellow COs, 'Well, old boy, at least nobody can say you suffer from promotionitis.'

Nemesis, however, was round the corner. *Contest* was due for her Annual Inspection and I realised now that D was out to get me.

The Annual Inspection was a two day affair. Normally, the first day dealt with cleanliness for which the ship must be burnished till she shone. The second day would be given over to General Drills at sea. General Drills were designed to be totally unexpected and to catch out the ship's organisation by calling for surprise evolutions which gradually increased in tempo till Captain, Officers, sailors and organisation were reduced to a whimpering shambles and the Inspecting Officer could depart with unkind words for the chaos he had caused.

In our case, most unusually, the General Drills came first. This was because we operated at such a tempo that the only way to fit the Inspection in was to catch us the day after we came out of a short refit and had to sail for Rothesay in the evening. Obviously, it would be pointless to inspect for cleanliness when we were still covered with dockyard grime so that must await our return from Rothesay. As it was, it seemed pretty hard even to do the General Drills under the circumstances.

Anyhow, we had to and, knowing how D excelled at this sadistic game, I flinched at the coming ordeal. Then, the night before, my Gunner came to see me. He was a bosom friend of D's Staff Gunner who didn't like his boss. Both, of course, knew of my bomb exploit and D's reaction so they had got together to help me. Guns now knew the secret of all the drills and surprises that D had prepared for the next day.

The result was splendid. D came on board minutes before we were due to sail.

'Land an armed platoon . . .'

He hoped that this unexpected order would cause a delay while a platoon was unexpectedly mustered and provided with arms; then he could start me off on the wrong foot by rebuking me for being late slipping from the jetty. But the platoon had long been ready to go and we sailed on time. 'Ah well,' thought D, 'at least he's lost half his seamen and will have to struggle through the day shorthanded.' But a hidden truck had whipped them through the yard to a waiting boat and they rejoined us as we went down harbour.

And so it went on. A line was already rigged to hoist the postman's bicycle to the yardarm and the components of a boxing ring had been hidden under the torpedo tubes since dawn. Even a stage was ready to be rigged and the ship's 'funny man' briefed to be ready to do a turn. Whatever unlikely evolution D demanded, *Contest* was prepared.

He did his worst, was foiled and finally forced to utter words of grudging approbation. The sailors hugged themselves with sinful pride and we went straight on to Rothesay, dropping off our frustrated tormentor in the Solent as we left. His last words were to remind me of what would be waiting for us on our return. After beating him at General Drill, he was going to be out for blood when he came to do the cleanliness inspection.

In Scotland, we had winter gales and rain. Every day and many nights we spent steaming round the Kyles of Bute, exercising with the submarines. By the time we were due to return south, we had just managed to paint the ship's side and clean the messdecks but the upper deck was far from ready for even a sympathetic inspection.

We left the Clyde on a Friday afternoon after one last, enormous exercise and we were due in Portsmouth on Monday evening. The Inspection was scheduled for the Tuesday and we were not ready for it. The thought of D's easy triumph was gall and I sat on the bridge on the Saturday afternoon, thinking gloomily of how much still needed to be done. The weather had, at last, improved and we were sailing south in sunshine and a flat calm. If only we'd had such conditions in Rothesay . . .

As I sat, I noticed a party of hands painting. We had very few defaulters in *Contest* and it seemed funny to see so many working during a well earned 'make and mend'. I looked aft. The whole upper deck was full of busy sailors. It seemed as if the First Lieutenant was working the Ship's Company on a Saturday afternoon and this was really too much, even before the Inspection. At the pace we had been working, the hands needed their rest, even if only at sea between watches.

However, No.1 assured me that no orders had been given to turn to. These were all volunteers. Even as he was speaking, more men appeared and started in. All the way south, the freak calm continued and, over the whole weekend, the Ship's Company painted and cleaned. On Monday evening, we secured alongside in Portsmouth but only a very few of the older married men went ashore. The whole Wardroom had already joined in and the spirit in the ship was rather like that of a houseproud young married couple, working late, determined to finish decorating the parlour before mother-in-law arrives the next day.

At midnight I finished painting the screen door outside my cabin and flopped into my bunk exhausted. I heard afterwards that some of the sailors never turned in at all but worked throughout the night.

By the time D arrived on the Tuesday morning, there were some very tired faces at Divisions but *Contest* looked like a yacht.

As a result, the Inspection for cleanliness was also a success and this time, at least, the praise was fairly earned. I was intensely grateful to my Ship's Company and, standing on the capstan, I told them so. My words were greeted by a throng of grinning faces and almost audible giggles. Something was obviously hanging in the air between us but I couldn't guess what so I just grinned back and left it at that.

Then I sent for my No.1 and, as delicately as I could, I probed him. Laughing at my not having known, he explained what had happened on that journey south. The sailors, of course, had all heard about my exploit in *Boxer* and they knew perfectly well the implications behind our cleanliness Inspection. They were determined that their *Contest* was going to be in spotless condition and that D was going to have no excuse to be rotten to me. They had certainly succeeded in frustrating any unworthy ideas he might have had and that was why they had been hugging themselves when I had thanked them so innocently.

The thought struck me that they had looked after me just like their predecessors had so long ago when I was only a Midshipman in charge of a boat and I knew then that I had the best, most marvellous Ship's Company in the world and that the spirit we had built up between us was beyond price.

Many fortunate Captains of HM Ships have probably felt the same over the past few hundred years. Many more, as yet unborn, will know the feeling as long as the Royal Navy puts to sea. It is an experience of total exaltation beside which nothing else in one's whole career can matter at all.

Chapter 20

ROYAL NAVAL BARRACKS

After leaving *Contest* I thought that any appointment must be a let-down but, once more, the Admiralty came up with substantial consolation in the form of the best job available to a Lieutenant Commander – First Lieutenant of a Barracks. It was particularly gratifying because in those days, such an appointment suggested that the incumbent was clearly marked for promotion.

Devonport Naval Barracks, HMS *Drake*, was an odd mixture of beauty and austerity. Lying beside the dockyard, with the Hamoaze beyond, the Wardroom, inside and out, must be one of the loveliest buildings in England and the big tree-lined cricket field in front was our arena for everything from Armada Night pageants to all the pomp and ceremony of Beating Retreat on Navy Days. The sailors lived in vast bare dormitory blocks, designed for hammocks, and inherited the Barracks tradition that authority was there to impose unwanted discipline and bull and sailors were there to evade authority.

The idea of a Home Port Barracks was really that of a human refit cum maintenance cum transit camp. Ships returning to pay off would discharge their companies full of genial seagoing bad habits and with half their kit missing or substandard after a couple of years in the close confines of a messdeck. As soon as they had had their leave, they returned to Barracks where the shaking up process began. Ceremonial, discipline, snappy saluting, smart turnout and a full, clean kit were the first essentials in RNB. Courses were provided for those who required them, arms were stuck full of inoculations, teeth were inspected, extracted and drilled and the slaphappy seagoing sailor rejuvenated, polished and generally sharpened up, ready to start his next commission on the top line of Barracks standard. Then he went off to his new ship, relaxed on his messdeck, and the whole cycle started again.

In Barracks, the sailor waged war with the Commander and the First Lieutenant. The Commander was responsible for discipline generally and the transformation process in particular. The First Lieutenant was responsible for organising everything from fire drills to Navy Days and for the general cleanliness of the whole enormous establishment. To maintain this cleanliness he had a large number of civilian workmen and the hands in Barracks who were awaiting draft.

To the sailor, his time in *Drake* was his rest at home between sea going appointments to the far corners of the world. His only idea was to do the minimum of work during the day and get out to his beer or his wife at night. As the time for draft drew near, the married men would return on board in the mornings and make an anxious beeline for the dread noticeboard to see if their names were on the list. If not, they had another twenty-four hours to relax.

Particularly before the War, venal Regulators could sometimes be bribed to adjust draft orders to the recipient's liking even, at a very high price, arranging the ultimate ambition of every married man which was to become a 'barracks stanchion' – a rating whose peerless draft chit actually appointed him to a permanent job in the Barracks complement. There were some old 'stripeys' who, by luck, skill, or subtle greasing of palms were believed to have held their jobs, limpet like, for years. In the meantime, out of the huge, shifting complement, the First Lieutenant's one idea was to acquire the maximum of working hands. The one idea of the 'working hands' was to avoid work and the First Lieutenant.

Before the War, one First Lieutenant decided to clear out a room where were stowed from floor to ceiling the hammocks of men believed to be on leave. After considerable labour, he found, in the very middle, a small nestlike cave of hammocks where lived four elderly Able Seamen. They had fixed a Regulator so that their cards had been removed from the Drafting office and they were, to all intents and purposes, lost for ever as far as the Drafting machinery was concerned. They emerged to eat, draw pay and go ashore but otherwise they hid in their pit, sleeping the idle hours away. Anything was better than working and they had beaten the machine. They had no other ambition in the Navy and they were perfectly happy.

Now such stories were still prized memories but the new, young generation of modern sailors had a rather more constructive attitude. Shortage of manpower meant minimal time in Barracks anyhow. I would face several hundred men in the Drill Shed every morning, but by the time those on joining and leaving routines had fallen out, there would only be a mere handful left. We lacked enough working hands even for our own necessities. It made the standard expected of a Barracks difficult to maintain but, at least, with the end of pointless idleness, it brought a new spirit to the place. Moreover, there was a purpose in life. Ships commissioning were likely to find themselves in Korea and, even at home, the possibility of war with Russia was also in our minds.

The Barracks was many worlds in one. We had our own theatre and our own printing shop. There was a Gunnery school tucked away in one corner, a

Seamanship school in another. We ran our own magazine, *Guzz Gazette*, which went to West Country ships all over the world. In the cell establishment we had our own prison.

The Commander spent most of his working forenoons seeing defaulters. Men who, in ships, accepted the community requirements, played up in Barracks. The discipline and the chasing provoked the congenital 'skates' to insubordination when they lacked the strength of spirit of a good ship. Others were deliberately trying to 'work their ticket' anyhow.

The 'ticket workers' were a difficult problem. These were the sailors, usually misfits in the first place, who had grown to hate the Navy. Starting with minor punishments, increasing in severity to cells and then Detention, their only idea in life was to go on fighting the machine till they achieved their goal – a sentence of civil imprisonment and discharge from the Service.

The Admiralty policy of keeping such men was extremely short sighted. There were very few. They were a curse to the Navy and, for both their sake and that of the Service, they would have been better out of it. But the argument ran that if all any bloody minded sailor had to do to get out was to fill in the nearest Petty Officer, nobody in any position of authority would be safe. It had to be made clear that it was not as easy as all that.

The Barracks Regulating Staff could easily have quoted a list of about twenty men in the Devonport Port Division whose loss would have been an asset to the Navy and to themselves. If such men had been thrown out everybody would have been thankful. With the general spirit in the Fleet, it would have been accepted that they were not good enough to have the honour to serve and, even if a few more had taken the easy way out after them, they would have been no loss compared with the worms we insisted on retaining in our apple.

However, these few dramas bore no relationship whatever to the general spirit in Devonport Barracks as a whole. Our Field Gun's Crew, suitably sponsored by young ladies from the Windmill Chorus, were determined to achieve for their greatly liked young Field Gun Officer what his father had once achieved before him – the collection of all the three cups available. Tough looking rascals, some with gold earrings to set off their beards (a rarity in those days), they got down to training and the whole of Plymouth marked their progress.

When they arrived at Earl's Court for the Tournament, a big blackboard was mounted at the Barracks' gate where the day's results, phoned down from London, were immediately inscribed. It was barely necessary. On one occasion, boarding a bus the far side of the city at a time when the board could hardly have been made up, I found the whole crowd of passengers avidly discussing the day's new record which our Field Gun had just put up that afternoon.

They broke their own record, they brought back the three cups for the Champion team, the fastest run, and the best aggregate time and the Lord Mayor of Plymouth dropped everything to give them a Civic reception on the Hoe. From there they marched back to the Barracks behind our Royal Marine Band, towing on the gun carriage a six foot 'tiddyoggy' (Cornish pasty), symbol of the West Country Port Division. Cheering crowds lined the pavements all the way and, in Barracks, we lined the roads with the Barracks guard presenting arms till they reached the biggest cake we had ever made, surmounted by a Field Gun in icing and surrounded by an individual crest for each man with his name on it – crests which were retained as mementoes for life of their epic achievement. No football team ever had such support in their native city. Plymouth was the Royal Navy.

The spirit showed again when King George VI died. Overnight it became necessary to raise some hundreds of adequately trained armed sailors for street lining duties along the funeral route and this was achieved by sending all available hands to the Barracks Parade Ground to be tried out. From ships all round the dockyard they came to join with our own men and, as they drilled, the Parade staff went round picking and discarding. There followed the astonishing sight of young sailors who had failed to make the grade sitting at the edge of the Parade Ground literally in tears because they had not been considered smart enough for the honour.

Those who were went to London and put up a performance of which the Navy could well be proud but, quite properly, it was our own regular Barracks guard who gained the greatest accolade. Paying their salute at Windsor, they were told by Royalty that theirs was the smartest piece of ceremonial ever seen in that ceremonial old town. We felt honoured indeed.

Altogether, there was never a dull moment in Barracks. Royal funerals, court martials, thousands of sightseers milling around at Naval Days, Balls, pageants mounted on the Hoe and our own Armada Pageant on the lawn in front of the mess – all were grist to the First Lieutenant's mill. It was a busy, stimulating life of which I enjoyed every minute and, if it was cut short after only a year, I had no cause to complain.

In the summer of 1952 I was promoted to Commander and my relief joined a week or so later. I had a longstanding appointment to visit Princetown gaol on Dartmoor to see what happened to our ultimate failures – those, Officers as well as ratings, who were dismissed the Service and sentenced to a term of imprisonment. I took my relief with me on the afternoon before I was due to depart and it was too good an opportunity to miss. Standing on the gallery of D Block, I asked if he would take over at that moment. He would. It must have been the only time a Royal Naval Barracks was turned over in Dartmoor prison.

Chapter 21

USA

Perhaps by now I had become thoroughly spoilt. I had had so many interesting and enjoyable jobs that I just could not see how, even as a Commander, I could look forward to anything better. But, as usual, the Admiralty had an ace up its sleeve and, after doing the Staff Course, I found myself faced by the last thing I had ever expected – an appointment to the United States of America.

The job was as Staff Officer (Plans) to the British Joint Services Mission (Navy Staff) in Washington DC but I had a second, more important, hat as the Assistant UK National Liaison Representative to the Supreme Allied Commander, Atlantic (SACLANT) in Norfolk, Virginia. My Admiral was the nominal UK NLR but, as he was more than fully employed in Washington, the actual leg work fell to me and I found myself a sort of nautical Ambassador to the big NATO headquarters to which most of the Royal Navy was allocated in time of war. I had to keep the British Officers up-to-date with Admiralty news and views and give the Admiralty prior warning of the way SACLANT's mind was working.

Before sailing, I was well briefed in the Admiralty on all aspects of RN thought and policy, ending with a session in the Trade Division with a Commander who probably knew more about shipping, convoys and general trade problems than any other two people in the world. He occupied an office in the oldest block of the Admiralty, overlooking Whitehall, and through his grimy open window came the muffled roar of the traffic below. On the sill, about half a dozen pigeons sat cooing, stepping onto his desk at intervals and hopping into his otherwise unused In basket in which he provided a veritable pigeon cornucopia of breadcrumbs and grain. As pigeons are birds careless in their personal habits, window sill, desk, In basket and dockets all bore obvious marks of their passing.

Some weeks later in the Pentagon, I found myself in a vast, air conditioned room. It had no windows but strip lighting made it as bright as day. About twenty Naval Officers arrived at half past seven every morning and beavered away till four o'clock in the afternoon. It was the USN equivalent of my Commander in Trade Division. They gave me a 'Presentation' which took most of the forenoon and they were good enough to speak kindly of the Admiralty's expertise and efficiency in their particular field. How, they asked, were we so good? What great organisation did we have to equate with theirs? I thought of the sheer, comparative civilisation of a man and his birds but I evaded answering their question. They could never understand.

The US Navy has an odd love-hate relationship with the Royal Navy. They admit we build better ships than they do. They give us full credit as the inventors of the Angled Deck and the Mirror Landing Sight which, alone, have made it possible for them to fly the British inspired jet aircraft onto their vast nuclear carriers. They also have a tremendous, rather envious admiration for our traditions and our mystique. But, equally, they look to their astonishing wartime campaign in the South Pacific which we could never have achieved and from the sheer, overwhelming size of their Fleet they know that they have long overtaken us as the greatest Navy in the world. Their contribution to NATO is so immense compared with ours that, much as they may respect us as we are and particularly as we were, they are not prepared to tolerate any interference by us in their affairs. They adore a British Admiral who is courteous and cooperative and they bask in his praise but they become very prickly indeed if they suspect he is criticising or trying to lay down the law. The British Admiralty is something to be revered but it also bears the image of the interfering incompetents of PQ17 and 'Steer North' and no American Naval Officer would ever risk US ships under its command. The net result is rather like the relationship between an affectionate but thrustful young man and his formidable maiden aunt. The sentiment is there and the respect. Praise from her is indeed an accolade to be appreciated. But the old lady *is* rather past it and can not be allowed to interfere with the real business of the day.

British Officers, on the other hand, feel an equivalent admiration for the size and very real achievements of the US Navy. It is truly a formidable force. But, in America, to join the Regular Service as an Officer is to suggest that you are not good enough to try and earn big money in the market place or, even worse if this should be possible, that you are so undemocratic as to relish having your fellow citizens salute and call you 'Sir'. We have a quaint, old fashioned pride in being 'Commander' So-and-so. An American car salesman would make a point of calling you Mister, paying the compliment of pretending that he thought of you as a proper man of commerce and not as one carrying the brand of services rank. In Norfolk, Virginia, the car salesman might well, in the evenings, be a Naval Commander himself, making a fast buck in the Dog Watches.

With this national attitude to the forces, the best men do not join. It was

Pam and the boys arrive in the USA.

quite normal to find US Naval Captains who wrote in capital letters because they found cursive difficult. One such issued an edict to his Division that all orders from SACLANT should be couched in NATO language. By that, he explained, he meant it should be like real diplomatic language – dignified and not easy to understand. A signal came from the Admiralty requesting confirmation that British escorts turning round convoys at American ports in wartime could count on obtaining oil fuel and provisions. It was a routine signal for the record only and one of the many British Commanders on SACLANT's staff simply signalled back the one word 'confirmed'.

The US Captain intercepted the signal before it was transmitted and cancelled it. It was a good example, he said afterwards, of the sort of practice he intended to stop. One word had no dignity . . . He had actually substituted, 'Review of subject requirements indicates compatibility with the concept of SACLANT logistic responsibility for earmarked forces.' Yet, at the same time as this Officer pursued his quest for esoteric sesquipedalianism, a US Marine General in Washington was claiming, in his Press handout, that he was famous for being able to spit further and more accurately into a cuspidor than anyone else in his Corps.

British Officers usually started by loving America and the Americans. Then the feeling changed to revulsion which, in turn, was replaced by objectivity as the time drew near to go home and one remembered how awful Britain and the British can be. For perhaps it is true to say that everything we're good at they're bad at and everything we're bad at they're good at. If only we could combine the best of both nations and Navies what an unbeatable combination it would be.

It was while I was in the United States that the Royal Navy tore itself in half. For some time it had been obvious that, with fewer and fewer ships in commission and more and more NATO and other shore jobs requiring large numbers of Senior Officers, there could not be enough time in sea command for all the Captains and Commanders concerned to get adequate experience. To add to the difficulty, the Navy was completely air orientated. After the lessons of the American campaign in the South Pacific, the Admiralty was determined that the future lay with the aircraft carriers. Carriers should be commanded by aviators and, to qualify them to drive these enormous ships, they must have learned their trade by driving smaller ones earlier in their careers. This took up even more of the few remaining billets for professional seamen and we therefore faced the lunatic prospect that, in order to find sea command for professional airmen, professional seamen had to be denied ships.

All executive Captains and Commanders were therefore divided into two lists, known as Post and General but immediately christened Wet and Dry by the Fleet. In America, nearly all the British Officers were executive Commanders and were therefore concerned. Many, like myself, had had their own commands, others were Navigators. We took it for granted that all our expertise was hardly likely to be thrown away and that we should be on the Wet List. We imagined that, if there were not enough commands to go around, the idea of giving totally inexperienced aviators sea time would obviously be abolished first and then numbers on the Dry List would be made up by picking the sort of Gunnery or other specialist Officers whose careers had been essentially in back room nuts and bolts rather than on the bridge. It would be hard luck but it was the obvious way of making the best use of the skill available with the least loss of Fleet efficiency.

The blue envelopes all arrived together and the shock as we opened them was staggering. Out of the many Commanders in Washington and Norfolk nearly all were placed on the Dry List.

It was not so bad for me because, as a Salt Horse, I had had command and in wartime. I was lucky. But, for those who were reckoning on their next job being their first command, the carpet had been swept from under their feet almost as they stepped hopefully forward. For all of us, our world was overturned. We had joined the Navy to go to sea and now the sea was being taken away from us for ever.

In Norfolk, Virginia, British habits required a bar and, as a NATO mess, the Americans had allowed it. Now the British contingent, the largest, most directly affected group of Commanders in the world, stepped up to it and commenced some really serious drinking. Two hours later they turned to their American colleagues and announced that they were going home to continue drinking. They would not be back until next day. One Officer went further. A bachelor Navigator, he intended drinking alone and he announced that he would not be back for at least two days. Then he would consider whether he would be returning at all. He had no love but the sea and now that had been denied him.

The US Navy were appalled and sympathetic. As sailors they understood what we felt. As Americans they supported our solution. For ourselves we did not care. We turned to the bottle.

When we had recovered from our hangovers, we read the letter again. Signed on behalf of the Second Sea Lord, it assured us that our chances of promotion to Captain would be 'little different' on the Dry List from what they had been before. As over half the Commanders were now Dry and we guessed, correctly as it turned out, that the great majority of promotions would go to those on the Wet List, this was an obvious untruth. The letter ended on the traditional note: 'The Second Sea Lord is confident that any personal disappointment you may feel will be tempered by the realisation that this serious measure is for the good of the Service.'

Naval Officers have, indeed, always been idealists but there is a limit beyond which demands on their loyalty are greeted with a reaction of sudden bitterness. This limit had now been over reached and the smug, complacent ending of a letter which seemed to have wrecked all our lives and careers was really the last straw. Even if such a scheme were necessary, the psychology behind its implementation was lamentable and, indeed, if proof were needed of how totally the Admiralty had failed to appreciate the results of what it was doing, one last humiliation was added. As if the word 'Post', with all its traditions, was not enough to underline our shame, the lucky Officers who would actually be allowed to go to sea were marked in the Navy List by a special symbol of crossed swords. Nothing could have been designed to rub in the implications more crudely. It was at this point that the selfless dedication of pre-war Naval Officers first began to be thrown aside.

Letters of resignation were written, culminating, when the Golden Bowler was announced, in a flood of volunteers to retire. Ten years later recruitment was to suffer greatly when the same Officers tried to discourage sons from joining a Service which, they reckoned, had treated them so shabbily. It was a tragedy because it could have been dealt with so differently. But, out of all the bitterness and heartbreak, perhaps one lesson was learned. The Mutiny of Invergordon had shown that Whitehall could not treat sailors as cyphers. Now the Admiralty learned that even Officers are human and could not just be accepted as loyalty machines. At least, when the shocks which then lay in the future were announced, nobody was crass enough to say ever again that 'Their Lordships were confident' that the latest disaster would be cheerfully accepted 'for the good of the Service'.

Out of travail, progress is born.

Chapter 22

NAVAL INTELLIGENCE DIVISION

There was one great consolation about the Dry List. I now had three boys aged fourteen, eight and six. These are delightful years for a parent and even the delectable prospect of my first sea job as a Commander had been marred by the thought of leaving them at such a period in their lives. Now I knew that partings were over. Wherever I went my family could come too. And, having no specialist qualification, I need not fear years spent in dull, technical appointments. Whatever I did from now on would at least be interesting.

In actual fact, our return from America and my obvious professional disappointment led to the most interesting job of my entire Naval career. I was appointed to head Section 2 of the Naval Intelligence Division.

Section 2 dealt with the whole world outside the Far East and the Soviet Block. The desk Officers each had a group of countries of their own and were responsible for making themselves experts on those countries' politics and Navies. From the Commander-in-Chief, Mediterranean, down to the CO of a frigate, Officers taking up new appointments overseas would come to us for detailed briefings and we sent out views and comments on their local situation to Fleets and ships from Iceland to the Persian Gulf. More importantly, we played a full part in the Intelligence machine which briefed both the Chiefs of Staff and, through them, the Government.

The Joint Intelligence Committee in those days came officially under the Chiefs of Staff although it had a Foreign Office chairman. It consisted of the Heads of all Intelligence agencies, including the three Services, and there was obviously considerable duplication of effort with so many different departments studying the same information, from clandestine sources to the mass of daily diplomatic telegrams from our posts abroad. On the other hand, this very duplication was the whole strength and justification of the system.

Once a week, at our level, the Service Heads of Sections and their equivalents from other Ministries met together to draft a Weekly Intelligence Summary for the Cabinet and those concerned in Whitehall. Although the same intelligence information was available to all of us our interpretations frequently varied widely. The Foreign Office were always reluctant to commit to paper any firm forecast. It was part of their congenital weakness that they would prefer any 'form of words', as they loved to call it, that would duck the awful responsibility of taking a decision. The Services' whole training being entirely different, we tended to go in exactly the opposite direction. We reckoned that the point of acquiring Intelligence was to use it to warn our masters of what was likely to happen. It was the logical conflict of the differing objectives of those concerned. Diplomats are there to influence foreigners. The Services are there to kill them.

Perhaps it would be kindest to say that the Services' over enthusiasm was kept in check by Foreign Office *savoir faire* whilst the Foreign Office's dislike of committing itself was gingered up by the Services' practical approach to problems. However you put it, the net result was that an excellent balance of varying brains interpreted the Intelligence available and the guidance given to the Cabinet was balanced and good.

Meanwhile, our primary bread and butter job was keeping the Admiralty fully briefed on actual or potential trouble spots.

The process involved an unceasing procession of blue dockets, marked 'Top Secret' – 'Most Immediate' in which, from our current knowledge, we would insert a quick brief for those concerned in taking the actual decision.

Looming behind all our daily activities, however, the biggest docket coming round again and again, was labelled 'Arab/Israel'. Obviously trouble was going to break out. The only questions were How and When?

The Intelligence appreciation was clear and simple. Whenever it happened, the Egyptian Army was totally useless as a military force and the Israelis could make mincemeat of it. No query was ever raised. It was too self evidently true.

Then, after a long period in which British endeavours concerning a loan for the Aswan Dam were totally frustrated by the obstructionism and indecision of the American Secretary of State, John Foster Dulles, Nasser got fed up and nationalised the Suez Canal.

Whitehall's immediate reaction was that it was unthinkable that Nasser should be allowed to get away with it. Operation Musketeer was ordered.

With this development, the situation changed overnight. 'Arab/Israel' was no longer of academic interest. When Musketeer was mounted, British troops would be involved and so the reputations and responsibilities of the British Commanders of the forces concerned. The Intelligence appreciation that the Egyptian Army posed little threat was no longer acceptable. Meanwhile, Section 2 was handed a crisis of our own.

The Labour Opposition, which had originally supported Eden's ideas of firm action, had now lost their nerve and changed their tune. After a typically bad tempered exchange in the House, the Prime Minister was asked why, when we seemed to be on the brink of going to war with Egypt, we were about to provide that country with two newly refitted destroyers. Eden, caught short, replied off the cuff, 'I'm sure we can leave that to the Royal Navy.' The fastest buck in Whitehall whizzed round in ever decreasing circles and ended up on the desk of the Head of NID 2. 'Do something,' I was told. 'Do anything but do it at once.'

Sabotage was the obvious answer. It could easily be arranged but, apart from being crude, it was too obvious. I shuddered to think of the meal the media would make of it. Then I suddenly saw a solution. Because NID 2 looked after the interests of all the foreign Naval Attachés in London, the Egyptian NA and I had been cooperating closely on the refit of the two destroyers concerned. Everyone had known about them. The sale might be ill timed but we were not yet at war, a contract was a contract and it seemed we needed the money. So the refit had been allowed to go ahead and the Egyptian NA, a conscientious man, had fussed over every detail.

Now, with the two ships about to sail, it was his very perfectionism which gave me the answer to the sudden crisis. A frantic phone call to Portsmouth elicited the news that the ammunition barges were actually on their way to the two destroyers. 'Send C-in-C's barge if you have to,' I begged, 'but for God's sake, get them back.' Portsmouth managed it and the NA came to see me in a state of great anxiety. What had gone wrong?

I reminded him that he had asked me to ensure that all the ammunition was new. We were now doing so but it had involved unloading the barges to check the serial numbers of each individual shell. Obviously this took time . . . the next day he was back. The job must have been done? Ah, yes. It had indeed but, unfortunately, a further delay had arisen. The Home Fleet had returned to Portsmouth and had to deammunition before the ships went up harbour. Obviously he would understand that this must have priority for the barges . . . He came back for the last time. 'We're not going to get the ammunition, are we?' Feeling an absolute heel, I mumbled some other excuse. We had already checked that only one factory in Czechoslovakia could produce the 4.5 shells required and even that would require some retooling which, apart from the time factor, the Russians would be unlikely to allow. That night, the two destroyers sailed unexpectedly for Egypt. They were in beautiful nick except that they couldn't fire their guns. Eden had been proved right.

Suddenly the Intelligence appreciation was no longer acceptable. Egyptians, we were assured, were the most formidable fighters. The First Sea Lord, Admiral Mountbatten, coined the new slogan. 'The Egyptians,' he said 'will fight like the old Indian Army.' To support his opinion, he quoted the case of some Egyptians surrounded in a desert fort by tanks who resisted most gallantly to the last man. My military colleague was more practical. 'Of course they did,' he said. 'But if you attack rats you shouldn't be fool enough to trap them in a ring. Make it a horseshoe and watch them run!'

Generals like to have a sledge hammer to crack a nut and, to justify the provision of such a weapon, the nut must be portrayed as savage and dangerous. Whatever its view the JIC came under the Chiefs of Staff and if the Chiefs of Staff were suddenly no longer prepared to accept our intelligence assessment there was nothing much we could do about it except watch the Government being misadvised.

It now became obvious that the might of Britain was insufficient to deal even with the Egyptians without major disruption of our affairs. Reservists were called up. Merchant ships were commandeered and taken out of their normal service. It takes time to plan such an operation and even longer to mount it. Eventually, all was arranged and then the problems of Musketeer entered a new phase. The plans were ready. The troops and ships and aircraft were ready. But the assault which had been prepared could not be launched because there was no excuse. We had not been organised to go in immediately after the Canal was nationalised which would at least have been a reasonable reaction. Now, months later, such an action could hardly be justified and everything was being held in abeyance.

In Cyprus, the reserve troops became restless.. They wanted to return to civilian life. The economy was suffering from the loss of the commandeered ships. It was obvious that, unless the assault had been carried out by mid November, we should have to stand down and give up the whole idea.

Then a series of small hints and portents appeared in the Intelligence picture. We looked and we thought and, on the Tuesday at the Heads of Sections meeting, the Navy tabled a paragraph for the Weekly Summary. Based on five factors ranging from the Israeli double harvest to the estimated progress of Egyptian military preparedness, it warned that Israel would probably attack Egypt within seven days.

The Foreign Office representative objected violently. It appeared that the Israeli Ambassador had assured the British Foreign Secretary only that morning that Israel had no intention of attacking Egypt.

'Do you believe him?' I asked sceptically.

'I think,' said the indignant diplomat, 'that when a Foreign Ambassador gives a categorical assurance to the Secretary of State we can accept his word. It is at least more likely to be dependable than a piece of pure supposition such as the Navy seems to suggest.' Our warning was not accepted for the Summary.

On the Friday morning, Section 2 was more worried than ever and I decided that, even if nobody else wanted to know, we must warn our own people of the probable imminence of hostilities. A quick brief was drafted for the Board of Admiralty and a signal to Commander-in-Chief, Mediterranean, and I took them in to the Director of Naval Intelligence. He approved them.

I was just nipping out for a quick lunch when he sent for me.

'I have stopped your brief and your signal,' he said. 'Something very odd is happening but nobody has been good enough to tell me what it is.'

Apparently, Lord Mountbatten had disappeared to his country retreat at this vital moment and was incommunicado. The other two Chiefs of Staff had similarly disappeared. The Vice Chief of Naval Staff who, as the First Sea Lord's Deputy and the Officer responsible for operations, should certainly have been in the picture, knew nothing. On the Friday afternoon, at a time of possibly acute crisis, the three Officers responsible for the Nation's armed forces had suddenly gone to ground leaving their Ministries completely in the dark as to what was happening.

'I don't know whether Commander-in-Chief, Mediterranean, is aware of what's going on,' said DNI. 'But I do know that, in his wildest moment, it would never occur to him that I am not. Anything we send could therefore be misunderstood and it's wisest to send out nothing. No signals or briefs are to go out from this Division till further orders.' So we entered the weekend.

By Monday it was apparent that, whatever was in the air, it was being handled personally at the very top. This entire machinery of Government, military and civil, had been bypassed. Nobody at any level knew what was going on.

That evening I was watching the Goon Show on TV when a typewritten ticker tape crossed the screen. 'Israeli forces', it read, 'have invaded Egypt.' I just had time to think that this was a joke in exceptionally poor taste under the circumstances when the 'phone rang. The news was all too true and I was to attend an Emergency Heads of Section meeting at seven o'clock the next morning. The Naval forecast had been right inside twenty-four hours of our original deadline.

The next morning the Heads of Sections met. The Foreign Office representative who believed Ambassadors was not present. He had, it appeared, been transferred rather suddenly to other duties. We were there, the FO Chairman explained, because the Cabinet and the Chiefs of Staff required an urgent appreciation of Israeli intentions. In particular, were they likely to stop on the Canal? (With hindsight, this was a particular interesting requirement. We now know that the Prime Minister and the Foreign Secretary had arranged the whole scenario in secret talks in Paris with the French and Israeli's Ben Gurian and General Dayan – talks so secret that, to his great chagrin, even the British Ambassador was excluded. Also, it has always been thought that the others never fully trusted us and so, to the end, we were unsure of their final intentions. The brief for this meeting seems to confirm it.)

We finished by about nine and I returned to the Admiralty. Obviously, Musketeer could now be launched. At last we had a flimsy excuse. Looking back, I remembered odd snippets which had come in on the Friday evening about troops embarking in Malta. At the time they had made no sense. With hindsight they did. Somebody had known on that day what was to happen. Somebody had issued orders. Now the assault was well on the way and Eden had only to issue his ultimatum.

With action imminent, high level cries of despair became hysterical. Everybody wanted caution but caution, like happiness, meant different things to different people. The Generals wanted any possible opposition obliterated beforehand to make the landings safe for the troops. The politicians, on the other hand, wanted an assault which would cause no Egyptian casualties. Impasse.

A signal was received at the last minute from the Field Commander warning that, if Port Said was not pulverised, we must expect casualties on the beaches on the same scale as in the Normandy landings. The Minister of Defence flew out to Cyprus and calmed the General down. An aircraft flying low over an assault convoy reported that Royal Marines in the landing craft had waved and seemed cheerful. An almost audible sigh of relief passed over Whitehall . . .

After the troops had been committed and the assault launched, the Government and the Service Ministries required coordinated operational and political intelligence on an immediate basis. Nobody had thought of this and an ad hoc emergency Joint Intelligence centre was set up on the Tuesday afternoon with the Heads of Section effectively in permanent session. That night, bedless, we slept on the floor.

The next day we were better organised but the trouble was that not only had the Intelligence and operational people been physically apart in their own Ministries, but now the combined Intelligence authority for the whole business had been set up in a building quite separate from all the Ministries and Headquarters concerned, which were themselves spread all over Whitehall. We therefore wasted hours trotting backwards and forwards to our own offices and we soon found that the only way to keep ourselves up-to-date with the military situation on the Canal was to listen to our portable radios and buy the evening papers off the streets.

However, in spite of every difficulty, at six o'clock every morning we produced an intelligence summary to be laid on every Very Important Desk before the incumbent arrived for the day's work.

The intelligence required was concerned mostly with the intentions and activities of other countries which might be involved. There had been those who had feared a general uprising against our interests throughout the Arab world with the possible murdering of British nationals and even armed intervention. We hàd dismissed this threat on the grounds that Arabs respect force and would wait to see what happened. The Russians would obviously capitalise on the situation but, we reckoned, would not actually do anything. In fact, they used the opportunity to invade Hungary whilst the spotlight was elsewhere.

But the situation rapidly worsened from the Government's point of view. Russian talk of the possible use of missiles was taken seriously. On Friday 2 November, led by Dulles, the UN passed a resolution calling for an immediate ceasefire and the setting up of a UN Emergency Force (UNEF). There was now a major Opposition-led peace movement in the country and in the Press. On the Sunday afternoon, a mass protest was held in Trafalgar Square against what the *Daily Mirror* called 'Eden's War'. Thousands of people marched down Whitehall and tried to get into Downing Street while the Cabinet was meeting in No. 10. The north end of Whitehall became the stage for some of the ugliest scenes London had ever witnessed while the south end was kept clear by mounted police charges. It was a lovely, misty autumn evening but it was horrible.

Finally, and perhaps most important, were the financial implications. The actual expense would have been acceptable but there was now a threat to the pound sterling and, worse, the discovery that the US Administration was preventing our drawing our own money from the IMF. We needed it to protect our currency from the speculation which, it was thought, was being stimulated by the US Treasury. The whole combination was too much and the Government lost its nerve. At 1700, 6 November, eight days after Israel invaded, a ceasefire was ordered.

Even then, things went wrong. A freak incidence of radio interference cut off communications for five hours. Optimists in Whitehall hoped that, by the time the order was received, our troops would have reached Suez. It fact, they had only advanced 23 miles down the canal.

That was the end. The UNEF took over and stayed ten years. The British and French withdrew, leaving the Canal blocked. Eden resigned, having demonstrated the remarkable power which lies in the hands of a British Prime Minister should he care to use it. Dulles actually told Selwyn Lloyd that we should have gone on and overthrown Nasser. The JIC was removed from its subservience to the Chiefs of Staff. The Heads of Sections returned thankfully to their own Ministries having learned a lesson which was to be incorporated in the new, integrated MOD. The US Naval Attaché's team, good friends who had kept shamefacedly away while it was all happening, appeared deprecatingly in NID 2's doorway to be greeted by a roar of welcome when it was seen that they were rolling in a barrel of beer.

And we wrote finis in the latest chapter of the Arab/Israel docket which was taken away to our Top Secret registry by a self effacing Soviet spy called Vassall . . .

Chapter 23

FLEET AIR ARM

Suez had made it clear that it had been difficult to raise the resources for a minor war with Egypt. Now the Government decided to reduce the Armed Forces even further and inaugurated the first of the many cuts which were to follow in subsequent years as Britain subsided to the status of a second class power. The scheme was christened 'The Golden Bowler' and the terms leaked in advance. Financially, they were generous because they were designed to compensate Officers driven out into the cold of civvy street prematurely in their careers and against their will. In the event, nearly everyone wanted to go and Whitehall, still out of touch with feeling in the Fleet, was shaken by the flood of applications to retire.

I drafted my own letter. Although my work in the Naval Intelligence Division had been interesting and, indeed, stimulating, I had not enjoyed living by myself in a grubby London bed sitter which was all I could afford. School fees and the mortgage on my house absorbed my modest pay like a sponge. I was being expensively entertained by foreign Naval Attachés yet suffered the embarrassment that I could afford to offer no hospitality in return. My resources just allowed me one five-shilling bottle of wine a week which I drank by myself in my own room before going out to the cheapest supper I could buy in the local Greek restaurant. Even a cinema was hopelessly above my means.

There was no prospect of ever going to sea again. If I must spend the rest of my life behind an office desk I reckoned I might at least find one where I got paid decently and could live at home with my family. It was going to be a tremendous wrench but the Navy seemed to have nothing left to offer and, like all my friends, I decided the time had come to make the break.

At this moment of crisis, I was appointed Commander of the Naval Air Station at Yeovilton.

We had a farewell party in the office which cost me a good many months equivalent of my weekly bottle of infuriator and ended in a pub across Trafalgar Square. Section 2 were envious of my luck in getting back to the

Navy. In London, we all reckoned, nobody cared. My bowler hat was old and greasy. My umbrella had been second hand when I started. I pulled the hat rim round my neck, leaving the crown perched on my head, and turned my umbrella inside out. Holding it at the slope, I crossed Trafalgar Square, Northumberland Avenue and Whitehall. In all the hurrying crowds nobody looked, nobody even noticed. I put my umbrella and both parts of my bowler hat in the wastepaper basket and fled the capital. My moment of weakness was over and The Letter was never posted.

Yeovilton Air Station was set in the wilds of rural Somerset but, being Naval, was officially known as Her Majesty's Ship *Heron*. It was the centre for All Weather Fighters and, in my day, flew Sea Venoms with a two man crew of pilot and observer. There was one Squadron, 766, which formed the All Weather Fighter school but the other Squadrons were operational and had either just flown in from or were about to embark in their carriers.

I knew that aviators constituted a self contained, exclusive club which regarded all 'fishheads' (non aviators) with suspicion. Many good Commanders had been broken in Air Stations when they tried to be too 'pusser'. So I went into the wardroom my first evening with some trepidation. A number of competent looking young men propped up the bar, each with a pint tankard in his hand. I found myself under searching but affable scrutiny and, after the ice had been broken, I was just beginning to relax when one of them said, 'I'm going up to thirty thou tomorrow, sir, to try out the radar. Would you like to come along?'

Now I had always been terrified of going up in aeroplanes and, even after many hours of flying in commercial comfort, I still was. The thought of racing about in a jet fighter appalled me. I had reckoned my job as Commander would be firmly on the ground. It had never occurred to me I should have to get airborne.

The silence was lengthening. The young aviators were looking at me oddly. It was the moment of truth. Choosing my words carefully I replied, 'Thank you, but no. I am extremely frightened of travelling in aeroplanes. I will do all that's needed here provided I can stay on the deck but, please, never expect me to go up in one of your dreadful machines.'

I went through the next day's turnover in a state of dumb misery. My fishhead predecessor told me happily how he and all the other Air Station Commanders had learned to fly. 'It shows we're trying and they do appreciate that,' he explained.

By lunch time I had realised that, in all fairness, I must go to the Captain and suggest that the appointment be cancelled. I was obviously the wrong man for the job.

I slunk into the Mess for a much needed gin. For a moment, nobody noticed me. Then they did. A cheer went up and I was propelled to the bar by many willing hands. 'Thank God,' cried 'Wings', the Commander (Air). 'At last we've got a proper fishhead. All the Commanders in the other stations start yammering to learn to fly and it always ends in tears. Some poor sod comes back to make an emergency landing and just as he's going to touch down the bloody Commander paddles across in front of him in a Tiger Moth.' I had inadvertently produced the best possible gimmick and the Fleet Air Arm worships gimmicks. Like the goat in front of the Welsh Fusiliers, they had adopted me as a perfect mascot – a real twenty-two carat fishhead who cheerfully admitted he was afraid to fly. As far as Yeovilton was concerned, the new Commander was all right.

The flying and operational side came under 'Wings' and was no concern of mine. My responsibility was to run and generally administer the station as a whole – to look after its cleanliness, discipline, welfare and efficiency as a Naval establishment. On the other hand, since the only object of the whole vast organisation was that aircraft should fly from ships, The Task, as it was always known, was naturally paramount. The Commander of an Air Station was therefore in the odd position that, although Second-in-Command and Executive Officer, he had no say in any of the things that really mattered. It was rather as if an actor manager suddenly found himself, in his own theatre, relegated to taking charge of the ticket office, cleaners and usherettes.

However, it quickly became obvious that I should have my hands full. The station, as such, was big enough to keep the Commander usefully occupied even if we had had no aircraft at all. But, apart from the static ship's company and the buildings, we had the problem of the permanently rotating squadrons. A carrier, returning from abroad, would fly off its aircraft as it came up Channel and the fighters would come to Yeovilton. On arrival, the whole squadron would proceed on leave and return a couple of weeks later having lost the edge of the expertise which is vital to land some ten tons of jet aircraft at over a hundred miles per hour onto a carrier's flight deck in the dark. They would therefore have to start getting their hands back in, day and night, at Yeovilton before their ship left its home port and re-embarked them as soon as it got to sea. Apart from the natural hazards of aviation, pilots who made mistakes killed themselves. It was as simple as that.

The result of such a life was that there was a terrific sense of urgency about everything. The normal Naval shore establishment has an eight to four mentality. Life folds up during what are well known as the Silent Hours. There were no silent hours at Yeovilton. All day and most of the night, the jets screamed down the runways, taking off and landing. Complaints came from local citizens and I used to call personally on every letter writer to explain that we did not operate from a sense of fun or cussedness. Indeed, we even liked quiet sleep too. Finally we invited the local Council to visit us. They came and, in the briefing room, they met the pilots and observers they were about to watch flying. One old chap sidled up to me afterwards looking stricken. 'They're so young,' he said. 'So terribly young . . .'

In his briefing, the Captain made the point clearly to a reporter from the local paper who was accompanying the visit. 'Tell your readers,' he said, 'that we feel very unhappy about keeping them awake at night. We could easily avoid it by sending the squadrons back to sea insufficiently practised to land on. They would then kill themselves. Is that the alternative the complainers would prefer?' Complaints dropped off sharply.

Knowing that, even for the best and most competent pilots, death always stood in the background I was still unprepared for it when it came. The signal arrived early one morning. One of our Sea Venoms had crashed as it was catapulted from the carrier. Pilot and observer had both been killed.

Death in war is normal but, in peacetime and particularly with young men, it shocks. The observer had only his parents as next of kin. The pilot had recently married a charming girl and, unlike most families who lived in Married Quarters on 'The Patch' just up the road, they had bought a small cottage in the country nearby. They had a St Bernard dog and shortly before, at the Squadron's pre-embarkation cocktail party, I had been teasing them by suggesting that this splendid animal should be trained to march in front of our station band.

Now, feeling sick and miserable, I drove out to the cottage to break the news. The young widow opened the door of their new home. The pilot had been building bookshelves along one wall but had not had time to finish them before he had to fly out. The St Bernard had a bandage around its neck.

I told her as gently as possible and she stared at me as if she was not listening. She said, terribly casually, 'My mother died of cancer last Christmas and I've just learned the dog has it on his neck.' Then she looked at the bookshelves, put her head in her hands and started to cry.

We lost twelve pilots and observers in six months but it was never as bad again as it was that first time.

It was difficult to get to know all the Squadrons because they came and went so fast but, after this, I tried. It would be too awful not to be able to put a face to the name when another such signal arrived. It also made it much easier to be patient with bad behaviour in the Mess. The Squadrons reckoned their real work was out at sea. Yeovilton was where they came home to have fun. They felt no particular loyalty to the Mess or the Station – we were there to provide facilities for flying and relaxation. They took no interest in Station activities such as the Amateur Dramatic Society or the Riding Club I had managed to start with the loan of some ropey old hacks from the local farmers. The Squadrons reckoned they hit Yeovilton with a bang and left with a bang and they never let up in between. Being President of the Wardroom Mess was, accordingly, an extremely thankless and difficult job.

I had heard horror stories from other Air Stations – particularly of Taranto Night dinners when the soup had hardly been served before the wretched Commander and Guest of Honour found themselves being soaked by well aimed rolls landing in their plates. Yeovilton, however, had been fairly well behaved until we had our Trafalgar Night dinner at which, by tradition, our special guest was always the Bishop of Bath and Wells.

The loyal toast had not even been drunk when there was a heavy explosion followed by four or five others. Thunderflashes in a confined room can be very noisy. Angry and astonished, I banged the table with my gavel and, without thinking said, 'Will the Officers responsible for that revolting exhibition kindly leave the Mess at once!'

A long silence ensued in which one overdilatory thunderflash exploded. A weak snigger came from someone. It was too much.

'Get out,' I said furiously.

Silence again and I suddenly wondered what the hell I could do if nobody moved. All my authority would have gone for ever.

Everyone was looking at me but, entirely without realising it, I was glaring at one particular Sub Lieutenant. He was one of the culprits and he had a guilty conscience. He thought I knew and, losing his nerve, climbed slowly to his feet. At once the other members of his newly arrived Squadron loyally rose too and they all trooped from the Mess. By Fleet Air standards a tough challenge had ended in total defeat.

I introduced the Bishop, remarking that, on Trafalgar Night, the smell of cordite was, perhaps, appropriate and he made an excellent and witty speech. The rest of the dinner passed placidly and enjoyably.

Next day I grounded the Squadron and, cap on head and telescope under arm, I tore them up in strips. I thought this would be the end of it and, as far as Mess discipline went, it was. We had no more trouble. But some weeks later when they were giving their farewell party I found myself talking to a most amusing young wife. When she found out who I was she surprised me by giggling. 'Gosh,' she said, 'you *do* dish out a good bollocking!'

I gaped and, seeing my face, she laughed out loud. The Squadron had guessed it was going to be good and I had been talking to a concealed microphone. The Squadron had given a special cocktail party for all their friends at which the *pièce de résistance* had been the playing of the tape of my blast. Aviators might be hell at times but at least they were never dull.

There are no half measures for fishheads with the Fleet Air Arm. Take against them, be stuffy, feel disgusted by some particularly nauseating and outrageous conduct in the Mess, wave your stripes and try to insist on normal Fleet standards, sob at the thought of some of them going to command HM Ships when they have not had five minutes of sea going watchkeeping and do not even know how to lower the whaler, turn on them in your justified wrath – do these things and the tightest Trades Union in the world will close its ranks against you and torment you till you are the one who breaks. Many good Commanders have had their careers thwarted as a result.

Or stand, as I did on a Somerset hillside at last light, looking up at the broken treeline where the plane first hit before it literally splashed apart on striking the ground. The Coroner particularly asked the Press at the inquest to use the words 'multiple injuries' because to describe what really happened would have been obscene.

Stand, again, on the airfield when the first Scimitar Squadron was embarking in its carrier for the first time. News had just come in of an arrestor wire failure when the CO, landing on first, had touched down. Man and machine had gone straight over the side and had never been recovered. Was the huge new aircraft too heavy for the wire to hold it? Was there an unknown, unexpected defect in the ship? If it had happened once, would it not happen again? We had no explanation but the flying on had not been cancelled. There would be a thirty minute delay while a new wire was rigged, then the Senior Pilot was to try. For half an hour, I stood beside him while we waited for the go and while we waited we talked of a lot of things. Then I said goodbye to a very brave man. He made it and so did the rest of the Squadron – that day and every day thereafter. It was all part of the job. But, once again, I had been privileged to share a little in the Fleet Air Arm's mystique – that superb amalgam of *esprit de corps*, morale, courage, dedication and sheer professional skill which makes Naval aviators unmatched by any other Force in the world. They were frequently exasperating but it was a privilege to serve them and I shall always feel that my life has been the richer for it,

Chapter 24

NAVAL ATTACHÉ, BONN

After Yeovilton, I was promoted to all the dignity of four stripes but hardly had the pleasure of wearing them because I had to spend another two years in Whitehall, about which perhaps the less said the better. Then, to make up, I was appointed Naval Attaché, Bonn. It was a very different role from my previous one and an equally different Germany. Now the *Wirtschaftswunder* had been completed and the standard of living was high. No longer the grey waifs amidst the ruins, these Germans were well fed, happy and prosperous. Everything which had been destroyed had been rebuilt. New houses, new cities, new factories, new railroads and, most important of all, a genuinely new mentality.

Everyone was tremendously pro British, especially the German Navy which, in spite of every kind of difficulty, had built itself into a very efficient little Service. The Senior Officers were all of wartime vintage. They had been defeated, had suffered the indignities of being 'demilitarised', and had gone through the shaming years of being unwanted, unemployed and, literally, often starving. Then, when the Cold War brought Allied forgiveness and recognition of the Federal German Republic, they had been called back and told to rebuild their Navy for NATO. They had done it well and they had shown remarkable flexibility of mind because not only had none of them any trace of bitterness but they had even come to accept and approve the new Navy that a new country and public opinion required. For behind the older Officers, roughly Lieutenant Commanders and above, came the gap of the missing years and then the new generation. The rating structure showed the same pattern.

In Kiel, I paid my calls on the German Navy. My accompanying Officer, who guided me round, was a delightful Korvetten Kapitän to whom I took an immediate liking.

I had been in MTBs. He had served in E-Boats. I had been in the Med. So had he. I had been in the Western Desert. He had been there too. I had been Executive Officer of the Naval Base in Mersa Maruh.

'I think,' he laughed, 'that it is just twenty years since I relieved you there.'

He showed me his photograph album that evening. There was the half ruined school that had been Navy House. In the background, with a German flag over her White Ensign, lay one of my old Flotilla which had been captured in the abortive Tobruk raid. In the foreground, leaning against a wall, was my motor bike.

He saw my face and smiled deprecatingly. 'So long ago,' he murmured. I agreed. It was. But, though we later became fast friends, I never liked to ask him if anything of note had happened in the loo at 0900 three days after he moved in. Some things are best left alone and, frankly, I would have been too ashamed.

The German Navy fascinated me. It was such a sharply divided mixture of the old and young generation, of idealism for NATO and its role of blocking the Baltic with, simultaneously, a determination to be democratic and unmilitaristic.

I went out for a big exercise in a German coastal minesweeper. They had already been working watch and watch for a week and four hours on, four hours off, day and night, becomes exhausting after even a few days. Right at the end, at two in the morning, the alarm bells went yet again and I stumbled, gummy eyed, from my bunk. I reached the cabin door as the young ship's company came racing down the central passage towards the Upper Deck. After the messing about they had had, a British ship's company would have been pretty chokker about it all. But as each German sailor passed I got a salute, a beaming smile and, '*Morgen, Herr Kapitän.*' They are a remarkable race.

The Germans have little tangible in the way of tradition as we have. Their barracks and their ships are not stuffed with silver and trophies and their Officers have no wardrooms ashore. They eat with their sailors, the same food, and return to their offices or cabins.

In Cuxhaven, the Naval Officer in Charge wangled a special room that he could use as an Officers' Mess. He had provided a series of tremendously happy and successful visits for HM Ships and I thought it would be a nice gesture if, in return, the Royal Navy presented the Cuxhaven Mess with some small piece of silver.

The Portsmouth Barracks trophy store raised a particularly ugly old rose bowl which they were prepared to lose and I sent it to my friend in Cuxhaven. I received an ecstatic letter of thanks. There must, he said, be some special tradition about this beautiful bowl if it came from the Royal Navy. Could he know what it was so that the German Navy could keep it up?

Obviously they would relish something suitably Germanic so I thought and then replied that it had always been used by the ships concerned as a special Honour Bowl for important guests. It was filled with champagne and the Guest had to drink it all without pausing to show that he was a true Man of the Sea. This harmless little invention appealed tremendously to the Germans as I had guessed it would. I reckoned they could worry about the fact that even two or three glasses of Sekt, the Germany champagne equivalent, leaves one feeling the next day as if one's eyeballs were hanging out with great hands squeezing them. What I did not reckon on, and should have, was that, of course, they invited me to be their first Guest of Honour in their new Mess . . .

Visits by HM Ships to Germany were always a terrific success. In all my two and a half years there we only had one minor incident with one Libertyman, probably because our sailors were simply collected by the Germans and taken into their homes. One sailor summed up his feelings for me. 'Wherever we went,' he said, 'people in the streets smiled at us and said hullo.'

When the aircraft carrier *Centaur* visited Hamburg a special switchboard had to be installed manned by six German sailors doing nothing except taking incoming calls offering hospitality. As a result, even the famous Reeperbahn was largely deserted. Jack had his feet under the table.

In Bonn, we lived the diplomatic life. There were over a hundred nations represented in the capital and nearly all had Service Attachés. This meant some two hundred National Days and Armed Forces Days to be celebrated by cocktail parties before one started on the normal diplomatic drinking.

However, our social life could be fun. Naval Officers from every country have an instinctive bond in common and my job was to be friends with other Naval Officers and, particularly, my German hosts. One had to do a certain amount of formal, diplomatic entertaining but the popular parties were those where the guests came to enjoy themselves. As Attaché, I was provided with a splendid house with a vast drawing room and even a tame deer in the garden. It had all the facilities for large scale entertaining.

My predecessor, a somewhat forceful Gunnery Officer, had told me during the turnover that he reckoned the British Naval Attaché should have one main function a year. 'Should be Trafalgar Night, of course,' he said, 'but the French would never forgive you. I thought of various other anniversaries but they'd all annoy someone. Trouble is, we've beaten all these damned foreigners at some time. Anyhow, there's the problem. If you can solve it, good luck to you.'

We solved it by having a party to commemorate the British victory at the Battle of Jutland which took place simultaneously with the German victory at the Battle of the Skaggerak. It is the only victory in history celebrated by both sides and we drank Scotch to celebrate Jutland till midnight and Rhine wine to celebrate the Skaggerak thereafter. It was a very successful party and greatly appreciated by the Germans who are not without humour.

Towards the end of my time, it was suggested from Cologne that the fiftieth anniversary of the Battle of Heligoland, in which the Royal Navy had sunk the city's 'name ship' *Köln*, should be marked by an Anglo-German Naval occasion to celebrate our new alliance and friendship.

The whole programme was a great success. The high spots were a ball, given by the City of Cologne to the visiting sailors of both nations, and a moving ceremony at the huge War Memorial when wreaths were laid by HM Ambassador, Admiral Zenker (the German equivalent to our First Sea Lord), and the Burgermeister, Herr Adenauer, (son of the famous old Chancellor).

But the stars were undoubtedly the Royal Marines Band sent from Deal. They left the Hook of Holland at 0400 and travelled overland, arriving just in time to put on uniform, grab their instruments and give an evening concert in the Rathaus square. Beside them, playing alternately, was a German Army band and the contrast between the drab appearance of the Germans and the British finery was most noticeable.

After the concert, the Royal Marines were borne off by the crowd and taken to bars and homes. They returned to barracks with the dawn for breakfast, followed by a forenoon tour of local breweries. In the afternoon they stood rock steady for an hour, in sweltering heat, and gave dignity and music to the ceremony at the War Memorial. In the evening, they played again in the Rathaus square after which they were taken off for another full night's carousing by the German Old Comrades' Association. The next forenoon there was another brewery tour, followed by yet another in the afternoon. (Cologne brews a lot of good beer!)

That evening they were to Beat Retreat in the Rathaus Square. A vast crowd turned up for the occasion and I sat on the rostrum with Admiral Zenker and the Burgermeister. No Royal Marines . . . had the strain told at last? I was just beginning to get really worried when a bus tore up with police outriders. Out of it tumbled the band and, exactly on time, they marched into the Rathaus square. White, gold knobbed helmets, leopard skins, crashing brass and perfect, glorious, marching and drumming. Their faces were green and I'll swear their eyes were shut. Some must have been virtually unconscious but they beat Retreat with all the panache of which only the Royal Marines are capable.

After the marvellous Sunset ceremony they marched off and the Burgermeister took the salute. Admiral Zenker turned to me and said, 'Herr Kapitän, that was the most superb piece of ceremonial I have ever seen in my life.'

'Herr Admiral,' I could only reply, 'you should see them when they're sober!'

Chapter 25

THE END OF THE ROAD

On return from Germany, I spent a year at the Imperial Defence College and then took over as Director of Naval Recruiting. There had been big changes since I had last known Whitehall.

DNR's office was the well-remembered room in which the Director of Naval Intelligence had told me to hold back the warning of the Israeli attack on Egypt. In those days, the original copy, and decode, of the Zimmerman telegram had hung on the wall, symbolising the great era when 'Blinker' Hall's NID had even been able virtually to bring America into World War 1. Now, where it had hung, were wall charts showing the depressing state of Naval recruiting and there was no longer a Vice Admiral in charge of the Naval Intelligence Division but only a Commodore heading the Naval section of a joint Services Intelligence set up.

Even 'the Admiralty' had disappeared into the maw of the vast new Ministry of Defence and our offices were in part of what, now known as the Old Admiralty Building, was soon to be taken over totally by the Civil Service Department who, finding the lovely old place not to their liking, had it expensively tarted up in bright colours like some brash modern road house.

Fortunately DNR's department was able to keep clear of the worst horrors of the Main Building. We had enough troubles of our own. The 'swinging sixties' were a bad time for recruiters. Full employment cancelled our main prewar attraction. Flower power, CND, hippies and anti Vietnam war demonstrations were the day's vogue and the Armed Forces tended to be anathematised. Moreover, potential young Officer candidates were being discouraged by fathers and uncles of the Golden Bowler generation while possible young sailors who asked their serving mates what the life was like were told of the strain of hard work, long partings from home and general turbulence. (The Indonesian 'confrontation' had drawn most of the Navy to the Far East.)

Then the heavens fell in. The whole future fleet had been predicated on our having a new generation of aircraft carriers. Now it was decided we must do without. The RAF had long waged a bitter campaign against Naval air power, claiming that they could provide the requisite air cover anywhere needed. Nobody could foresee the Falklands war where tragically unnecessary casualties would occur because we lacked the Airborne Early Warning that a proper carrier could have provided. The Navy, with harsh memories of the empty skies during World War 2, did its best to fight its corner but the politicians found the potential financial savings too attractive to resist and the carrier got the chop, leaving the Fleet we had planned without its major component. Hamlet without the Prince.

Finally came the withdrawal from East of Suez. We were giving up the last of Empire and we no longer needed such large Forces. To add to all our other recruiting problems we faced the stigma of redundancy.

It was obviously time for the Navy to pause and take a very long, hard look at itself and its problems. Much had been done to improve conditions of service but, obviously, not enough. The 'turbulence and overstretch' had been no fault of the management but, even so, it must be stopped. If impossible demands were made on our surviving ships then these must be refused and the politicians simply told that the force required was not available.

New types of ships would be needed to build a new concept Fleet. To man it we should need to revolutionise all our thinking on conditions of service in order to attract enough of the type of man we required and keep him of his own free will because he liked what the Service had to offer. The new Navy must be a *corps d'élite* in which it would be a desirable honour to serve.

There was obviously need for fundamental change and, luckily, we had an Admiralty Board of the calibre required. Nothing was inviolate, nothing was left unchallenged nor taken for granted. The corridors of the Ministry of Defence echoed to the frenzied mooing of Sacred Cows galloping unlamented into oblivion.

In the late sixties, the foundations were laid for the revolution which has come since.

Certainly my own conditions of service underwent a considerable and unexpected change. A year before I reached the top of the Captain's list, a letter from the Naval Secretary informed me that my name was on the short list for promotion to Flag rank. My chances of selection, he considered, were 'fair'.

'Fair', of course, could be taken in the barometric sense or that of the sailor's conduct sheet – which meant pretty mediocre. It must have been the former because, after six nailbiting months of wondering, I was told that I was to become the Flag Officer, Admiralty Interview Board. I was to end my career on the other side of the table across which, so many years before, I had rebuked the Parson.

The AIB sits in HMS *Sultan* at Gosport and, although today's Board uses the sophisticated techniques evolved during the last war, it is still the lineal descendant of 'The Admirals' of my day and the original Committee set up by Jackie Fisher at the beginning of the century. Indeed, in a very old file, I stumbled on one of the Committee member's pencilled notes to himself as he considered how the new system should best operate.

'We have before us,' he wrote, 'A report from his schoolmaster as to his general attributes and we have the boy before us to ascertain (I suppose):-
a) If he is a gentleman
b) If he is a sharp and intelligent one
c) If he is observant and enthusiastic
d) If enthusiastic and keen about Navy and patriotic
e) If fond of manly sports
f) What his relatives and ancestors have been.'

On second thoughts, he ruled out (f) but went on to show his concern by commenting, 'I am not quite clear as to whether his social fitness is entirely left to the Committee or whether invitations to appear before the Committee are only extended to those whose birth is considered suitable. If it is left to the Committee, it seems a large question to say where to draw the line. It seems only right that it should be possible for every Englishman of whatever class to serve his country in the Navy either as an Officer or on the Lower Deck.

'What about the sons of Engineers and Paymasters etc., and merchant class – and of clergymen, who themselves are of widely different classes?'

The terrible problem of class distinction appears to have been solved by asking questions such as with what foods various sauces were eaten (which 'showed whether a boy dined properly at night – a sure test of a gentleman'.) The notes end:-
'Who are your Godfathers and Godmothers?
N.B. V. good question for finding out if a gentleman by birth!
Also detected a boy of Jewish faith last time!! (he got in!)'

The Admiralty Interview Board of my day faced very different problems. Instead of the little prep school aspirants we dealt with the whole spectrum from fifteen-year-olds seeking a scholarship or reserved place for Dartmouth, through eighteen-year-olds wanting Direct Entry or a paid place at University, on through Undergraduates already there and wishing to get in on the financially attractive scheme and, finally, to Graduates of any age up to thirty. These latter were usually Engineers who, finding the acquisition of a good job more difficult than that of a degree, hoped that a few years in the Navy would tide them over.

Class, of course, had long been forgotten but this raised a new problem. Before the war, the old master and man relationship could carry a bad Officer and made life relatively easy for the mediocre. Nowadays, a third of our Officers are, in any case, ex lower deck. Of the remainder, at least half come from the same background, indeed the same schools and streets, as many of their ratings. To maintain discipline, to earn and keep a position of respect, is therefore infinitely harder for today's young Officers than it was for their fathers. We had to select the lads who could do it, whatever their background.

The AIB procedure is careful, sympathetic, painstaking and thorough. We knew a lot about the candidate before we started from Headmasters' reports, psychological tests and the boys' own answers to a long questionnaire. The day began in the gym with each candidate taking charge of the rest of the squad and carrying out an evolution such as crossing a 'chasm' using spars, rope and oil drums. These drills were surprisingly effective in showing up qualities, or their lack, which might need detailed probing later. Bullying, skiving, bossiness, cowardice, courage, deceitfulness, humour, temper were only some of the characteristics unconsciously but clearly displayed by the candidates as they carried out the evolutions.

'The Scheme' posed a problem requiring logical thought to produce a solution. Having studied it carefully the candidates would argue their answers out in syndicate. Again, the fool, the muddled thinker, the born staff Officer, the leader, the shy and the bully would all stand out plainly.

The final interviews, one alone with the psychologist and one before all the rest of the Board, took three quarters of an hour and, with what had gone before, one was left with a very clear picture of a young human being.

Thus we tested them and thus we chose them – not for what they were when we saw them but for what we thought was their potential, which Dartmouth and the Navy would mould and develop into something good.

Dartmouth certainly did superbly well with those we sent there, and it was most rewarding to go back and meet some of my dubious ex-Candidates, now alert and self-confident Midshipmen or Subs. I went, as Flag Officer Admiralty Interview Board, bellwethering a group of Headmasters, and it was the first time I had been back since I had learned Mr Niblock's secret thirty-seven years before. It was an unexpectedly emotional experience.

I stepped, once again, onto the lovely old Quarterdeck. I visited the Eleventh Term gunroom from which the Exmouths had finally Gone To Sea. So little had changed. Now there were cabins where we ranged the chests every night in the big open dormitories but the flats between were as I remembered them. I stood on the exact spot where Nicholls had told me that wilfully obtaining five ticks was virtually mutiny and I bent slowly down, flinching mentally at the thought of the cane. Then I stood up, looked at the stripes on my sleeve and felt thankful.

I went into the war memorial chapel and thought of the fifteen-year-old boy looking at the Book of Remembrance and thanking God that there could be no war for his generation.

The whole of one wall has been turned into the Memorial for World War 2 and there are three times as many names carved in its stone as there were in the Book. So many Exmouths, nearly a third of the term, are there . . .

The Headmasters had an interesting day and they were very impressed by it all. Question time at the end was long and varied till, finally, one said, 'We have heard a lot about leadership and "fliers" and the development of Officer-like qualities whatever they may be. I have certainly met one of my old boys and you have done miracles with him. But what I want to know is this. How accurately can you foretell now what your present youngsters are actually going to make of their future lives? Are today's fliers really tomorrow's Admirals, or will the ones you disparage now amaze you all?'

This was obviously one for me to answer. 'In my term,' I said, 'we had two obvious fliers. Both were intellectually brilliant and effortlessly at the top of the Alpha class. Both were also good sportsmen and generally popular. Both were, inevitably, in our first promotions to Cadet Captain. One is now Commander-in-Chief of the Fleet and the other is about to become First Sea Lord. At the other end of the Term there was a cadet inexorably bottom, idle, poor at games and markedly lacking in a sense of responsibility or Officer-like qualities. He is answering your question now.'

Sometimes we got depressed, at the AIB, feeling that Industry was stealing the fliers and that the young men we were accepting lacked motivation and character. Perhaps it was inevitable. Age has always tended to denigrate youth so it was natural for us to wonder gloomily how those we passed would face up to the challenge of the revolutionary new Navy they would find when they, in their turn, finally Got To Sea. Happily, I have lived to see the answer. The Falklands and Kuwait have clearly shown that those to whom we handed on the torch have proved themselves more than capable of carrying it. The Royal Navy has never been in better hands.

The end of the road. Calling on the C-in-C in Victory.

EPILOGUE

My first day as Flag Officer, AIB, I paid my formal call on the Commander-in-Chief. He received me in his Flagship, HMS *Victory*. After the drab, plain clothes of Whitehall anonymity, I found it strangely moving to be received by a Guard and Band in the arena alongside the famous old ship and, as I went up the long brow and the side was piped and the bugle sounded the 'Still', my mind raced back over the years as it had that day when Pam and I came back to find Portsmouth in ruins.

Repulse and being passed over as a Midshipman, a Sub doing courses with his dog, *Forester* and wild oats in the A & B, the war, *Vernon*, *Hornet*, getting married, the city after the blitz, *Contest* and our first home – so much had happened in Portsmouth and now here I was suddenly at the centre of all this ceremonial. How little I had foreseen it at the beginning of my road . . .

Pam, too, had her moment when we dined in Nelson's Great Cabin on the eve of Trafalgar Day at the same table where Nelson had been seated exactly 164 years before when he wrote his famous prayer. She, also, had come a long way from being the young Wren refused her Leading Rate for being a bad influence on the messdeck . . .

Then, on my last day, the time came for me to interview my final candidate – an eighteen-year-old lad appearing before the Board for Direct Entry. He had the intelligence, the character and the motivation to go far.

I had just been reading a recruiting booklet. 'As an Admiral leaves the Service,' it said, 'a Cadet enters Dartmouth . . .' I was going and here he was. I was looking at my relief.

Silently I wished him luck and he may have wondered why I smiled at him so oddly as he left the room.

I was remembering how unthinkable was change when I joined. He would enter a Navy when change, fast and dramatic, is the only certainty.

If he ever writes a book, what story will he have to tell?